Cambridge Companions to Music

The Cambridge Companion to the Recorder

Cambridge Companions to Music

The Cambridge Companion to the Violin
EDITED BY ROBIN STOWELL

The Cambridge Companion to the Recorder
EDITED BY JOHN THOMSON

The Cambridge Companion to the Clarinet
EDITED BY COLIN LAWSON

The Cambridge Companion to Chopin
EDITED BY JIM SAMSON

Frontispiece   Virgin and Child surrounded by angels playing musical instruments. This is the centre panel of the Altarpiece of Our Lady of the Angels painted for the church of Santa Clara, Tortosa, by Pere Serra (c1390), and now housed in the Museu Nacional d'Art de Catalunya, Barcelona. For the significance of this painting see p. 22, note 8.

The Cambridge Companion to the Recorder

Edited by
JOHN MANSFIELD THOMSON

Assistant editor
ANTHONY ROWLAND-JONES

CAMBRIDGE
UNIVERSITY PRESS

Published by the Press Syndicate of the University of Cambridge
The Pitt Building, Trumpington Street, Cambridge CB2 1RP
40 West 20th Street, New York, NY 10011–4211, USA
10 Stamford Road, Oakleigh, Melbourne 3166, Australia

First published 1995

Printed in Great Britain at the University Press, Cambridge

A catalogue record for this book is available from the British Library

Library of Congress cataloguing in publication data

The Cambridge companion to the recorder / edited by John Mansfield
Thomson; assistant editor, Anthony Rowland-Jones.
   p.   cm.
   Includes index.
   ISBN 0 521 35269 X (hardback) – ISBN 0 521 35816 7 (paperback)
   1. Recorder (Musical instrument). I. Thomson, John Mansfield.
   II. Rowland-Jones, Anthony.
ML990.R4C35 1995
788.3'6–dc20 94–31992 CIP MN

ISBN 0 521 35269 X hardback
ISBN 0 521 35816 7 paperback

To Walter Bergmann
1902–1988
friend of recorder players

Contents

Illustrations

In compiling the illustrations for this book substantial use has been made of the series Musikgeschichte in Bildern, especially III/8, Edmund A. Bowles, *Musikleben im 15. Jahrhundert* (Leipzig 1977; referred to as 'Bowles, *Musikleben*'); III/9, Walter Salmen, *Musikleben im 16. Jahrhundert* (Leipzig 1976; 'Salmen, *Musikleben*'), and IV/3, *Haus- und Kammermusik* (Leipzig 1969; 'Salmen, *Kammermusik*'). Edmund A. Bowles's bilingual *La pratique musicale au moyen âge / Musical Performance in the Late Middle Ages* (Geneva 1983; 'Bowles, *Pratique*') has also been drawn upon. 'WB' followed by a number refers to the Walter Bergmann Collection (see p. xxi).

Plate acknowledgements
Frontispiece: Museu Nacional d'Art de Catalunya, Barcelona
1, 7: Alte Pinakothek, Munich
2B: su concessione dell'Assessorato BB. CC. AA Galleria Regionale della Sicilia, Palermo
3: Minneapolis Institute of Arts
4, 11A, B: Permission of the British Library
5: Freiburg im Breisgau University
6A, B: Reproduced by courtesy of the Musée du Berry, Bourges, and the Musée du Louvre, Paris

8: Bibliothèque Nationale, Paris
9: University Library, Heidelberg
10A: Musée de Cluny, Paris
10B: Royal Collection of Copperplate Engravings, Copenhagen
13: Musées Royaux d'Art et d'Histoire, Brussels
14: Reproduced by courtesy of the Archivio fotografico del Castello del Buonconsiglio. Monumenti e Collezioni Provinciali, Trent
15A, 27: Reproduced by courtesy of the Wallace Collection, London
15A (inset 1): © Prado Museum, Madrid
15A (inset 2): Palazzo Barberini, Rome
15B: Reproduced by courtesy of the Graf Harrach'sche Gemäldesammlung, Schloss Rohrau, Austria
17: Permission of the Syndics of the Fitzwilliam Museum, Cambridge
19: Presse-Bild, Munich
20A: National Gallery, London
20B: Bayerische Verwaltung der Staatlichen Schlösser, Gärten und Seen
21: Rijksmuseum, Amsterdam
22: Reproduced by courtesy of Sotheby's
23A: *Portrait of a Family Making Music.* Oil on canvas, 1663, 98.7 × 116.7 cm. Pieter de Hooch, Dutch, 1629–1684. © The Cleveland Museum of Art, Gift of the Hanna Fund, 51.355
23B: Reproduced by courtesy of the Noortman Gallery, London and Maastricht
24, 25: Reproduced by courtesy of the Syndics of the Cambridge University Library
28: Permission of the Britten-Pears Library and Colin Osman. Photo: Kurt Hutton
32, 38: Reproduced by courtesy of the National Gallery, Ireland
33: Reproduced by courtesy of the Bundespräsidialamt, Bonn
34, 35A: Reproduced by courtesy of the Dolmetsch Library; 35A photograph by Colin G. Futcher
35B: Permission kindly granted by the Master and Fellows of Christ's College, Cambridge
36: Photo: © Friso Keuris
37: Reproduced by courtesy of the Witt Library, the Courtauld Institute, University of London
40: Klášter Premonstrátů Na Strahově, Prague
Endpiece: Bayerische Staatsbibliothek, Munich

Music example acknowledgements

Page 58 (Ex.1): Permission of the Syndics of the Fitzwilliam Museum, Cambridge
Page 59 (Ex.2): Reproduced by courtesy of the Syndics of the Cambridge University Library
Page 69 (Ex.7): Reproduced by courtesy of the Library of Congress, Washington
Page 161 (Vetter, *Rezitative*): © by Moeck Verlag & Musik instrumentenwerk, D-29227 Celle

Notes on contributors

CLIFFORD BARTLETT studied classics at school and English literature at Cambridge. He worked as a librarian at the Royal Academy of Music and the BBC and played harpsichord and organ in Ars Nova, one of the pioneering early-music groups in the 1970s. Now he is an editor, writer and publisher. His firm King's Music issues facsimiles and editions of mostly baroque music and he has edited many works for performance and recording. His editions of Monteverdi's *Orfeo* and the 1610 *Vespers* have been performed throughout the world. Having edited several of Handel's major works, he has recently been commissioned by a leading publisher to prepare a new edition of *Messiah*. He is Associate Editor of *The New Oxford Book of Carols*. Between 1977 and 1994 he wrote a monthly survey of new editions and books about music in *Early Music News* (London); this has been superseded by his own publication *Early Music Review*.

HOWARD MAYER BROWN (1930–93), an accomplished recorder player and flautist, was born in Los Angeles and graduated from Harvard. He came to specialise in the late fifteenth- and early sixteenth-century chanson and in the instrumental music of the latter period. During his long tenure of the Chair of Music at the University of Chicago he conducted and played several instruments in the University's Collegium Musicum. From 1972 to 1974 he was King Edward Professor of Music at King's College in the University of London and became deeply involved with the early-music world at that time. His many publications include a pioneer study in bibliography *Instrumental Music Printed Before 1600* (1965), *Musical Iconography*, with Joan Lascelle (1972), *Embellishing Sixteenth-Century Music* (1976), *Music in the Renaissance* (1976) and, as editor, *The New Grove Handbooks in Performance Practice*, 2 vols., with Stanley Sadie (1989). His chapter in this book is one of his last published writings. He proved a source of inspiration for innumerable scholars, for his helpfulness, tolerance and humility, for the lucidity of his style and for the unique qualities of mind he brought to bear on the understanding and interpretation of the music of the past.

EVE O'KELLY holds B.Sc and B.Mus (Hons) degrees from the National University of Ireland and an M.Phil from the University of London. She is a native of Cork, Ireland, and worked in London for ten years as a specialist recorder tutor. Since 1990 she has been General Manager, and is now Director, of the Contemporary Music Centre in Dublin, the centre for promotion and documentation of contemporary Irish composition. She is the author of a highly successful book which concentrates on the contemporary scene, *The Recorder Today* (1990), and edited *The Recorder Magazine* from 1991 to 1993, at which time it ceased to be published by Schott.

DAVID LASOCKI was born in London and grew up in Manchester. While a student of chemistry at the University of London, he took recorder and baroque flute lessons from Edgar Hunt and summer courses with Gustav Scheck on the Continent. In 1969 he went to the University of Iowa in the United States where he studied the flute with Betty Bang Mather and obtained an M.A. and Ph.D. in musicology and an M.A. in library science. His Ph.D. dissertation, *Professional Recorder Players in England, 1540–1740* (1983), was awarded the Humanities and Fine Arts dissertation prize of the Council of Graduate Schools in the United States. As a musicologist he has specialised in the history of woodwind instruments (especially the flute and recorder), their repertoire, performance practices, social history and bibliography. He has published six books and about seventy articles, and has edited 100 editions of eighteenth-century woodwind music. At present he is Head of Reference Services in the Music Library at Indiana University, Bloomington, Indiana, USA. (For his most recent books see pages 210 and 222).

ANTHONY ROWLAND-JONES is one of the best known of today's writers on recorder playing. After taking his degree in English at Oxford, he became a university administrator at London, Newcastle upon Tyne and Leeds, and then the first Registrar of Essex University. After a period of overseas consultancy work in Africa, Asia and the South Pacific, he was Vice-Principal of what is now Anglia Polytechnic University in Cambridge. He studied with Walter Bergmann at Morley College, and since early retirement in 1984 has continued teaching recorder at Anglia, conducting groups and running weekend courses. With Mary Bonsor he co-founded the West Riding Branch of the Society of Recorder Players and is currently President of the Cambridge Branch and a Musical Adviser to S.R.P. He was a founder member of the editorial board of *The Recorder Magazine*. Until the publication of his most recent book, *Playing Recorder Sonatas: Interpretation and Technique* (1992), he was most known for his *Recorder Technique* (1959, rev. edn 1986).

ADRIENNE SIMPSON, musicologist and opera historian, was the 1993 J. D. Stout Research Fellow in Cultural Studies at Victoria University of Wellington, New Zealand, engaged in writing a history of opera in New Zealand. She edited the *Lute Society Journal* in 1971–2 and was assistant editor of the *Recorder and Music Magazine* to which she contributed several articles, as she did to *Early Music, Continuo* and other specialist journals. She was founder and editor of the quarterly *Early Music New Zealand* from 1985 until 1988. She made numerous contributions to *The New Grove*, mainly in the field of Czech baroque and early nineteenth-century music, and has published editions of recorder and lute music as well as three books on opera and many scholarly articles.

JOHN MANSFIELD THOMSON, founding editor of *Early Music* (1973–83), edited the *Recorder and Music Magazine* for two separate periods in the 1960s and 70s. His publications include *Your Book of the Recorder* (1968), *Recorder Profiles* (1972) and contributions to *The American Recorder*. He studied recorder in Wellington, New Zealand, with Zillah and Ronald Castle, the well-known instrument collectors, and in London with Walter Bergmann, with whom he later worked in the establishing of the Faber Music recorder list. For over a decade he was music-books editor, first for Barrie & Jenkins then Faber and Faber. He has a deep interest in musical caricatures and his collection of *Musical Delights* (1984) was voted by *The Times* as one of the ten best books of humour of the year 'for historical not hysterical reasons'. His other books include *A Distant Music: Life and Times of Alfred Hill (1870–1960)* (1980), *Biographical Dictionary of New Zealand Composers* (1990), *Musical Images: A New Zealand Historical Journal 1840–1990* (1990) and the *Oxford History of New Zealand Music* (1991). He is also editing the forthcoming *Cambridge Companion to the Flute*.

Foreword

by DANIEL BRÜGGEN
of the Amsterdam Loeki Stardust Quartet (See p. 179)

In reviewing the history of the recorder, there is little doubt but that one of the most spectacular chapters has been written during the past century. Since its rediscovery the instrument has shown a remarkable number of different faces.

To be able to observe the contemporary as well as the historic countenances, it seems appropriate to show its diversity with enlightening articles written by several authors, all experts in their own field. This book provides a detailed map of the extensive area of the recorder. One gets acquainted with it by taking adventurous walks, sometimes passing familiar sites seen, however, from different perspectives. It comprises background information, stimulating ideas about music-making, practical advice as well as elaborate research. Not only do the articles portray the instrument, they will nourish the musician as well.

As every instrument confronts its performer with limitations, some find this especially true of the recorder. The limitations of an instrument, however, are always far less interesting than its possibilities. In this respect I recall a movie scene with Fred Astaire where he dances with a hat-stand, bringing it to the point where it becomes his dancing partner. Although more adequate than a hat-stand the recorder can sometimes act straight and unbending, and it takes patience and creativity to make the gentle voice tell haunting tales.

Imagination is an important ingredient of the musical story yet difficult to learn. Like creativity it is after all stimulated by questions rather than answers.

For the recorder player wishing to acquire an insight into the many aspects of our instrument, and learn to see facts not only as 'how to do' but also as an inspiration, this book is warmly recommended.

Preface

'Flutes or Recorders are a brave noble Instrument, being skilfully handled'

Thomas Tryon,
The Way to Health, Long Life and Happiness
(London 1683)

The recorder has had a long and at times fragmented history, for although it did not entirely disappear from the scene in the nineteenth century as historical accounts might suggest, it was undoubtedly regarded more as a curiosity than as a serious musical instrument. It took virtually no part in domestic music-making but emerged from time to time in lectures and demonstrations on antiquarian topics. The art of playing and especially of making recorders died out. The flute became the favourite instrument of amateurs of the period and was well served by composers, publishers and manufacturers.

The effective revival of the recorder dates from the early decades of this century, in particular from what is now part of recorder lore, Arnold Dolmetsch's decision to replace his lost Bressan treble, an event fully described herein, by making one himself. At the Haslemere Festival in 1926 he threw down the gauntlet by presenting two recorders instead of the usual flutes in Bach's Brandenburg Concerto No. 4 with Rudolph Dolmetsch and Miles Tomalin playing the solo parts. The instrument's subsequent hold over the affections of amateurs culminated in Edgar Hunt's launching of the Society of Recorder Players in 1937, with colleagues such as Stephanie and Max Champion. There followed the creation of a contemporary literature of a singular grace and charm to counterbalance the gradual rediscovery and publication of the repertoire of the past. Notable performers began to emerge. Parallel developments took place in Europe, especially in Germany, where Gustav Scheck and others played a pioneering role. Austria and the Netherlands followed suit, the latter in particular producing a line of gifted artists. Each of these events has contributed to the instrument becoming a musical phenomenon of the age.

Recorder playing for a time had all the elements of a craze. Temporarily losing its earlier consort connotations, the descant became widely adopted in schools, a lucrative market for plastic recorders having been developed to make it the least expensive of all musical instruments. Although it provided almost instant access to the basics of music, at the same time it inevitably aroused ambivalent feelings on the part of children and also their parents because of the lopsided picture it presented, coupled with the dire effects it had when played *en masse* and out of tune. It tended to obscure the reality that the individual members of the consort were indeed expressive musical instruments in their own right, with a relatively small but often distinguished repertoire, and their own place in music history.

Affirmation of this has gradually come about not only through music historians, scholars, performers and the many dedicated makers in all parts of the world, but by the impetus of the early-music revival as a whole. Buoyed up by its enthusiasms and willingness to experiment, the recorder has been re-established as securely as the harpsichord, and a variety of other instruments once considered obsolete.

This has created a need for informed commentary and helpful publications that will stimulate both amateur and professional players, through a knowledge of the recorder's history, repertoire and general musical background. A number of important works in these fields have already appeared but, given the striking advances in scholarship over the past few years, it was felt that there had now arisen a need for more detailed studies of particular aspects of the recorder world. Such a symposium as that held in 1993 in Utrecht on the seventeenth-century recorder would have been unimaginable a few decades ago.

Accordingly, leading figures from four countries, many of whom had been colleagues at some time or other, were invited to write on subjects related to their own interests, which together would cover the main historical periods and illuminate areas still relatively unknown. We also wished to provide comprehensive reference material that would be of use to recorder players for some considerable time. Each contributor was given freedom to approach his or her topic from an individual point of view and in their own style, including the way in which they wished to use the notes at the end of chapters. This was a deliberate editorial decision so that if at times similar issues are discussed they nevertheless appear as through a different prism. The *Companion* does not attempt to be a technical manual: several admirable books in this field already exist. Nevertheless, readers will find here much to lead them to aspire to higher levels of performance, as in Clifford Bartlett's essay on playing from facsimiles. 'Many recorder players may think that the suggestions made in this chapter are too demanding', he writes. 'But those who have read the rest of the book are clearly taking the recorder and its music seriously. It is, of course, important to take great care of your instruments and work hard on your technique. But the complete recorder player needs to exercise his mind as well as his fingers and breathing.' It is to this end that the *Companion* has been compiled.

Howard Mayer Brown's challenging opening chapter on the medieval and renaissance recorder will sadly be one of his last published writings following his tragic sudden death in Venice in February 1993. A brilliant recorder player, as all who heard him demonstrating sixteenth-century divisions will recall, he contributed occasionally but effectively to the *Recorder and Music Magazine* as in his 'What makes Brüggen great' in the December 1973 issue. His approach to the art he so graced might be summed up by his article on 'Explaining and understanding music' in the February 1983 issue of *Humanities*: 'Music delights, intrigues, astounds, and even moves people just because – or perhaps in spite of the fact that – it casts its spell without needing verbal concepts, without words. Music is a kind of magic . . .'.

A special feature of the book is the way in which the illustrations have been integrated into, and frequently elaborate on, material in the text. Anthony Rowland-Jones, to whom I owe an immense debt for his enlightened contributions to this volume, not only provides intriguing captions to the illustrations but also gives the reader a visual history of the development of the recorder from medieval times onwards. He thus demonstrates not only the changes in recorder design but also shows how its role has altered in different periods, revealing the social and symbolic aspects of the instrument which range from angelic consorts to boat parties, bathing escapades and *la vie pastorale*. His aim is to make 'reading the illustrations' valuable in itself.

All who have worked on this book and watched it grow into something far more useful, admirable and comprehensive than its original conception could ever have been, a process in which Anthony Rowland-Jones's assistance has been crucial, hope that it will become a lodestar in the recorder world and have a long and companionable life. The book is dedicated to Walter Bergmann, for his musicianship, his generosity of spirit and his idealism.

JOHN MANSFIELD THOMSON
Wellington, New Zealand, September 1994

Acknowledgements

Many people in various parts of the world have given generous help in all aspects of this book. Both Anthony Rowland-Jones and myself owe a particular debt of gratitude to a mutual friend, the late Walter Bergmann, whose fine collection of pictures was made available to us by his daughter Erica Bendix. We thank Bruce Robertson of the Media Production Division of Anglia Polytechnic University at Cambridge for his skill and artistry in processing photographs, also Tony Bingham, Bruce Phillips of Oxford University Press, Bernard Thomas and Professor Peter Walls of the School of Music, Victoria University of Wellington, New Zealand. Dr Victoria Cooper and Penny Souster, our editors at Cambridge University Press, have been extremely supportive. Lisa Larkendale, my research assistant and secretary, not only managed a voluminous correspondence but read the entire volume and made a number of valuable suggestions. We gratefully acknowledge the assistance of the British Council in New Zealand and would also like to thank Anthony Goff of David Higham Ltd., London.

A note on terminology

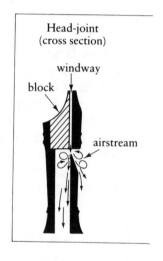

Head-joint
(cross section)

windway

block

airstream

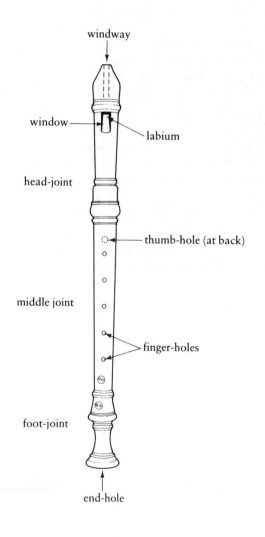

windway

window ——— labium

head-joint

thumb-hole (at back)

middle joint

finger-holes

foot-joint

end-hole

The parts of a recorder

There is an excellent short account of the design, characteristics and acoustics of recorders in Chapter 3 of Eve O'Kelly's *The Recorder Today* (Cambridge 1990) from which, with her permission, the above diagram is taken. This gives the names used in this book for the parts of the instrument; the end-hole is also called the 'bell hole'.

The soprano size of recorder is generally referred to as 'descant', and the alto size as 'treble', in accordance with normal British usage.

Larger sizes of renaissance-model recorders often have a perforated box or 'fontanelle' to protect the key-work for the bottom finger-hole. Some renaissance and early baroque recorders have a 'flared bell' or expansion of the instrument at its foot, not necessarily reflected in the bore design.

The presence of the thumb-hole and a hole or holes for the bottom little finger is regarded as a *sine qua non*. However, in his book *Music in the Middle Ages* (London 1941), p. 328, Gustave Reese confusingly says 'The long flute – the *flûte douce* in France, recorder in England, *blockflöte* in Germany – was a whistle-flute with a softer tone [than the rather shrill small whistle-flute] and usually with six holes'. This common instrument is referred to in the present book as a 'six-holed pipe' or 'flageolet'. Following Jeremy Montagu's terminology, the instruments of the fixed windway flute family as a whole are called 'duct flutes'.

For a full account of the physical processes which determine the recorder's sound, see *The Acoustics of the Recorder* by John Martin (Celle, Moeck, 1994).

1 The recorder in the Middle Ages and the Renaissance

HOWARD MAYER BROWN

The study of the early history of an instrument must begin with two simple questions: how early was it commonly used, and what sort of music did it play? If we concentrate our attention on the music that interests us the most – the fixed and written repertoires of European art music – we can ask a series of even more specific questions. Was the recorder ever included in performances of the kinds of music collected in thirteenth-, fourteenth- and fifteenth-century manuscripts? If so, when did it begin to be used regularly? Was it seen to be appropriate for all kinds of music or only for a certain portion? Who normally played the recorder? Was it used alone or with other instruments (and if so, which)? Such questions are easy to ask but not so easy to answer, for there is scarcely any literature before the sixteenth century dealing directly with them, or with the technical and musical aspects of the recorder's construction, playing technique or repertoire. Our answers must be based on circumstantial evidence, most of it taken from literary works of the imagination or pictures. Both kinds of information are enormously useful, but each has serious shortcomings. Literary works at times do not mean precisely what they say, and in any case it is not always a straightforward task to associate a particular technical word (such as 'flute') with a specific instrument. Pictures, on the other hand, hardly ever produce tangible and unambiguous evidence about the repertoires instruments played, and in the case of the recorder, the task of evaluating the evidence is complicated by the fact that one long tube looks much like another, and so there are inevitable questions about whether some of the pictures of wind instruments are in fact supposed to represent recorders, shawms or even trumpets (see the frontispiece and pls. 1–3 for problems of identification).

There can be no doubt that fipple flutes (or 'duct flutes' as Jeremy Montagu insists on calling them)[1] were known in the thirteenth and fourteenth centuries. Guillaume de Machaut, for example, enumerates a number of various kinds in his two long lists of instruments, in *La Prise d'Alexandrie* and *Remede de Fortune* (c1330?).[2] He clearly

Plate 1 Detail from the bottom of the circle of angel-musicians surrounding the Virgin in an *Assumption of the Virgin* probably painted about 1340 by an anonymous Sienese artist at Avignon, as it shows traces of the influence of Simone Martini. It has at times been attributed to Lippo Memmi, and to Gualtieri di Giovanni da Pisa who was active in Siena between 1380 and 1445. (Alte Pinakothek, Munich) See p. 5.

differentiated the *flute traverseinne* from the *flute dont droit joues* (a descriptive phrase that can only refer to a duct flute). He included as well a number of other sorts of duct flutes in his lists: *flajos, flajos de Scens, fistule, pipe, fretiaus, flëuste brehaingne,* and *muse de Scens, muse d'Aussay* and *muse de blef* (if the last three are in fact whistle flutes and not types of bagpipes). There are at least two major problems, however, in interpreting his list. In the first place, it is not clear whether he meant each of the instruments to be a distinctively separate type. Would a fourteenth-century musician really know the difference between a *fistule,* a *pipe* and a *fretiaus*? Was there a clear distinction between a *muse de Scens* and a *muse d'Aussay*? Is it possible that a 'Bohemian flute' (if that is, in fact, what *flëuste brehaingne* means) and a *flute traverseinne* are not completely different instruments, but simply two separate terms for the same instrumental type? Machaut, after all, regularly used as a standard rhetorical device, presumably for the sake of elegant variation, two more or less synonymous terms one after the other, as for example when he described his lady in the *Remede de Fortune* as someone who heals and restores his troubles, sorrows, afflictions and misfortunes:

> Ma dame, qui rest et qui ponse
> Mes mauls, mes annuis, mes durtes
> Et toutes mes maleurtes.[3]

   More important, it seems likely that Machaut's lists were not intended to be accurate reflections of musical practice, but instead offered a comprehensive catalogue of all the instruments the poet knew, simply as a rhetorical gesture of exuberance. On the one hand, it is true that Machaut offers us a social context for all these instruments. They are, according to him, those the minstrels played during and after banquets, the principal venues for courtly music-making in the late Middle Ages and the Renaissance. On the other hand, there is precious little corroborating evidence for the presence of some of the kinds of duct flutes and reed pipes – if we can even begin to guess what they might have been – at courtly functions in the fourteenth century. Therefore, it is at least possible that Machaut was engaging in literary hyperbole by naming all the instruments he knew in order to give us as vivid an impression as possible of the great luxury and variety of music-making at the courts of the very rich or noble.
   Whatever their meaning, Machaut's lists include many more duct flutes than we can trace in Italy during the fourteenth century. We have some idea of the Italian instrumentarium of that period by conflating various sources that appear to be at least partly comprehensive in intention: the instruments enumerated in the room of the palace set aside for music in the anonymous poem 'L'Intelligenza';[4] the instruments pictured in those trecento paintings that show crowds of angels adoring Christ or the Virgin Mary;[5] and the portrait of Landini which heads his madrigal 'Musica son' in the early fifteenth-century Squarcialupi Codex, and which appears to offer a conspectus of the kinds of instruments the artist would have included under the rubric 'Musica' (pl. 2A).[6] These Italian sources seem to show that (1) the only soft winds known in Italy until the very end of the century were short pipes played with tabors, and double pipes,[7] and (2) that recorders began to appear regularly in paintings only at and after the end of the fourteenth century, as one among the many kinds of instruments played by angels, and perhaps as one of those associated with Lady Music and Landini in the Squarcialupi Codex.[8]

We may even be able to document a little more closely the introduction of recorder-like duct flutes into Italian paintings, if not into Italian musical life. Their earliest depiction may be the anonymous Sienese *Assumption of the Virgin*, now in the Alte Pinakothek in Munich, dated about 1340, a detail of which is shown in Plate 1. Art historians seem to agree that it was painted by a follower of Simone Martini, who worked during those years in Avignon, and that it is the earliest surviving work to show the Assumption with a circle of musical angels surrounding Mary. The image was copied a number of times by later Sienese artists, but in most of the later paintings the instrument played by the angel in the right centre was badly copied or was transformed into something else (as though the Italian artists did not quite know what the original instrument was).[9]

It may be that Machaut included in his list of instruments suitable for courtly banquets (and played by minstrels) all those he knew, including the ones associated with shepherds and peasants. Even so, the comparison between Machaut and the Italians suggests two things: recorders (as well as transverse flutes) might have been known in France in the fourteenth century and not in Italy, and (2) there is little

Plates 2A and 2B   Problems of identification (opposite)
Plate 2A   The two details are from the foot of f. 121v and f. 195v of the Squarcialupi Codex, compiled around 1415–20. These two folios both show at their lower left-hand corners three instruments which look like recorders. The upper detail, which is from the first folio of the section of the Codex devoted to the music of Landini (c1325–97), has three instruments of equal size, while in the lower detail one of them is smaller, perhaps just to fit the space. On the Landini folio the artist illuminated the three instruments in gold and marked their windows and finger-holes in pen. Unfortunately, with the passage of time the black ink has almost rubbed off the gold surface. However, f. 195v, which starts a section of the Codex prepared for the music of another organist, Magister Johannes of Florence, has duct flutes without gilding, and dancers with two shawm players take the place of Lady Music. Each pipe has six holes, so these are not recorders, although Landini's golden ones may have been – we shall never know whether those critical extra holes were marked in. The Codex contains 354 pieces of secular vocal music from 1340 to 1415, of which 227 are ballatas, and 146 are by Landini. The two organist-composers are both shown playing portative organs, and the surrounds may imply that vocal music of the later thirteenth century which was intabulated for organ may also have been played on a trio of duct flutes, perhaps recorders.

Plate 2B   This figure appears at the bottom right-hand corner of Turino Vanni's *Virgin with Child and Angels* in the National Museum in Palermo. This Pisan artist was known to be active in Sicily from 1390 to 1427, and at first glance this seems to be an early depiction of a recorder, the window being very clear, the shape cylindrical and the hands held in a good thumbing position. Note, however, that the bottom two fingers are *under* the instrument. The right-hand fingers are aligned to the upper four holes. This 'four-plus-two' fingering, which gives good support, was in later baroque times a standard alternative way of playing the six-holed flageolet.

reason to suppose that the recorder played any active role in the performance of written art music before the very late fourteenth or early fifteenth century. There are no literary sources before then known to me that indicate unambiguously the use of recorders in the performance of high art music; and the evidence of the pictures reinforces that conclusion.[10] Some medieval shepherds play duct flutes (or some sort of reed instrument) in paintings and miniatures. A number of angels and minstrels also play double recorders or tabor-pipes. None of these musicians, however, can be associated convincingly with courtly song, let alone polyphonic courtly song.

The situation changes in the fifteenth century, when there is more reason to believe that the recorder began to take some part in the performance of courtly polyphonic music. While the evidence is

Plate 3   Detail (lower part of picture) of Mariotto di Nardo's *Coronation of the Virgin* (Minneapolis Institute of Arts). This Florentine painting has been dated 1408, and is one of the least ambiguous of early fifteenth-century representations of the recorder. The right hand is curiously depicted, but the left hand, with its stretched little finger, is well placed to cover the four lower holes of a recorder. Moreover, the instrument, like the extant Dordrecht recorder which is probably of the same period (see pp. 11 and 29), is cylindrical, but appears to be of alto rather than cantus (or soprano) size. The other two instruments are a large fiddle, bowed, and a psaltery, plucked with both hands – a convincing soft music ensemble.

mostly pictorial, Edgar Hunt cites a number of literary references to the 'recorder' in English literature of the fifteenth century, and he points out that Chaucer's young squire, described as 'singinge ... or floyting al the day' may well have played the recorder.[11] At least one French romance of the fifteenth century strongly suggests that recorders had by then become instruments appropriate for the upper classes to play, and there is surely other such written documentation still to be discovered. In the romance *Cleriadus et Meliadice*, the knight Cleriadus arranges a series of jousts with his fellow courtiers.[12] The losers are put into 'prison', which consists of an elegant large room furnished with all sorts of diversions for them, mostly games of chance and musical instruments, including 'flustes', a word more likely to mean recorders than transverse flutes, tabor-pipes (exclusively minstrels' instruments in the fifteenth century), double pipes (by the time of the romance virtually unknown in western Europe, if Tinctoris is to be believed),[13] or any of the other duct flutes associated with shepherds and peasants.

In contrast to the infrequent and ambiguous literary references, a number of pictures can be found that include what appear to be recorders in connection with courtly situations. Edmund A. Bowles, in his two anthologies of fifteenth-century pictures, reproduces several in which the recorder can be seen in contexts that imply music-making by or for the upper classes.[14] Those that seem to suggest some more or less direct connection with reality include the following: (1) several miniatures showing amorous couples singing and playing instruments, including a scene from the Chigi Codex showing four singers with music sheets and another of two courtly couples playing recorder and lute, and rebec (or small fiddle) and harp,[15] and also a tapestry from about 1500 showing two courtiers playing recorder and dulcimer;[16] (2) a series of boating scenes illustrating May[17] on the calendar pages of Flemish Books of Hours, showing some combination of musicians singing (some with music sheets), and playing recorder (or transverse flute) and lute or even viola da gamba (for one of them, see pl. 4);[18] (3) several scenes showing courtiers entertaining themselves, including a late fifteenth-century tapestry where the emperor and his wife play chess while several courtiers sing (from music sheets) and four play harp, lute, fiddle and a ? recorder (or tenor pipe);[19] and an early sixteenth-century tapestry where one courtly lady sings from a music sheet while two other courtiers play clavichord (!) (or virginals?) and ? recorder (or tenor pipe);[20] (4) a miniature showing the young patrician St Cecilia in her elegant Roman home being entertained by three minstrels with ? recorder (or a shawm played softly), lute and portative organ;[21] (5) a late fifteenth-century illustration of the carole from the *Romance of the Rose*, which in fact seems not to show a carole at all (surely in its primary meaning a line or circle dance) but rather a couple dance, accompanied by pipe and tabor as well as recorder and

Plate 4 The month of May from a calendar in a Flemish Book of Hours from about 1500 in the British Library (MS Add. 24098, f. 22v), one of a number of scenes of boating parties celebrating spring and regeneration – note the branches of new leaves decorating the boat and carried by people on the bridge.

Assuming the second lady in the boat sings, this ensemble is the common one of

harp;[22] (6) a miniature showing the ceremonial entrance into a city by Alexander the Great (as a fifteenth-century ruler), accompanied by a number of musicians including several groupings of recorder and lute or recorder and harp;[23] and (7) a copy of the statutes of a German university regulating students' music-making and illustrated by a drawing of two students playing lute and recorder (pl. 5).[24]

In these pictures the recorder is played either by well-born ladies and gentlemen or else by the sorts of minstrels who specialised in soft instruments and were hired either as household musicians to the nobility or as free-lance musicians. There is every reason to believe that the repertoires of the two kinds of players, both amateur and professional, overlapped in significant ways even if minstrels also could play music (and especially improvised or otherwise unwritten music) inaccessible or inappropriate for the well-born amateur. Our definition of what constitutes 'courtly' music should accordingly be broad enough to include both the music played by the upper classes and also the music played for them by professionals in upper-class contexts.

Almost all of the fifteenth-century pictures reproduced by Bowles depict scenes where the recorder is combined with harp, lute or fiddle, or some combination of the last three that served as the principal soft instruments for the performance of upper-class music throughout the fourteenth and fifteenth centuries. Indeed, the evidence of the pictures inclines me to believe that the recorder was one of the main new instruments added to the list of those suitable for upper-class amateurs in the fifteenth century,[25] and that professionals as well as amateurs began to play it regularly when they took part in entertainments at banquets, weddings and other upper-class celebrations. If my assessment is correct and the pictures do in fact reflect reality, then a single recorder was most often used in combination with other instruments. Given the ranges of recorders in comparison with those of harps, lutes and fiddles, the wind instrument must normally have played the top line of the texture, while the stringed instruments must usually have taken over the responsibility for the lower lines. That generalisation is surely oversimple, and needs to be tested picture by picture and piece by piece, and yet it must also contain at least a grain of truth, numerous exceptions notwithstanding. Moreover, the combination of a single

voice, recorder or flute (here a tenor recorder) and a plucked instrument, usually a lute (see pls. 15B and 22, and p. 32). These well-to-do citizens would be performing a chanson with the singer on the top part, the recorder playing the tenor line, and the lute plucking the contratenor (Bowles, *Pratique*, pl. 108). There is an almost identical Bruges miniature by Simon Bening (1483–1561) in a Book of Hours (c1540) in the Bibliothèque Royale at Brussels, but the gentleman there plays a flute, not a recorder.

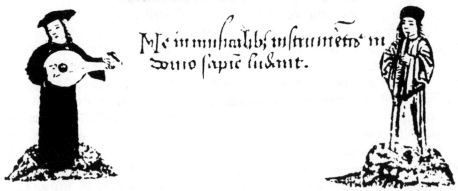

Plate 5 Student musicians at the foot of a page (f. 34v) of the Statutes of the Collegium Sapientiae in Freiburg im Breisgau, Germany. These date from 1497 (from Freiburg University Archives, Coll. Sap. 2a). The recorder is clearly in the tenor range. The other student plays a lute. (Bowles, *Musikleben*, pl. 144)

recorder with one or more stringed instruments or voices continues to be seen in sixteenth-century pictures, notably the boating parties illustrating the month of May in the calendars of Flemish Books of Hours. Such a combination can be inferred, too, from the frescoes by Francesco Cossa (1436–78) in the Palazzo Schifanoia in Ferrara, where one lady among the group of courtiers gathered together beneath the three Graces holds two recorders, while two other courtiers each hold lutes;[26] and from a mid-sixteenth-century Venetian painting now in Bourges showing three evidently well-born ladies and a gentleman playing out of doors, presumably for their own amusement, in an ensemble that consists of virginals and lute, bass viol and recorder (pl. 6B). A companion painting shows a similar group (or possibly even the same one) singing from part-books (pl. 6A).[27] If the two pictures in Bourges can be read to imply that the players and the singers are performing the same or a similar repertoire, we can imagine the instrumentalists playing a mid-sixteenth-century madrigal or chanson, with the outer voices taken by recorder and viol, and the entire polyphonic texture simulated by virginals and lute, a proto-baroque scoring not uncommon in the sixteenth century.

However normal such groupings continued to be, combining recorders in consort with each other appears to have been the principal new (or newly prominent) way to use the instruments in the sixteenth century. To be sure, there are some indications that recorder consorts were known already in the fifteenth century. It is at the very least suggestive that those wind instruments that might be recorders on the Landini page of the Squarcialupi Codex are shown there as a set of three, distinct from the set of three shawms which also appear on that page (see pl. 2A); and several Flemish and German paintings of the fifteenth century that show crowds of angels praising the Virgin Mary in Heaven include trios of recorders[28] (for one of them, see pl. 7, and, for an early sixteenth-century example, pl. 12).

The nature of the evidence about the character of the recorder and the way it was used changes radically in the sixteenth century, for we are no longer dependent solely on secondary sources that only incidentally reveal musical practices. Inventories of various collections, such as those of King Henry VIII of England (himself an avid recorder player), the Austrian Archduke Ferdinand, various other princes or wealthy collectors, and the Accademia Filarmonica of Verona, inform us about the number of recorders thought to be necessary for a musical establishment, from which we can infer how common they were, where and how they were used, and how they related to other instruments in regular use at that time.[29] Most of the inventories list recorders in cases of four or more instruments, suggesting they were made and tuned together for playing in consort. Actual instruments also survive, which allow us to examine at first hand how they were built and how they sound. Museums in Verona, Vienna and Brussels, for example, own unusually good sixteenth-century examples.[30] The earliest recorders to survive, however, one a fragment from fourteenth-century Würzburg, and another, almost entire, from fifteenth-century Dordrecht (see p. 29), may have been instruments more appropriate for simple tunes and folk music than for composed art music.[31]

In addition, a number of treatises appeared in the sixteenth century that offer technical information about the form and playing technique of the instrument. Martin Staehelin has described the earliest known treatise on the recorder, a manuscript booklet of five leaves, now in the Universitätsbibliothek in Basel, probably written out for the fifteen-year-old Bonifacius Amerbach about 1510.[32] The brief 'Introductio gscriben uf pfifen' includes a picture of a soprano recorder (called a 'Discant') in G (that is, with g as its lowest written note), with its fingerings, a brief explanation of mensural notation, and a series of exercises for the young man to practise. Amerbach's *Introductio* was probably written before Sebastian Virdung's *Musica getutscht* was published in Basel in 1511, for the young Swiss patrician (or his teacher) makes no mention of the printed work, and seems not to have been influenced by it.[33] The two works do not contradict one another, but Virdung includes rather more details about the instrument,

Plates 6A and 6B (opposite).   Musique Champêtre – both 'cantare' (singing) and 'sonare' (playing instruments). These could possibly be the same players in similar out-door settings, and they could perhaps be playing two versions of the same piece of music, although no one has yet succeeded in identifying the indistinct notes and words in the part-books in the upper painting. These pictures are by an anonymous Venetian sixteenth-century artist and, as suggested to me by Anthea Brook of the Courtauld Institute, are in the manner of Bonifazio de' Pitati. They show admirably how natural a step it was from the vocal chanson and madrigal to the instrumental canzona and solo sonata. Perhaps these four patrician players had learnt the music by heart when singing it, and were therefore able to play it instrumentally without music. Note that there is no audience – they are singing and playing just for their own enjoyment (see likewise pls. 4, 11A and B, 20A, 22, 24, etc.). It would be nice to imagine that the lady might have had recorder lessons in Venice from Ganassi (pl. 29), in which case she would have been adept at freely ornamenting her part. (Musée du Berry, Bourges) WB 104 and 27

including pictures of the three sizes that were normally used to play four-part music (with the middle size capable of playing both tenor and alto parts). Virdung also makes clear that the three sizes of recorder had as their nominal lowest notes *F* (for the bass), *c* (for the tenor), and *g* (for the soprano), although they sounded an octave higher (*f*, *c'* and *g'*). This was the disposition of the recorder consort that seems to have been standard throughout the sixteenth century.

Virdung's chief aim in publishing his little book was to explain to students and amateurs what instruments were called and how they looked, and also to instruct his readers in how to intabulate music for the three instruments (one from each of three principal families) he chose to write about in detail: clavichord (stringed keyboard), lute (fretted string) and recorder (wind with finger-holes). With each instrument, he offers a tablature notation. He may have invented himself the number tablature he presents in connection with the recorder, one that seems never to have been widely adopted. Moreover, for the purpose of his demonstration, Virdung did not feel the necessity either to supply pictures that are technically correct or intabulations that can actually be played.[34]

The German schoolmaster Martin Agricola used Virdung as a model for his own *Musica instrumentalis deudsch*, published in Wittenberg in 1529 and then re-issued in extensively revised form in 1545, but Agricola's treatise is much more practical in its orientation, directed as it is towards the needs of German schoolboys.[35] *Musica instrumentalis deudsch* offers much more detailed information about all of the instruments in common use in Germany in the early sixteenth century, although in his section on recorders Agricola tells us little more than Virdung. The Wittenberg schoolmaster explains the basic sizes of the instruments and how they are fingered; he adds a few details about their playing technique; and he makes explicit the connection (mostly the similarity of fingerings) between the recorder and other fingered winds, such as the cornetto and the crumhorn.

Plate 7 Detail of some of the angel-instrumentalists in the *Coronation of the Virgin* painted in Cologne about 1463 by the Master of the Lyversberger Passion (active *c*1460–1490). At that period recorders were commonly played as a trio (see pls. 2A, 12 and 13, and p. 37); this is not simply an emblem of the Trinity. Appropriately, the recorders' neighbours are plucked-string instruments, here citterns. (Alte Pinakothek, Munich) WB 58–9

The most advanced and sophisticated of all the sixteenth-century treatises on the recorder was the next to be published, Sylvestro di Ganassi dal Fontego's *Fontegara*, issued in Venice in 1535.[36] Ganassi, a member of the official wind band of the Venetian state, was patently a better musician than a writer. Some passages in his treatises are difficult to understand, but he raises questions of real interest to musicians, far beyond the elementary explanations of Virdung and Agricola. His is a book that should be studied carefully by all wind players. *Fontegara*, along with Ganassi's two-volume treatise on viol playing, the *Regola rubertina* (1542–3), form the best starting point for any serious study of sixteenth-century performance practice. In *Fontegara*, Ganassi purports to explain how the player must learn to control his breath, his tongue and his fingers. He is especially interesting for what he has to say about articulations (and hence about how to phrase), and for his tables of ornamentation. From Ganassi, we learn how much attention sensitive musicians paid to the number of different ways a player can attack and leave a note, and we can infer from what he writes that every note in even the fastest passage-work was articulated (a view of the way sixteenth-century music was played that is supported by various musicians later in the century). Moreover, it is clear from *Fontegara* that Ganassi and his contemporaries quite regularly ornamented the music they played with divisions or *passaggi* of the most exuberant flamboyance.

Ganassi has nothing to say, unfortunately, about the differences between simple and elaborate ornamentation. It would be helpful for us to know the circumstances when one or the other would have been required, desirable or even merely tolerated according to the tastes of the time; but he makes no distinction, as so many later sixteenth-century writers did, between the more subdued practice of lightly ornamenting consort music and the greater freedom to embellish allowed a soloist.[37] By far the largest amount of space in his treatise is devoted to details about ornamentation, which suggest a high level of extravagant embellishment in a remarkably rhythmically free manner. Indeed, Ganassi reminds us that ornamentation plays a very large role in the elementary technical training of the instrumental musician, and that many of the treatises, including Ganassi's own, were in fact intended to teach their readers the rudiments of performance in general, and not merely one specialised technique.

After Virdung, Agricola and Ganassi, treatises on performance, and especially on ornamentation, appeared irregularly throughout the sixteenth century. Only Philibert Jambe de Fer's *Epitome musical* in Lyons in 1556 gives some elementary technical information about the recorder.[38] The others – notably those by Dalla Casa (1584), Rogniono (1592), Conforto (1593), Bovicelli (1594) and Bassano (1585 and 1591)[39] – are devoted principally to an exposition of the techniques of ornamenting the written notes; their precepts may be adapted for use by recorder players, but their authors make little distinction between vocal and instrumental embellishment, and give very little space to the question of differences in ornamenting technique among various instruments. Relevant, too, to any study of the recorder in the Renaissance are several seventeenth-century treatises, among them Aurelio Virgiliano's useful manuscript *Il Dolcimelo* (*c*1600), Michael Praetorius's monumental three-volume *Syntagma musicum* (Wittenberg and Wolfenbüttel 1614–18), Pierre Trichet's erudite (but not very practical) manuscript *Traité des instruments de musique* (after 1630), Marin Mersenne's *Harmonie universelle* (Paris, 1636–7) and even Bartolomeo Bismantova's *Compendio musicale* of 1677.[40]

Recorder consorts appear to have been a pan-European phenomenon in the sixteenth century. By implication, the German writers Virdung and Agricola seem to imply that the recorder was normally played in consort, if only because they both describe the three principal sizes which they explain as appropriate for normal four-part music, and because their discussion seems to take for granted that the tenor recorder plays tenor and alto parts and the bass, bass parts. The impression that consort playing was common in Italy as well is reinforced by the frontispiece of Ganassi's *Fontegara* (pl. 29), which shows two youths and a man playing recorders (a tenor and two basses?) from part-books, while a fourth person sings (evidently sharing his part-book with one of the tenor recorder players) and a fifth man directs (he holds a small recorder, probably a soprano, and he may also sing from the cantus part-book). A French consort of four recorders of various sizes decorates the title page of a collection of dance choreographies probably published in Lyons by Jacques Moderne in the 1530s (pl. 8).[41]

That the Spanish also played recorders in consorts in the sixteenth century is demonstrated by the archival notices published by Robert Stevenson.[42] A regular band of instrumentalists was hired to play at sacred services in some Spanish cathedrals as early as the 1530s. They were expected to play from written notes, as is clear from the number of notices recording purchases of volumes of motets or even Masses for their use. Although they are normally listed as shawm or sackbut players, it is clear from some of the notices that they were also expected to play recorders. Thus, the chapter in Seville asked one of its canons to buy a new chest of recorders in 1565 unless he found that the old set could still be used after repairs were made; and in 1586 the choirmaster Francisco Guerrero set down rules for the instrumentalists at the cathedral of Seville to observe about where and when they could embellish their parts (the most important of them being that the two treble players should not both do so simultaneously, lest harsh dissonances result), and he made clear that recorder consorts were to perform regularly at solemn sacred services.[43]

Some anthologies of music printed in the sixteenth century state that they are suitable for instrumental ensemble. Girolamo Scotto, for example, indicated on the title page of the first volume of Nicolas Gombert's four-part motets, published in Venice about 1539, that they were appropriate for 'lyribus maioribus ac tibiis imparibus', instruments I would identify as viols and recorder consorts (interpreting 'large lyres' as the Latin equivalent of *violoni*; and 'tibiis imparibus' as consorts since the instruments are said to be of unequal sizes), although Scotto might have intended a more general meaning of 'strings and winds'.[44] Giovan Tomaso Cimello suggests that his first book of four-part madrigals, published by Gardano in 1548, would include all the information necessary to play the compositions on instruments, or to

Plate 8   A four-part recorder consort plays basse danses – 'some well known and some not as you can see inside', this being the title page of a book probably published by Jacques Moderne in Lyons in the 1530s. It is revealing of performance practice of that time and place that a recorder consort is shown playing the music. This early representation of a recorder quartet (compare it with pl. 14) is all the more interesting as the instruments seem to be treble, two tenors and a basset bass (a 'direct-blow' model). Renaissance basses were also played with a crook or 'bocal' as is shown in a French woodcut of *c*1570 on p. 96 of Georg Kinsky's *A History of Music in Pictures* (London, Dent, 1930). From Howard Mayer Brown and Joan Lascelle's *Musical Iconography* (Cambridge, Mass., 1972, and Oxford 1973), p. 89 – see *Early Music* 2/1 (Jan. 1974), pp. 41, 43 and 45. The original is in the Bibliothèque Nationale, Paris.

perform them in combinations of voices and instruments. His title page states that the volume would supply 'le più necessarie osservanze instromentali, e più convenevoli avvertenze de toni accio si possano anchora sonare, et cantare insieme'.[45] The volume does not live up to its promise – it contains no such information – but at least it reveals that similar kinds of performances were envisaged at that time.

Chansons, too, were published in anthologies that suggested they were appropriate for performance by either voices or instruments. Tielman Susato of Antwerp, for example, quite regularly described the contents of his anthologies of chansons as 'convenables et propices a jouer de tous instrumens' (or something similar).[46] And Pierre Attaingnant of Paris published two collections in which the tables of contents indicate which compositions are best for recorder consorts, which for flute consorts, and which can be played by either kind of ensemble.[47] His advice about which sorts of instruments to use appears to depend on the ranges of the voices in particular compositions, and whether or not they place emphasis on notes difficult to play in tune. Obviously, Attaingnant had a didactic intent in aiding his readers to make the best use of the music he offered them. The implication seems to me inescapable that he supposed all the anthologies of chansons he published to be appropriate for instrumental consorts, and especially those of flutes or recorders, even though none of his other collections singles out particular instruments in this way (except, of course, for his volumes of music for keyboard instruments and lutes, which required special parts that combine all of the voices of a composition into a kind of short score).

From the clues given us by Attaingnant and the other sixteenth-century publishers, it seems clear that consorts of recorders, like all other instrumental ensembles of the period, regularly performed a repertoire that consisted in the main of vocal compositions, in all known genres. The evidence suggests that recorder players, like those of viols, transverse flutes, lutes, keyboard instruments, and even shawms and sackbuts, mostly played motets, chansons, madrigals, Lieder, and even Mass movements. To this central core they added a much smaller repertoire of autonomous pieces – preludes, fantasias, ricercars and the like – especially from the 1530s and 40s on, when composers began to write instrumental music in imitation of vocal styles.

In addition, of course, professional ensembles of minstrels earned an important part of their living by playing dance music. While much of this repertoire was improvised or at least not written down, a large number of dances survive, some of them probably intended for an audience of amateurs, so that they could perform themselves the music they had found attractive on social occasions. Such collections were published by Attaingnant in Paris, Jacques Moderne in Lyons, Pierre Phalèse in Louvain and Tielman Susato in Antwerp, among others.[48]

In England, Anthony Holborne's collection of pavans, galliards and other dances, published in 1599, was intended for 'viols, violins or other musicall winde instruments', that is, for either strings or winds, suggesting that idiomatic distinctions among various kinds of instruments were either unknown in the sixteenth century, or at least not yet fully exploited by composers.[49] That conclusion appears to be challenged by another English collection published in 1599, the same year as Holborne's: Thomas Morley's *First Booke of Consort Lessons*.[50] It, too, consists mostly of dances (along with some ballad tunes), arranged for the fixed combination, apparently unique to England, of lute (playing mostly fast passage-work), pandora, cittern, bass and treble viols, and 'flute'. Scholars do not agree on whether Morley's 'flute' meant recorder or traverso, or either, but in any case, Morley's collection, along with Philip Rosseter's *Consort Lessons* of 1609,[51] contradicts the idea that sixteenth-century music for instrumental ensemble did not take into account the idiomatic capabilities of each instrument. The apparent disinterest in making distinctions between the kinds of music appropriate for strings and winds, or recorders and viols – which we suppose to be a characteristic of sixteenth-century composers because of the number of volumes said to be appropriate for various kinds of consorts – may in any case be deceptive. In arranging 'vocal' music for their own purposes, and in devising appropriate ornamentation, performers surely took advantage of the special qualities of their own instruments, and indeed of their own musical personalities. In this respect, we ought certainly to imagine a contrast between what we see on the page and what sixteenth-century listeners actually heard.

The proliferation of ornamenting treatises in the second half of the sixteenth century suggests that virtuoso instrumentalists flourished then, soloists capable of playing the most flamboyant passage-work, and interested more in displaying their own skills than in revealing in performance the intentions of the composers. Various writers of the late sixteenth century complain about the emphasis placed on virtuosity in singing, and various composers of the time criticise singers for the way they distort the written music.[52] A number of treatises describe the way an ensemble should lightly embellish the polyphony they played, each part adding modest *passaggi* no more than four or five times in the course of a composition of moderate length, with the bass having the fewest and the top line the most opportunities for embellishment. Writers agree that the more important cadences ought to be decorated, a precept that seems to have as much force as the baroque convention of adding trills to leading notes at cadences. Many treatises of the later sixteenth century also spend considerable space in explaining how soloists might add much more elaborate *passaggi* to the compositions they play, simply in order to demonstrate their virtuosity. Most such treatises, if they single out particular kinds of performers, mention singers and players of viol and cornetto, but there is every reason to suppose that their rules apply to recorder players as well, especially since the earliest tables of elaborate ornamentation to appear in print where those in Ganassi's treatise on the recorder, the *Fontegara* of 1535. The desire on the part of performers to astound listeners with their virtuosity seems to have grown in the later sixteenth century, and even in the absence of tangible evidence, we can imagine that recorder players were as affected as every other sort of instrumentalist. Certainly, the collection of pieces for solo descant recorder in *c″* by the blind carillon player of Utrecht, Jacob van Eyck, *Der fluyten lust-hof*, published in Amsterdam around 1644–c1655, demonstrates a continuing interest in virtuoso display.[53] Van Eyck's sets of variations on Dutch, English, French and Italian songs reveal a highly developed technique for applying ingenious passage-work over a given melody, and require extraordinarily nimble fingers to perform.

In sum, it would appear that the recorder was not regularly used in the performance of written music of high culture before the fifteenth century (a tendentious statement that should continue to be discussed and debated during the coming decades). At that time the recorder first begins to appear as an instrument appropriate both for members of the upper classes and also for those minstrels specialising in soft instruments who entertained them. Presumably both groups used the recorder in the performance of the same repertoire of secular music. From pictorial evidence, it would appear that in performances a single recorder was most often combined with harp, psaltery, lute or fiddle, hitherto the principal soft instruments used for courtly music (see pls. 11A and B).

In the sixteenth century, a single recorder continued to be combined with strings and keyboards, but the characteristically new way of using the instrument was in combination with other recorders of various sizes as a consort. Evidence for the prevalence of recorder consorts comes not only from pictures and treatises, but also from the music books themselves. It seems clear that they were capable of playing all genres of vocal as well as autonomous instrumental music and also dances. To judge from instruction books on how to embellish written music, especially those from the second half of the sixteenth century, some players of wind instruments – including almost certainly recorders – developed their virtuosity to a high degree, though on occasion at the expense of the composer.

The Renaissance can be said to close when recorders ceased to be played in consorts. The Roman nobleman Vincenzo Giustiniani, in his

Discorso sopra la musica of 1628, offers us a personal view of the change that took place at the beginning of the seventeenth century when he writes:

Formerly the pastime of a concert of Viols or Flutes was much in vogue, but in the end it was discontinued because of the difficulty of keeping the instruments in tune ... and of getting together the many persons to make up the concert. Then, too, experience has shown that such diversion, with the uniformity of sound and of the consonances, became tiresome rather quickly and was an incentive to sleep rather than to pass the time on a warm afternoon.[54]

By this time the era of the solo sonata had begun, and the Renaissance was over.

Notes

1. See the review of *The New Grove* by Jeremy Montagu in *Early Music* 9 (1981), pp. 513–17, where he rejects the term 'fipple flute'. The best history of the recorder remains Edgar Hunt, *The Recorder and its Music*, rev. edn (London 1977).
2. One list appears in a modern edition in Machaut, *La Prise d'Alexandrie*, ed. M. L. De Mas Latrie (Geneva 1877), pp. 35–6, and the other is in a modern edition in Machaut, *Le Jugement du roy de Behaigne* and *Remede de Fortune*, ed. James I. Wimsatt and William W. Kibler (with English translation) (Athens, Ga., and London 1988), pp. 390–1.
   On these lists, see also Joscelyn Godwin, ' "Mains divers acors": some instrument collections of the ars nova period', *Early Music* 5 (1977), pp. 148–59. For other late medieval lists of instruments, see the studies cited in Howard Mayer Brown, '[Medieval] instruments', in *The New Grove Handbooks in Music: Performance Practice: Music Before 1600*, ed. H. M. Brown and Stanley Sadie (London 1989), p. 32, note 6.
3. This example, picked at random from among many similar examples, appears in Machaut, *Remede*, pp. 374–5.
4. 'L'Intelligenza' has most recently been published in a modern edition in *Poemetti del duecento: Il tesoretto, Il fiore, L'intelligenza*, 2nd edn, ed. G. Pegronio (Turin 1967). The passage describing instruments is also in *Poeti minori del trecento*, ed. N. Sapegno (Milan 1952), pp. 650–1, and in *La cronaca fiorentina ... e l'Intelligenza*, ed. D. Carbone (Florence 1871), pp. 196–7.
5. On the instruments seen in pictures with crowds of angels, see H. M. Brown, 'Trecento angels and the instruments they play', in *Modern Musical Scholarship*, ed. Edward Olleson (Stocksfield 1980), pp. 112–40. For brief descriptions of trecento paintings showing musical angels, see H. M. Brown, 'Corpus of trecento pictures with musical subject matter', *Imago musicae* 1 (1984), pp. 189–243 (Instalment 1), and in the following volumes: 2 (1985), pp. 179–281 (Instalment 2); 3 (1986), pp. 103–87 (Instalment 3); and 5 (1988), pp. 167–241 (Instalment 4 – final).
6. Landini's portrait in the Squarcialupi Codex is reproduced, among other places, in *The New Grove*, *The New Oxford Companion to Music* and *Die Musik in Geschichte und Gegenwart*. The composer and Lady Music both play portative organs. In addition, the following instruments are pictured in the margins of the page: lute, gittern, rebec, harp, psaltery, three recorders or pipes and three shawms.
7. For pictures of trecento pipes and tabors, see Brown, 'Corpus', nos. 167, 208, 217,

219, 316, 325, 350, 355, 510, 535–6, 643 and 685; for pictures of double pipes, see Brown, 'Corpus', nos. 8, 14, 16, 27, 34, 36, 41, 45, 81, 100, 110, 112, 123–4, 126, 143–5, 175, 188, 192, 208, 213, 217, 219, 225, 228, 237, 243, 283, 291, 297, 312, 316, 321, 336, 340, 350, 355, 357, 362, 379, 398, 405–9, 417, 421, 431, 436, 452, 473, 486, 489, 494, 499, 510, 512, 516, 518, 522–3, 536, 540, 552, 573, 637–9, 663, 665, 685 and 688. A few manuscript illuminations show trecento shepherds or peasants with duct flutes, but they are most commonly depicted holding or playing bagpipes.

8. Recorders are pictured among the angels in the late fourteenth- or early fifteenth-century paintings listed in Brown, 'Corpus', as nos. 167, 215, 217, 219, 286, 315–16, 325, 379, 452, 529, 540, 633 and 658. [A further example is the altarpiece by Pere Serra, the frontispiece of this book. Jaime and Pere Serra were influenced by Sienese painters, including Simone Martini and others who worked at Avignon, and perhaps the recorder was invented in the sophisticated musical ambience of the papal court there. Pere Serra is noted for his realism and accuracy, and subject to two uncertainties this may be the earliest representation in art of a recorder. Pere Serra's *retablos* were painted in and around Barcelona between 1363 and 1405; there are, however, no records of payment for the Tortosa altarpiece which would have given an exact date, such as is the case with his great altarpiece of 1394 in Manresa Cathedral. Nevertheless, the art historian Rosa Alcoy believes on stylistic grounds that it preceded the Manresa altarpiece. It probably therefore dates from about 1390. The other uncertainty is that it is always difficult to tell whether a cylindrical duct flute in a picture is a recorder or a six-holed pipe, although here the hand positions, remarkably similar (though 'left-hand down') to those illustrated much later in Hotteterre's recorder tutor of 1707 (see p. 127), are perfect for recorder playing, allowing coverage of the octaving thumb-hole which, together with bottom little-finger holes, differentiates recorders from other duct flutes. The recorder was a remarkable innovation in duct-flute design, for the complication of having to use two more holes, including a thumb-hole, did not result in any increase in the instrument's range or improvement in its tone – what it achieved was that high notes could be played more softly (see p. 29). The remaining instruments in this picture are lute, portative organ, psaltery, mandora and harp, creating a credible 'soft music' ensemble. A R-J]

9. On the Munich *Assumption*, which has been attributed to Lippo Memmi (active between 1317 and 1357 in Siena), see the bibliography of studies cited in Brown, 'Corpus', no. 350. On the transformation of the instruments, see Brown, 'Trecento angels', pp. 132–4. On the image and its later history, see Michael Mallory, *The Sienese Painter Paolo di Giovanni Fei (c1345–1411)* (New York 1976), pp. 177–91.

10. On fifteenth-century literary works that may refer to recorders, see notes 12–13 below. The most extensive set of medieval pictures showing musical instruments are those decorating a thirteenth-century copy of Alfonso el Sabios's *Cantigas de Santa Maria*. The miniatures with instruments, reproduced, among other places, in Rosario Alvarez, 'Los instrumentos musicales en los códices Alfonsinos: su tipología, su uso y su origen. Algunos problemas iconográficos', *Revista de musicología* 10 (1987), pp. 15–28, decorate every tenth *cantiga*: those praising the Virgin (as opposed to the majority of poems that recount her miracles). This series of miniatures depicts double 'recorders', and pipes and tabors, and a few other winds that may be duct flutes (though many are supplied with pirouettes, which implies a double reed). Thus, the *Cantigas*, too, appear to uphold the idea that recorders were not used in the performance of courtly song in the late Middle Ages. In any case, it is doubtful that the evidence of the *Cantigas* should be applied to repertoires other than Spanish.

11. See Hunt, *The Recorder and its Music*, pp. 4–5, for several fifteenth-century literary references that may refer to the recorder.

12. See *Cleriadus et Meliadice. Roman en prose du XVe siècle*, ed. Gaston Zink (Geneva and Paris 1984), pp. 224 and 250.

13. See Anthony Baines, 'Fifteenth-century instruments in Tinctoris's *De Inventione et Usu Musicae*', *Galpin Society Journal* 3 (1950), p. 21, who translates Tinctoris's

description of the double tibia: 'Though a single player is sometimes able to perform two parts of a composition on *double tibiae*, these suffice for but few, or rather scarcely any, songs, and they are considered the least perfect [of wind instruments]'. Tinctoris may refer to instruments with reeds rather than ducts.

14. Edmund A. Bowles, *Musikleben im 15. Jahrhundert*, Musikgeschichte in Bildern III/8 (Leipzig 1977), and his bilingual *La pratique musicale au moyen âge / Musical Performance in the Late Middle Ages* (Geneva 1983).
15. Bowles, *Pratique*, pls. 103 and 154.
16. Bowles, *Musikleben*, pl. 80.
17. Sometimes April.
18. Bowles, *Musikleben*, pls. 92 and 93; and Bowles, *Pratique*, pls. 107, 108, 110 and 111. Bowles, *Pratique*, pl. 100, shows a similar scene not taken from the calendar of a Book of Hours.
19. Bowles, *Pratique*, pl. 112.
20. *Ibid.*, pl. 109.
21. *Ibid.*, pl. 76.
22. Bowles, *Musikleben*, pl. 77.
23. *Ibid.*, pl. 22.
24. *Ibid.*, pl. 144.
25. See Howard Mayer Brown, 'Songs after supper: how the aristocracy entertained themselves in the fifteenth century', in *Festschrift for Walter Salmen* (forthcoming), for the suggestion that lutes, harps, psalteries and fiddles were the principal instruments suitable for upper-class amateurs (and minstrels specialising in soft instruments) throughout most of the fifteenth century.
26. Reproduced, among other places, in François Lesure, *Musik und Gesellschaft im Bild* (Cassel and Basel 1966), fig. 76, pp. 174–5. On the frescoes, see also Paolo d'Ancona, *I Mesi di Schifanoia in Ferrara* (Milan 1954), and Kristen Lippincott, 'The frescoes of the Salone dei Mesi in the Palazzo Schifanoia in Ferrara: style, iconography and cultural context', 2 vols. (Ph.D. Diss., U. of Chicago 1987).
27. The two paintings in Bourges, Musée du Berry, are reproduced in Lesure, *Musik und Gesellschaft im Bild*, figs. 11–12, pp. 46–7.
28. Three angels playing recorders can be seen, for example, in the painting of Mary, Queen of Heaven, attributed to the Master of the St Lucy Legend and dated *c*1485, now in Washington, National Gallery of Art. It is reproduced and the music described in Sylvia W. Kenney, *Walter Frye and the Contenance angloise* (New Haven and London 1964), pp. 153–4, pls. 6–8. Plate 7 is a detail of the *Coronation of the Virgin*, dated *c*1463 and attributed to the Master of the Lyversberger Passion, now in the Alte Pinakothek in Munich. See *Alte Pinakothek München: Erläuterungen zu den ausgestellten Gemälden* (Munich 1983), pp. 323–4.
29. Henry VIII's instruments are listed in Canon Francis W. Galpin, *Old English Instruments of Music: Their History and Character*, 4th edn rev. Thurston Dart (London 1965), pp. 215–22. The inventory of the Austrian Archduke's collection at Ambras and several others are printed in Julius Schlosser, *Die Sammlung alter Musikinstrumente* (Vienna 1920; repr. 1974), pp. 11–20. Inventories of the Verona collection may be found in Giuseppe Turrini, *L'Accademia filarmonica di Verona dalla fondazione (Maggio 1543) al 1600 e il suo patrimonio musicale antico*, Atti e Memorie della Accademia di Agricoltura, Scienze e Lettere di Verona, Series 5, vol. 18 (Verona 1941), pp. 26, 88, 134, 180, 187, 199–200; see also Marcello Castellani, 'A 1593 Veronese inventory', *Galpin Society Journal* 26 (1973), pp. 15–24. For other inventories of sixteenth-century collections, see Alfred Berner, 'Instrumentensammlungen', *Die Musik in Geschichte und Gegenwart*, vol. 6, cols. 1297–8, and Laurence Libin, 'Instruments, collections of', *The New Grove Dictionary of Music and Musicians*, vol. 9, p. 253. Anthony Baines, 'Two Cassel inventories', *Galpin Society Journal* 4 (1951), pp. 30–8, includes a further list of sixteenth-century inventories of instruments.
30. The Verona recorders are illustrated in Turrini, *L'Accademia filarmonica*, pl. XXI following p. 242. The Vienna instruments are described in Schlosser, *Die Sammlung alter Musikinstrumente*, pp. 76–80. The Brussels instruments (some of

them from the sixteenth-century Contarini–Correr collection) are described and illustrated in Victor-Charles Mahillon, *Catalogue descriptif et analytique du Musée Instrumental du Conservatoire Royal de Musique de Bruxelles*, 2 vols. (2nd edn Ghent 1893; repr. Brussels 1978), I, pp. 285–92; and in *Catalogue de l'exposition: Instruments de musique des XVIe et XVIIe siècles appartenant au Musée Instrumental de Bruxelles* (Brussels 1972), pp. 120–9. On the character of the early surviving recorders and English flutes, see Robert Marvin, 'Recorders and English flutes in European collections', *Galpin Society Journal* 25 (1972), pp. 30–57.

31. The Dordrecht and Würzburg instruments are listed and briefly described in Frederick Craine, *Extant Medieval Musical Instruments: A Provisional Catalogue by Types* (Iowa City 1972), pp. 39–40, where earlier studies are cited. On these instruments, see also Rainer Weber, 'Recorder finds from the Middle Ages, and results of their reconstruction', *Galpin Society Journal* 29 (1976), pp. 35–41.

32. The *Introductio* is described and three pages reproduced in facsimile in Martin Staehelin, 'Neue Quellen zur mehrstimmigen Musik des 15. und 16. Jahrhunderts in der Schweiz', *Schweizer Beiträge zur Musikwissenschaft*, Series III, 3 (1978), pp. 62–4 and figs. 4–5. See also John Kmetz, *Die Handschriften der Universitätsbibliothek Basel: Katalog der Musikhandschriften des 16. Jahrhunderts* (Basel 1988), pp. 322–4.

33. Virdung's treatise is published in facsimile by Leo Schrade (Cassel 1931) and by Klaus Wolfgang Niemöller (Cassel and Basel 1970).

34. A point made in the introduction to Beth Bullard's English translation, *Musica getutscht: A Treatise on Musical Instruments (1511) by Sebastian Virdung* (Cambridge 1993). In her introduction she cites earlier studies.

35. Both the 1529 and the 1545 editions of Agricola's treatise are published in quasi-facsimile, ed. Robert Eitner, in the series Publikationen älterer praktischer und theoretischer Musikwerke vol. 20 (Leipzig 1896). William E. Hettrick has edited and translated into English *The 'Musica instrumentalis deudsch' of Martin Agricola* (Cambridge 1994).

36. Ganassi's *Opera intitulata Fontegara* (Venice 1535), is published in two facsimile editions (1934 and 1970), translated into German by Hildemarie Peter (Berlin-Lichterfelde, 1956), and into English by Hildemarie Peter and Dorothy Swainson (Berlin-Lichterfelde 1959).

37. On this point, see Howard Mayer Brown, *Embellishing Sixteenth-Century Music* (London 1976).

38. Philibert Jambe de Fer's *Epitome musical des tons, sons et accords, es voix humaines, fleustes d'alleman, Fleustes a neuf trous, Violes, & Violons* (Lyons 1556) is published in facsimile, ed. François Lesure, in *Annales musicologiques* 6 (1958–63), pp. 341–86.

39. Bibliographical citations for these and other treatises may be found in Brown, *Embellishing Sixteenth-Century Music*, p. x; and in *Performance Practice: Music Before 1600*, ed. Brown and Sadie, pp. 267–71.

40. All these seventeenth-century treatises are listed in *Performance Practice: Music Before 1600*, ed. Brown and Sadie, pp. 267–71, except Bismantova's *Compendio*, published in facsimile, ed. Marcello Castellani (Florence 1978). On Bismantova, see also Castellani, 'The *Regola per suonare il Flauto Italiano* by Bartolomeo Bismantova (1677)', *Galpin Society Journal* 30 (1977), pp. 76–85.

41. The title page of *S'ensuyvent plusieurs basses dances tant Communes que Incommunes* (n.p., n.d. [c1530–8]), is reproduced in Howard Mayer Brown and Joan Lascelle, *Musical Iconography: A Manual for Cataloguing Musical Subjects in Western Art Before 1800* (Cambridge, Mass., 1972), pp. 88–9, after the unique copy in the Collection Rothschild of the Bibliothèque Nationale, Paris.

42. Robert Stevenson, *Spanish Cathedral Music in the Golden Age* (Berkeley and Los Angeles 1961), pp. 139, 144, 149, 152, 157, 167, 298 and 302.

43. The chest of recorders is mentioned in Stevenson, *Spanish Cathedral Music*, p. 152. Guerrero's extremely interesting set of rules is printed in English translation, p. 167.

44. The title page of Gombert's volume is given in Nicolas Gombert, *Opera Omnia*, ed. Joseph Schmidt-Görg, vol. 5 (American Institute of Musicology 1961), p. i.
45. The title page of Cimello's volume is given in Emil Vogel, Alfred Einstein, François Lesure and Claudio Sartori, *Bibliografia della musica italiana vocale profana pubblicata dal 1500 al 1700*, 3 vols. (Staderini 1977), vol. I, p. 383, no. 578.
46. See the volumes listed in Ute Meissner, *Der Antwerpener Notendrucker Tylman Susato*, 2 vols. (Berlin 1967), vol. II [1543]^{15}, 1543^{16}, 1544^{Susato}, 1544^{10}, [1544]^{11} and so on.
47. The contents of the volumes are briefly described in Howard Mayer Brown, *Instrumental Music Printed Before 1600: A Bibliography* (Cambridge, Mass., 1965), as 1533^2 and 1533^3, and in Daniel Heartz, *Pierre Attaingnant: Royal Printer of Music: An Historical Study and Bibliographical Catalogue* (Berkeley and Los Angeles 1969), pp. 250–3. On the distinction between the chansons for flutes and those for recorders, see Anne Smith, 'Die Renaissance Querflöte und ihre Musik – Ein Beitrag zur Interpretation der Quellen', *Basler Jahrbuch für Historische Musikpraxis* 2 (1978), pp. 9–76; and Howard Mayer Brown, 'Notes (and transposing notes) on the transverse flute in the early sixteenth century', *Journal of the American Musical Instrument Society* 12 (1986), pp. 5–39.
48. The anthologies of dances for instrumental ensemble published in the sixteenth century are listed and described in Brown, *Instrumental Music*, as 1530^4, 1530^5, [1538]^3, 1547^6, 154?^{6}, 1550^5, 1550^6, 1551^8, 1553^2, 1555^2, 1555^3, 1555^5, 1557^3, 1557^4, 1559^1, 1559^2, 1559^3, 1564^2, 1571^5, [1573]^6, 1578^8, 1583^7, 1589^1, 1590^8, 1596^1, 1597^1, 1597^2, [1598]^7 and 1599^5.
49. The contents are listed in Brown, *Instrumental Music* as 1599^6, and modern editions are cited.
50. The contents are listed in Brown, *Instrumental Music* as 1599^8, and modern editions are cited.
51. On this fragmentary collection, see Ian Harwood, 'Rosseter's *Lessons for Consort*, 1609', *Lute Society Journal* 7 (1965), pp. 15–23. For a modern edition of some of the pieces, see Warwick Edwards (ed.), *Music for Mixed Consort*, Musica Britannica 40 (London 1977), pp. 130–51. On English music for mixed consort, see also Warwick Edwards, 'The sources of Elizabethan consort music' (Ph.D. Diss., U. of Cambridge, 1974). See also pp. 168–9.
52. See Brown, *Embellishing Sixteenth-Century Music*, pp. 73–6.
53. Van Eyck's anthology is published in a modern edition ed. Winfried Michel and Hermann Teske, 3 vols. (Winterthur 1984).
54. The passage is printed in English translation in Carol MacClintock (trans.), *1. Hercole Bottrigari: Il Desiderio.... 2. Vincenzo Giustiniani: Discorso sopra la musica* (American Institute of Musicology 1962), p. 79. See also p. 74.

2 The recorder's medieval and renaissance repertoire: a commentary

ANTHONY ROWLAND-JONES

What is 'repertoire'?

It is difficult to be precise about what constitutes the repertoire of an instrument, particularly a melody instrument such as the recorder. It can be argued that your repertoire is the music that you are able to play, to yourself or to others, and which interests you. But one would not readily accept Stravinsky's *Rite of Spring* as recorder repertoire even though the Cambridge Buskers used to perform a spectacular abbreviated version on a recorder and concertina. At a less bizarre level is Varèse's *Density 21.5* (being intended for a platinum flute) which is played on a tenor recorder – including the final third-octave B – with such aplomb by Walter van Hauwe and his brilliant pupils, as well as Debussy's haunting *Syrinx* flute solo. Some people enjoy playing Mozart and Weber flute music on tenor recorder or voice flute. And can there be a recorder repertoire from a period when the recorder did not exist? 'Interest' is a very subjective criterion. Many consort players are not interested in music later than Bach, or even Gibbons, ignoring a substantial repertoire of twentieth-century re-corder music.

One therefore has to see 'repertoire' as a continuum ranging from the most specific, where the composer intends the recorder rather than any other instrument, to the most far-fetched arrangement. Within this continuum it is possible to identify 'categories' of repertoire, which inevitably overlap:

(1) Designated repertoire. At best this comprises music where the composer has given recorder or 'Flauto' (baroque) as the sole designation. Twentieth-century composers may write music which, with its particular avant-garde effects, cannot be played on any other instrument. More frequently composers – or publishers in order to increase sales – designate the recorder among a range of instruments, although the composer may have had the flute (baroque 'Traversa') or violin in mind when composing the piece.[1]

(2) Probable repertoire. This includes those many cases, especially in eighteenth-century French, early seventeenth-century Italian and sixteenth-century consort music, where a formula implies that the music may be played on any instrument, or, in the Renaissance, instruments or voices (texted or untexted – if they did not know the words renaissance singers could use the six solmisation syllables of the gamut, or just 'la'). Probability is, however, confined by the range of the parts, for the piece may not suit recorders of the period even if transposed, and also by what we know about performance practices from iconographic, literary and other sources.

(3) Extended repertoire. This encompasses music that was probably not originally played on recorders, but which nevertheless sounds right to the player and convincing to a critical and informed audience. It opens up a wide field where the sound of the recorder so resembles that of other instruments that pieces from their repertoire become open to appropriation. The effect of a baroque flute played with precise articulation and a limpid tone-quality is closer to a baroque recorder than to a modern concert flute, and in the later eighteenth century some pieces designated for transverse flute were played on the voice flute in D provided they were not unsuited by range, idiom or technical difficulty.[2] The Amsterdam Loeki Stardust Quartet have recorded a Bach organ fugue (BWV 560)[3] with such consummate qualities of ensemble, articulation, intonation and tone-quality that it is easily mistaken for a performance on a very beautiful pipe-organ, and this same sound is evident in their recording of English renaissance consort music,[4] emphasising that this music is suitable for all kinds of musical instruments. And there could not have been much difference in sound between an early fifteenth-century duct flute with eight holes (i.e. a recorder) and one with six holes, the flageol(l)(e)(t).[5]

(4) 'Arranged' repertoire (which may be without changes from the original notes; or the arrangement could be by the composer himself, or at least known to or permitted by him). This term is used here to cover the considerable part of the recorder's repertoire, drawn from music of any period, where the recorder version, designed primarily for the delectation of recorder players, is manifestly less effective than the composer's conception of the original. On the continuum it clearly overlaps with (3) above, but at the end of the spectrum includes questionable (or downright bad) arrangements perhaps designed for educational purposes.

Medieval music

For the sake of convenience 'medieval' may here be regarded as 'up to about 1400'. The best-known fourteenth-century composers are Guil-laume de Machaut (*c*1300–1377) and Landini (*c*1325–1397); the early renaissance composers Dufay and Binchois were both born about 1400, and Dunstable *c*1390. 'Renaissance' encompasses the fifteenth and sixteenth centuries, although if 'baroque' music is characterised by the regular presence of a thorough or figured accompanying bass line the change in style takes place later in England than in Italy. Italian music of Monteverdi's 'Seconda Prattica' type[6] ('Prima Prattica' being the old polyphony) was being written about 1600, but the polyphonic fantasia persisted in England even up to Henry Purcell's time in 1680.

If 'medieval' means up to the end of the fourteenth century, it has to be assumed that the recorder as such has no medieval repertoire in

Plate 9   A Minnesinger in company with a flute and fiddle (vielle). The Manesse MS from which this illustration comes (f. 423v) is in the University Library of Heidelberg (MS Pal. Germ. 848). It was probably produced at the monastery of Ötenbach near Zurich around 1340, and contains fifty-four songs by the Minnesinger Johannes Hadlaub. Other singers are depicted such as Heinrich Frauenlob (with two vielles, shawm, duct flute and percussion), Reinmar der Udille (with vielle) and Wolfram von Eschembach. While the vielle may have played soft chords during a song, the flute probably only played before, after, and between the verses.

categories (1) and (2) above, as there is no conclusive evidence that it existed much before 1400. The recorder is a sophisticated instrument designed to meet special needs. A three-holed duct flute such as the tabor-pipe can play two octaves by overblowing its fundamentals three times, inevitably becoming louder and more piercing with each successive increase in breath-pressure; even the more aristocratic tenor three-holed pipe in D (Bowles, *Pratique* (see note 7), pls. 109 and 112) has a compass of an octave and a fifth. The six-holed duct flute, by far the most common of its type among folk instruments, can play one octave without overblowing but second-octave notes have to be over-blown and are therefore louder. The presence of a thumb-hole which can be used as a 'speaker' to facilitate the production of second-octave notes makes it possible for the recorder to play up through its range without becoming louder, and this dynamic flexibility gives it a considerable advantage in imitating vocal music where, in order to express the meaning of the text, high notes may need to be sung more softly than low notes. As Ganassi puts it in Chapter 1 of *Fontegara* (1535), 'with this instrument only the form of the human body is absent'. Moreover, the recorder is especially sensitive to varied articulation – 'it is possible with some players to perceive, as it were, words to their music'.[7] Except for keyboard and plucked-string compositions (in tablature), most renaissance music was conceived with the human voice in mind. As a soft instrument participating in courtly entertainment this ability of the recorder to imitate the voice was of paramount importance. In fact its repertoire derived from chansons and related vocal genres was probably more important to renaissance recorder players than their participation in the relatively small amount of later renaissance music actually designated for performance by ensembles of melody instruments.

As Howard Mayer Brown has pointed out, graphic representation even in three dimensions cannot easily show the thumb-hole under the instrument that distinguishes the recorder from other duct flutes, although the presence of the paired little-finger holes (to accommodate left- or right-handed players with the unwanted hole being filled with wax) provides an adequate identification[8] taken together with playing stance and finger positions. Elsewhere[9] Brown says that the first two unambiguous representations of a recorder in art date from the early years of the fifteenth century (see pl. 3). He also mentions (p. 11) the one recorder that exists from that period with its windway, lip, thumb-hole and eight finger-holes intact.[10] It was discovered in 1940 in the moat of a large fortified house (a castle in all but name) by a river near Dordrecht in Holland. The house was occupied only from 1335 to 1418 when it suffered severely from an assault; in 1421 the whole area was flooded and long remained so. The recorder may have been discarded at the time of the assault as metal utensils which could have been part of a soldier's kit were found in the same excavation. The bottom part, from hole 5 downwards, of a very similar instrument was found in a well in Würzburg where the strata suggest a fourteenth-century dating. Both instruments are cylindrical in bore. Many representations of pipes in art that have been called recorders look conical in bore,[11] but they may be shawms without the mouthpiece pirouette being evident. If recorders are made with a bore of more than slightly expanding conicity they require impracticable fingering techniques.[12] Unequivocal literary evidence of the use of the word 'recorder', which is confined to English ('pipe', '*pfeife*', '*pifa*', etc. were generic terms)[13] does not predate 1400.[14]

The medieval repertoire for recorder players must therefore be either in the 'extended' category, or 'arranged'. But, however unsuited or unauthentic to the instrument, this provides them with pleasurable and invigorating excursions into realms that would otherwise remain undiscovered.

The extended repertoire is mainly the music of the medieval 'jongleurs', professional entertainers of a lower social caste who made their living at fairs, pageants, festivals, mystery plays and other occasions of entertainment including banquets and dancing in noble households, where they might acquire permanent status as minstrels. They played a variety of instruments such as the vielle (medieval fiddle), shawms and other 'pipes', especially the pipe and tabor for dancing, and had even more diverse accomplishments such as juggling and tumbling. Some became attached as occasional vielle accompanists to a troubadour or trouvère (who could be aristocratic persons) providing a drone background and/or short instrumental interludes to the singing; vielles with their only slightly curved bridge, as well as double duct flutes (sometimes referred to as 'double recorders'), were well suited to such functions. Medieval and early renaissance singers expressed their music partly through the vowel sounds of the words and through nuances of intonation which would have been smothered by anything other than a light non-melodic accompaniment. Plate 9, however, shows a flautist joining the vielle in providing interlude-type variety in a Minnesinger's performance. But the jongleurs' staple was of dance-type music. They acquired and extended their skills and repertoires at occasional gatherings of their fraternity, and developed them by improvisation. Their music is as lost to us as 1920s jazz would have been without recordings and even without the possibility, however inadequate, of trying to write it down in notation. Nevertheless forty-seven dance pieces from the period have been preserved, and the complete collection has recently been published.[15] They should be played extrovertly with a strong rhythm but with plenty of improvisation and freedom within the pulse; drone basses and percussion do not come amiss.

In a refined and courtly environment, recorder players may (un-authentically) take an instrumental part in a fourteenth-century motet with mixed voices and instruments, for example, singer, recorder and plucked strings.[16] Some of Machaut's motets lend themselves to instrumental performance. The Squarcialupi Codex which has two pages with friezes containing groups of wind instruments such as shawms and pipes (pl. 2A) at least suggests that some of the music of Landini's period may have been played consort style, even though the Codex dates from some twenty years after his death. Decorative friezes such as this and the spectacular margins of the *Cantigas de Santa Maria* of Alfonso X (*d.*1284) do not, however, provide conclusive evidence that the instruments that appear in them were actually used in the music they surround. Nevertheless, professional groups have no compunction in playing the *Cantigas* and other medieval music with mixed voices and instruments, and the results are often enjoyable and effective.

Even as early as the twelfth century, polyphonic organum or conductus by composers such as Pérotin at Notre-Dame in Paris was occasionally intabulated for keyboard and used in motet versions in non-ecclesiastical surroundings. At some places and times, duct flutes may have taken part in playing medieval motets, and such a conjecture should encourage recorder players to delve into this fascinating repertoire. Enterprising 'desk-top' publishers such as Hawthorns Music are producing recorder editions.

Renaissance music

Recorder players are fortunate in having available the London Pro Musica's playing editions, including its 'Early Music Library' with 168 issues (by 1994), published by an experienced performer and musicologist, Bernard Thomas. These editions provide an overview of the recorder's medieval[17] and renaissance repertoire. Informative introductory notes by the publisher or other scholar-performers such as Michael Morrow and Peter Walls are careful to indicate how each piece might have been performed and its suitability for recorders. The same applies to the Moeck editions of music of this period. Bernard Thomas has edited *The Schott Recorder Consort Anthology* (1991) in six volumes, mainly divided by country, with an exemplary introduction and notes which together with the music provide the best available survey of the recorder's renaissance repertoire. There is no point in repeating here what can be gleaned from these editions and from chapters in Hunt's and Linde's books (see the Guide to further reading, p. 210).

In principle, the recorder's fifteenth- and sixteenth-century repertoire is enormous. Although certain instruments might be more appropriate than others on some occasions, composers rarely specified particular ones except for keyboard and plucked-string music, normally in its own tablature. Moreover, most vocal music was open to instrumental or mixed performance, *per cantare o sonare* (see pls. 6A and B).[18] Instrumentalists are attracted to untexted pieces in renaissance song-books, though the lack of a text does not imply they were not sung. A particularly challenging piece is 'The Cat's Paw' in the *Glogauer Liederbuch* of *c*1455,[19] where the three parts dart across each other in an early piece of descriptive music.[20]

There is therefore very little 'designated repertoire' for recorders from the Renaissance, but in the category of 'probable repertoire' we may attempt to arrive, from iconographic, literary and other sources, at what sort of music might have been played on those recorders that appeared in such large quantities in the possession of royal or ducal courts or of town waits (see Hunt, pp. 24–5). We may subjectively put our conclusions to the test by listening to the many excellent recordings and concerts of music of this period which involve recorders, and by trying out pieces ourselves.

Castiglione's *The Courtier* (1528) suggests that music is to provide pleasure and entertainment, especially 'in the presence of women'[21] – no baroque affective catharsis here! Renaissance pictures suggest that this was particularly the case with recorders, played by refined amateurs[22] in delightful surroundings. The recorder is seen in boating parties in calendar illustrations for the month of May (pl. 4); it accompanies the delights of the bath, where food and drink was also served (pls. 10A and B, and 42), and symbolises the pleasures of life

Plates 10A and 10B – The recorder and bathing

Plate 10A (opposite top) Soft music, as well as food and drink, accompanied the pleasures of the bath, as shown in *Le Bain* from *La Vie seigneuriale*, a series of early sixteenth-century tapestries in the Musée de Cluny in Paris. The oddly crooked shape of the instrument's flared foot is found in some other depictions of this period identified as recorders; does it perhaps reduce little-finger stretch? Or is it just artist's aberration? Again a lute, with its dynamic flexibility and its ability to play two parts of a chanson, completes the ensemble, unless the lady herself, as her gestures might suggest, sings in her bath. Another Cluny tapestry shows a splendidly arrayed nobleman playing a tenor recorder accompanied by a damsel with a dulcimer. (Bowles, *Musikleben*, pl. 80)

Plate 10B (opposite bottom) This woodcut from the first half of the sixteenth century shows mixed bathing being thoroughly enjoyed in a warm spa bath. The artist is Hans Sebald Beham and the picture is in a collection in Copenhagen (Salmen, *Musikleben*, p. 102). Music, some especially written for these social occasions (*Bade Lieder*), accompanied the bath, or you could bring and play your own instrument, like the rather lonely young recorder player on the balcony, or the bearded fiddler on the left by the towels hung out to dry, dangling his feet in the warm water. For the men's bath, see plate 42.

(see note 8, end); at banquets it provided the informal relaxing soft music towards the end of the meal when the trumpet pomp and ceremony of the earlier stages had come to a conclusion. Perhaps with more symbolic significance, music with duct flutes accompanied the bride to the porch of the church, and soft music may even have taken place in a private chapel. But recorders did not commonly participate in the music within a church.[23] Stone, wood or stained-glass angels played their recorders (along with a cacophony of other instruments) in silent worship. Nevertheless, clerical gentlemen, even bishops and saints,[24] were not denied the pleasures of music with recorder and flute in a library (pl. 11A) or in a garden (pl. 11B). Whether they are playing sacred or profane music is anyone's guess.[25] Outside churches, pieces from Masses and other sacred music were occasionally performed by a recorder consort,[26] although the purpose of the music as a word-setting is diminished, together with the effect of the tonal interplay of the vowel sounds of the familiar Latin words. But we should bear in mind Bernard Thomas's points in his introduction to *The Schott Recorder Consort Anthology* (vol. I, p. vi):

A recorder consort's relative purity of sound makes it suitable for the kind of abstract music whose effect is dependent on a strong sense of interval, such as the English 'In Nomine' repertoire. In fact there is much pre-Counter-Reformation sacred music which works especially well on recorders. This is music where the relationship between music and text is not an intense and intimate one, as it is in madrigals, but where exquisitely crafted polyphony, well-controlled melodic climaxes, or subtle cross-rhythms are of more importance. Sections of masses by Josquin des Prés, Heinrich Isaac, Jacob Obrecht, etc., often make surprisingly good instrumental pieces, especially the Benedictus, or Agnus Dei II, which were traditionally set in three rather than

Plates 11A and 11B – Ecclesiastical recorder playing

Plate 11A (opposite top)   Part of a miniature from Valerius Maximus's *Histoires* (French *c*1475) from the British Library (MS Harley 4375, f. 151v); see also Bowles, *Pratique*, p. 104. Three clerical gentlemen relax with music in a library, playing a rather slender-looking recorder, a lute (or possibly mandora, the small lute) and harp. While they may be indulging in a secular chanson, it was a common practice for music originally composed to a sacred text to be transformed into an instrumental piece. Recorders sometimes feature on the decorated title pages of psalm settings (see p. 47, note 25).

Plate 11B (opposite bottom)   This illustration – unfortunately damaged – of monks playing in a monastery garden (but not Ketelby!) is actually from a psalter – Flemish, fifteenth century (British Library, MS Add. 15426, f. 86, and see also Bowles, *Pratique*, p. 111). The combination of flute and recorder is especially interesting. The other instruments are rebec, psaltery and lute, again the common ensemble of blown, bowed and plucked instruments which were later so well combined in the so-called 'English consort' of around 1600 (see p. 19). The symbolic harp of the psalms is visible in the foreground, whatever music this assortment of monks (from different religious orders) is playing.

four parts. Here the structure and shape of the music is relatively independent of the words. Should anyone think that performing this music on instruments is an historical solecism, there are many early-sixteenth-century manuscripts which contain such sections taken from masses, and some examples are included in the present volume. [i.e. vol. I of the *Anthology*]

The association of the recorder in renaissance literature and art with pleasurable occasions suggests that we should look to dance music for part of our repertoire. Arbeau's statement in *Orchésographie* (1589) that recorders were among 'all sorts of instruments' that could accompany pavans and basse danses,[27] linked with the clear evidence of Plate 8, is encouragement, if any is needed, for recorder consorts to play renaissance dance music – Attaingnant, Susato, Phalèse, Gervaise, Jacques Moderne,[28] Bendusi, Mainerio, Zanetti and, above all, Praetorius. But the literary and iconographical sources on the whole suggest that recorder groups were not commonly used to accompany dancing, although a recorder could be part of a mixed ensemble.[29] Louder instruments such as bagpipes or shawms[30] were needed for outdoor dancing – modern shawms (*tiple* and *tenora*) are still used in the Catalan cobla band for sardana dancing, although the piercing pipe and tabor was sufficient in itself, as it is for today's morris dancing. For indoor dancing the pipe and tabor was also usual, even for the stately basse danse, although plucked-string instruments were a suitable addition or alternative. By Arbeau's time when, as he says, both the basse danse and the pipe and tabor were out of fashion for courtly dancing, the recorder consort, when used, might have been reinforced by substituting a strong instrument such as a dulcian for the weak-toned bass recorder.

Recorders 'sound right' playing a pavan for courtly dancing; they sound just as persuasive, with infinitely more musical interest for all the players, in the pavan as an art form – of course without the percussion. In practice most of the refined English dance-based music of the late Renaissance would probably only have been played on recorders as an occasional change of sound from the normal viol or violin consort associated with the music of Holborne, Dowland, Simpson and Brade, or to suit the availability of players. It was not, it appears, customary to change instrumentation during the course of a pavan (e.g. for the repeat of a strain) though it might well have been changed for the more lively galliard. The 'other Musicall Winde Instruments' in Holborne's title (p. 19) may include recorder consorts as well as the cornett and sackbut group, for Holborne's music, much more than Dowland's, has a clarity, a mixture of lightness and gravity, that suits recorders, especially when the pavans are played on a 'great consort' with a tenor on the top line. It is interesting that the example of recorder consort music given by Mersenne in his *Harmonie universelle* (1636–7) is a dance – a gavotte (Hunt, p. 33, Linde, p. 86) – which gives us further encouragement to take dance-type music of the late Renaissance and early seventeenth century into our repertoire, including masque dances (Adson), intradas (Franck, Demantius and other German composers, often written in five or six parts), and early

Plate 12   This detail from Gangolf Herlinger's *Coronation of the Virgin* altarpiece from the Cistercian monastery of Osseg (Osek) in northern Bohemia dates from about 1520, the time when consorts of like instruments were in the process of development. At bottom right is a four-part crumhorn consort; and at bottom left a consort of three cornetts (played from the side of the mouth) with a huge bass sackbut. But the recorder consort in the centre still consists of only three players, here it seems, rather oddly, two soprano instruments and one large tenor or possibly basset bass. The players look distinctly unangelic, but they do have wings. WB 90

dance suites (Peuerl, Schein, etc.), even though they too were intended more for strings than wind.

Very soon after their appearance around or before 1400 the recorders, like the shawms, were made in different sizes, constituting a three-part recorder consort; and they were then also able to participate in mixed ensembles at either cantus or tenor levels. Although musical angelic hosts represent glory[31] rather than performance practice, the frequent appearance of three like instruments together (e.g. pls. 7, 12 and 13) confirms the extent to which fifteenth-century three-part music was performed on recorders.[32] Towards the end of the century four-part music became more common, and more music was intended primarily for instrumental performance, but the three-recorder consort seems to have persisted, for Plate 12, from about 1520, shows a four-part cornett and sackbut ensemble, a four-part crumhorn consort, but only three recorders. Throughout the Renaissance the motet, then the chanson and the frottola, and (with reservations) the Italian madrigal, could all be played by a recorder consort or by voices and instruments mixed. The instruments and voices might alternate, repeating the music of each verse or section. Bowles (*Pratique*, p. 198) quotes the phrase 'Un chançon convient fleuter', and Virdung in *Musica getutsch* (1511) advises on choosing sizes of recorders to fit vocal music.[33] In referring to Attaingnant's 1533 chansons marked for recorders, flute or either (see p. 18), Bernard Thomas (*Anthology* introduction) says that those marked for recorders, four of which are published (ed. Brown) in American Recorder Society edn 52, cover

a reasonably wide emotional span ... including lively, saucy pieces as well as melancholy ones...

The most striking feature of these pieces is how conventional they are: there is nothing to distinguish them from the several thousands of chansons printed during the first half of the sixteenth century. They should not, therefore, be regarded as exceptional, rather as a pointer to a whole repertoire. Chansons of this particular period make good instrumental pieces, because they are more 'abstract', and less intimately connected with the texts, than madrigals, for instance. In fact, the *canzoni da sonar* of many late-sixteenth-century Italian composers, like Gabrieli and Maschera, developed directly from the chansons of musicians such as Thomas Crecquillon and Clemens non Papa, so there is good historical precedent for playing this music instrumentally.

One of the surviving copies of Georg Forster's *Frische teutsche Liedlein, ersteer Theil* (Nuremberg, 1552) has manuscript additions indicating recorders (*Flödt*) and flutes (*Pfeiff*) for certain pieces. Once again, there is nothing remarkable about these particular Lieder, and one is quite justified in exploring the whole repertoire of German song of the period.

We can deduce from the above that recorders were considered by at least some renaissance musicians as quite acceptable instruments for music of certain commonly established genres.

Despite their name 'Carmina' (= 'songs') are a genre intended more to be played ('s(u)onar(e)') than sung ('cantare'). This repertoire from around 1500 provides wonderful music for the instrumental consorts which are a feature of early sixteenth-century music with its ever-larger bass recorders. It has long been well represented in recorder publications by (among others) Schott – *Liber Fridolini Sichery* – and Bärenreiter – *Carmina Germanica et Gallica* – containing music by composers such as Josquin, Ockeghem, Obrecht, Isaac, Senfl, Brumel, Agricola, Arcadelt and Jannequin.

The great and grave consort fancies and *In nomines* of Elizabethan England by composers such as Tye, Parsons, Byrd, Gibbons and Alfonso Ferrabosco II, though they remain central to many recorder consorts' repertoires, are more properly viol music. They may occasionally, for variety or in response to circumstances – including financial ones, for viols were expensive – have been played on the lighter-toned recorders. Michael East's *Ayerie Fancies* suit recorders admirably, as

Plate 13 Detail from an early sixteenth-century series of four tapestries representing the Victory of the Virtues, in Brussels, Musées Royaux d'Art et d'Histoire. This is part of the *Tapestry of Dance*. Despite the rather relaxed hand position of the gentleman in front, this representation of three singers mingled with three recorder players almost certainly has performance practice significance as a basse-danse group. Do all six performers play together, doubling each of three parts, or do singers and instrumentalists alternate? (See p. 48, note 32.)

do those of Richard Mico. The music composed by members of the court recorder consort, such as successive representatives of the Bassano family (see p. 167) is suggestive of the repertoire played at the time; it includes pavans, galliards, almans and fantasias in up to six parts.[34]

The consort music of the last half of the sixteenth century and the early seventeenth century can be more deeply satisfying to recorder players if by transposition (but without 'doctoring' lines to suit compass) it is played with no recorder higher than a treble on the top line and no notes higher than treble second-octave E flat or its equivalent appearing in any part. It sounds best on renaissance-type recorders with their open tone, especially when Ganassi's articulations and suitable breath-delivery and inflections are used to imitate the vocal style of most of these compositions. Later consorts, such as those of William Lawes, Tomkins and Jenkins,[35] are, with their angular leaps and wide range, less vocal in style, and many – but by no means all – are impracticable on recorders even when transposed. Purcell's 1680 *Fantasias* go awkwardly on recorders – Locke's Suites fare somewhat better,[36] but Purcell's two *In nomines*, à 6 and à 7, provide for recorder players an elegiac close to a 'consort era' that had developed from two centuries earlier.

In his *Anthology* introduction (p. vi) Bernard Thomas refers to a point made by Jerome Cardan (1501–76) – doctor, philosopher and recorder player – that the recorder's tone-quality 'does not blend well' with the voice, and in 1627 Francis Bacon (*Sylva Sylvarum* cent. II, 278), having said that 'the recorder and stringed music agree well', adds that 'the voice and pipes alone agree not so well'. But at a much later period it was the *contrast* of cool recorder tone,[37] particularly with two recorders playing in thirds, with the warmth of the voice that led Purcell, Bach and others to write the finest music composed for our instrument. The striking beauty of this contrast was not lost on renaissance musicians. The majority of renaissance works of art depicting a performance with recorder show it with voice[38] (see, for example, pls. 4 and 13), and in most of the others the recorder plays with other instruments (pls. 6B, 10A, 11A, 11B and 42). Other than in angel-choirs, pictures of recorder consorts are less common (but note pls. 8 and 14). Even the frontispiece of Ganassi's recorder tutor (pl. 29) shows the players with a singer, as does that of Hudgebut's tutor over a century later, where three fat putti play recorders and one sings (pl. 30), although in both cases there is a spare recorder on the table to make up a consort. Perhaps recorder players do not give enough attention to the consort song repertoire.[39]

Some pictures, including Ganassi's frontispiece, include the music being played, though it is not always decipherable. In those sixteenth-century paintings with recorder or flute where the music is legible, it is

Plate 14 Daniel Brüggen and his colleagues came across this charming and rare fresco of a recorder quartet when his twentieth-century recorder quartet (pl. 36) was performing at Trent in northern Italy. It has been used on their 1993 CD 'Capriccio di Flauti', which includes Italian renaissance music (L'Oiseau-Lyre 440 207). The painting, dated 1531, is by Girolamo Romanino, and adorns a lunette in the loggia of the Castello del Buonconsiglio at Trent. The quartet is of descant, two trebles and tenor. There is no bass (compare this with pl. 8 which belongs to the same decade). This should encourage present-day quartets without bass to seek out suitable music from this period, largely from vocal originals.

usually identified as a chanson or frottola. Plates 15A and B, 16 and 17, for example, show two popular French chansons, an Italian frottola and (probably) a madrigal – in each case the music links with the significance or symbolism of the painting. All this emphasises the importance of this type of music as the main 'authentic' source of sixteenth-century repertoire for recorder players. It is well represented in London Pro Musica publications and in *The Schott Recorder Consort Anthology*.

It is interesting that where a work of art depicts what appears to be an actual performance with recorder the scene is rather more frequently out of doors than indoors, even in north-European climes (e.g. pls. 4, 6B, 10A, 11B, 13, 24, 27, 31, 32, 33 and 41). Often recorders play by water[40] (pls. 4, 10B, 31 and 42). Renaissance recorders with their narrow windway and lip often require a strong breath-pressure to achieve their optimum tone,[41] so making them less susceptible to tone-degradation by passing breezes. They would therefore have been well fitted to play the soft music required for visions of heaven in mystery plays performed on wagons or in front of a church, and for the serenades and night-time patrol music played by the town waits,[42] and

Plates 15A and 15B   The music in two sixteenth-century paintings

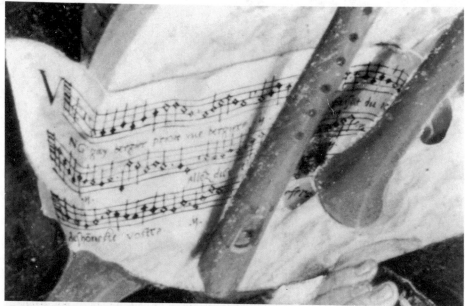

Inset 1   El Greco   **Inset 2   Carlo Magnone**

Plate 15A and insets   One of the best-known representations of recorders – three of them – is in Pieter Pourbus's *An Allegory of True Love*, dated 1547, in the Wallace Collection, London, also known as *An Allegorical Love-Feast* (see, for example, *The Recorder Magazine* 4/5 (June 1973)). The two recorders on the table side by side represent marriage, or at least an amorous partnership. The words of the music, 'Ung gay bergier prioit une bergiere …', bear this out more boldly, and also reflect the recorder's association with the pastoral and shepherds. The music in this inverted detail is the tenor part of Thomas Crecquillon's popular four-part chanson published by Susato in Antwerp in 1543. It is available to sing or play in LPM edition PC 6. The recorders are of a common sixteenth- and seventeenth-century 'choke-bore' design which has a cylindrical or very slightly tapering bore but then expands towards the bell, though not with as much flare as the exterior often suggests (see also pls. 21 and 37). The front covers of *The Schott Recorder Consort Anthology* and of LPM's Renaissance Chansons series use the Pourbus *Allegory* in colour, which shows up the curvaceous outline of these recorders (and the red wax stopping up an unused little-finger hole). They are also seen in El Greco's *Annunciation* of 1597–1600 (for detail, see inset 1 – WB 12; and see also p. 48, note 31), and, to perfection, across the foreground of a variant copy of Caravaggio's famous *Lute Player* made in 1642 by Carlo Magnone for the Barberini family at Rome (inset 2). This design prevailed for over 200 years, twice the lifetime of the, to us, more familiar baroque recorder, for the flared bell can be seen in the two recorders symbolically clutched by a lady in Francesco del Cossa's *The Triumph of Venus* fresco at the Schifanoia Palace in Ferrara, dated *c*1470 (see *The Recorder Magazine* 8/11 cover (Sept. 1986)) as well as in the fifteenth-century Psalter of King René II of Lorraine, and the principle was still applied by Dutch makers until late in the seventeenth century. Renaissance instruments so constructed are sometimes termed 'Ganassi recorders' as his fingerings respond to this bore profile.

Plate 15B   This is the music which gives its name to the exquisite picture (*c*1520) by 'The Master of the Female Halflengths' entitled *Jouyssance vous donneray*. It is often reproduced, for example in Raymond Meylan's *The Flute* (London 1988). Two ladies play flute (it could just as well have been a recorder) and a lute, and a third sings. Both the symbolism of the instruments and the tender words of the poem indicate that the promised *jouissance* is as much erotic as aesthetic. This extremely popular chanson was composed by Claudin de Sermisy (*c*1490–1562) to words by Clément Marot (1496–1544). It was published by Attaingnant in Paris in 1529. The picture was painted about 1530–40 by an unknown Dutch artist and is now in the Harrach Collection near Vienna. The artist shows only the singer's music, transposed to suit the instrumentation to a C clef on the second line up, a routine practice of the time (see p. 204). The music is available, in more familiar clefs, in Bärenreiter HM 137, no. 14, and in *The Schott Recorder Consort Anthology*, vol. 2 no. 4.

later to produce the 'stil music of records' in supernatural or funereal contexts in the Elizabethan theatre.[43] Did they play soft pavans? Such conjectures are as impenetrable as Sir Thomas Browne's question 'What song the Syrens sang?', or our own curiosity as to what recorder music it was that so ravished Pepys 'when the angel comes down'.[44]

Plate 16 Portrait of a man with a recorder by the Brescian painter Giovanni Girolamo Savoldo, *c*1548, now in a private collection in New York. The picture is the subject of a fascinating article by H. Colin Slim in *Early Music* 13/3 (August 1985), pp. 398–406, for the music pinned to the wall represents a letter, although the words turn out to be the artist's signature (a not uncommon device). The notes – difficult to make out – form the tenor line of a four-part frottola setting of a sonnet in dialogue of *c*1524, *O Morte? Holà!*, later published in Rome in 1531 and attributed to 'F. P.', probably Francesco Patavino from Padua who was working in Udine at the same time as the artist. The elegant young man is discreetly practising in his room the treble part of the same piece from the music book in front of him, on a cylindrical model descant recorder.

Notes

1. See Edgar Hunt, 'The right instrument', *The Recorder Magazine* 9/6 (June 1988), pp. 150–1.
2. Douglas MacMillan, 'The recorder in the late eighteenth and early nineteenth centuries', *The Consort* 39 (1983), pp. 489–97.
3. 'Extra Time', Decca 425 222; and also 'Baroque Recorder Music, L'Oiseau-Lyre 421 130.
4. 'A Concorde of Sweete Sounde', L'Oiseau-Lyre 436 155.

5. As Howard Mayer Brown pointed out in the preceding chapter, citing Guillaume de Machaut, the early nomenclature of duct flutes in various languages is inconsistent and confusing (see also note 13 below).

6. See Monteverdi's preface to his Fifth Book of Madrigals (1605).

7. Sylvestro Ganassi, *Opera intitulata Fontegara* (Venice 1535), ed. Hildemarie Peter, trans. Dorothy Swainson (Berlin-Lichterfelde 1959), pp. 9 (Chap. 1, both quotations) and 13–14 (articulation). Ganassi may well have been biased, but he is not the only renaissance writer to comment upon the expressive potentialities of wind instruments (see Edmund A. Bowles's bilingual *La pratique musicale au moyen âge/Musical Performance in the Middle Ages* (Geneva, Minkoff, 1983), p. 195 – references to Bowles in this book are either to *Pratique* or to his 1977 *Musikleben* volume in German, see p. xii). It is fallacious at any time to assert that the recorder is markedly less flexible than other wind instruments, but expressivity and dynamic contrast are technically much harder to achieve on the recorder without going out of tune or prejudicing tone-quality. *Fontegara* confirms that renaissance recorder players were expected to master these techniques. Bernard Thomas has commented to me how much easier it is to express dynamic nuances on the renaissance transverse flute than on the recorder when accompanying voice.

8. The two little-finger holes are clearly shown in the Dürer woodcut in plate 42, in plates 17 and 29, and even in the recorder which appears in the blind organist Conrad Paumann's gravestone (1573) in the Frauenkirche in Munich. They are also very clear in *The Flautist* attributed to Murillo (1618–82) in the Museum of the Old Bishop's Palace at Chartres, in *St Francis* by a follower of Botticelli (*c*1445–1510) in the National Gallery (London), and in Steenwyck's *Vanitas* (*c*1640) in Leyden where the right-hand hole is stopped with wax; they do not appear in *Vanitas* by Steenwyck in the National Gallery (London) where the bottom three holes of the instrument are hidden by a skull – but the London painting shows a maker's mark and the instruments may be the same. The Steenwyck *Vanitas* of ?1654 in the Prado in Madrid shows the whole recorder. See also *Vanitas* (1664) by Jan Davidsoon de Heem in the Beaux-Arts Museum in Brussels (reproduced as the cover of the March 1992 issue of *The Recorder Magazine*). The recorders in these *Vanitas* paintings symbolise the passing of earthly pleasures, so 'gather ye rosebuds while ye may'.

9. See p. 21, note 5. In Brown's 'Corpus' all representations of instruments before 1400 which could be recorders (p. 22, note 8) are indicated as doubtful. In *Early Music* 16/2 (May 1988), pp. 238–49, Jeremy Montagu described 'The restored Chapter House wall paintings in Westminster Abbey' including one, unfortunately damaged, which shows the lower part of a cylindrical wind instrument looking rather like a recorder; these paintings are dated 1390–1404. But if the instrument in the painting by Pere Serra shown as the frontispiece of this book really is a recorder and if a dating of *c*1390 is correct for this altarpiece, this confirms Howard Mayer Brown's conjecture (p. 5) that the earliest recorders appeared in north-west Mediterranean regions.

10. Pictured in Edgar Hunt, *The Recorder and its Music* (London 1962 and later edns), pl. III. The information that follows here is drawn from Rainer Weber, 'Recorder finds from the Middle Ages, and results of their reconstruction', *Galpin Society Journal* 29 (May 1976), pp. 35–41, which includes a report on the excavation by Dr Clemens von Gleich of the Gemeentemuseum at The Hague where the recorder is exhibited. I am indebted to my wife for her suggestion that the drinking mug, beer-pitcher, plate, bowl and frying-pan, one of each and *all* in metal, might have been a soldier's kit. Some recent evidence suggests that the Dordrecht recorder might possibly be 100 or even 200 years older than has always been generally believed.

11. One has to allow for perspective and foreshortening. Moreover, artists are rarely disposed (or able) to depict instruments and their manner of playing (especially hand positions) accurately, all the more so if such exactitude were adversely to affect the composition or balance of the picture. Some artists, such as Grünewald in his Isenheim altarpiece, carry such licence to excess for deliberate effect. Artists also tend to copy from each other rather than from actual instruments and players.

12. This statement is the outcome of meticulous experimentation on my behalf by Albert Lockwood, recorder-maker of Bridlington, Yorkshire. While the iconography suggests that some early renaissance recorders and other duct flutes did have a slightly expanding bore – though the appearance of conicity may be largely due to thickening of the wood at the bell end (see pls. 1, 2A and perhaps 12 – but this could be an effect of perspective) – anything more than a slight outward conicity causes the fundamental to overblow to less than an octave. This means that second-harmonic fingerings, equivalent to the complex third-octave fingerings of a baroque recorder, have to be employed to produce an uneven-toned sequence of second-octave notes. The additional breath-pressure then required defeats the purpose of the recorder's 'speaker hole' to play second-octave notes softly. I am extremely grateful to Mr Lockwood for his help.

13. 'Pipe' and its equivalents were used to cover a wide range of wind instruments other than flutes, including shawms, bombardes and even trombones. The town waits were 'Pfeiffen' or 'Pifarri'; they 'pipeth the watche' (see note 42). 'Flute' and its equivalents embrace transverse flutes, flageolets, recorders and related soft instruments ('Flasoz, fleutez et douchaines' – Bowles, *Pratique*, p. 195).

14. Chaucer (*c*1340–1400) frequently mentions musical instruments and often refers to 'flutes', but never 'recorders'. The literary history of the word is delightfully expounded in Christopher Welch's *Six Lectures on the Recorder* of 1911 (reprint of the first three, with an introduction by Edgar Hunt, Oxford 1961); he traces the word back to a lexicon of *c*1400 (p. 18 of Hunt edn). See also note 24 below.

15. Timothy J. McGee, *Medieval Instrumental Dances* (Bloomington, Indiana U. Press, 1989). He quotes (p. 25) – but not in full – Guillaume de Machaut's list in the mid-fourteenth-century *Remede de Fortune* (see p. 2) of a large number of instruments used in association with dance, including the flageolet.

16. Scholars differ on the role of instruments in medieval music, especially in conjunction with song – see, for example, Christopher Page's book *Voices and Instruments of the Middle Ages* (see p. 214).

17. Examples of pre-1400 composers represented in the EML series are Machaut, Landini, Adam de la Halle, Johann Vaillant, and pieces from the Bamberg Codex from around 1260–90.

18. See, for example, Wendy E. Hancock, 'To play or to sing', *The Consort* 42 (1986), pp. 15–28, and Gustave Reese, *Music in the Renaissance* (London, Dent, 1954) pp. 411, 636, etc. Tess Knighton in 'The *a cappella* heresy in Spain: an inquisition into the performance of the *cancionero* repertory', *Early Music* 20/3 (Nov. 1992), pp. 561–81, discusses the role of instruments in Spanish polyphonic songs of the late fifteenth and early sixteenth centuries – the presence of recorder players in the illustrated margins of the 1527 edition of the *Cancionero general* lends some support to the conjecture that recorders were involved in chansons from this great Spanish collection. In Howard Mayer Brown's article 'On the performance of fifteenth-century chansons', *Early Music* 1/1 (Jan. 1973), pp. 2–10, there is a perceptive consideration of the part played by the recorder in the iconographically common setting of voice, recorder or flute, and harp or lute.

19. The date given for the *Glogauer Liederbuch* is from Linde, *The Recorder Player's Handbook*, p. 58. It is a treasure-trove for recorder players – Reese, *Music in the Renaissance*, p. 635, says that sixty-one of its 294 pieces are apparently intended for instrumental performance. Linde also mentions that Arnt von Aich in his Lieder-buch of 1519 suggests that for several of the songs 'flutes or fifes and other kinds of instrument may be used'. Linde lists six other German song-books from the first half of the sixteenth century where instruments (such as recorders) might have played in parts other than the cantus-firmus tenor, the only part-book with a text; and even that part may be played instrumentally so long as it dominates. The meticulous research carried out by Keith Polk ('Voices and instruments: soloists and ensembles in the 15th century', *Early Music* 18/2 (May 1990), pp. 179–97, and his book *German Instrumental Music of the Late Middle Ages* (Cambridge 1992)) indicates that the recorder featured only rarely, if at all, in *mixed* voice and instrument ensembles in Germany, but was more likely to be used as a consort of three recorders, or, more

usually (especially when played by waits on civic occasions), five instruments, employing different sizes of recorder, their soft timbre providing an occasional contrast with other ensembles. It must be remembered, however, that performance practice, like speech and dress, varied from one country and region to another.

20. Rhythmic complexity is a feature of late medieval and early renaissance music, and also of some later sixteenth-century music. Recorder consorts who have mastered Byrd's *Browning* and Brade's difficult six-part pavans might attempt the ultimate complexity of the 'rhythmic games' pieces from the Baldwine manuscript (Zen-On, ed. Kees Boeke).

21. '*The Book of the Courtier* by Count Baldassare Castiglione Done into English by Sir Thomas Hoby' 1561 (London, Dent, n.d.), p. 101.

22. Castiglione says (p. 100), 'And for all he be skilfull and doth well understand it, yet will I have him to dissemble the studie and paines that a man must needes take in all things that are well done'. Upper-class amateurs therefore cultivated soft instruments such as lute or recorder for secret practising (see pl. 16). They would not descend to playing noisier instruments such as shawms, associated with lower-class professionals. The latter, as town waits and players at dramatic performances, also played the recorder, but as a 'second-study' instrument. Although, as is evident from *Fontegara*, an amateur recorder player was expected to 'do it excellently well' making it 'much esteemed of other men', he had to 'make semblance that he esteemeth but little in himselfe'. If he achieved professional standards he would be censured for devoting too much time to music to the detriment of acquiring excellence in the other pursuits. This attitude applied later to the eighteenth-century amateur who played the recorder or flute, but rarely the professional oboe – and a gentleman would never blow his own trumpet.

23 But see p. 16. Also Leslie Korrick, 'Instrumental music in the early 16th-century Mass: new evidence', *Early Music* 18/3 (August 1990), pp. 359–70.

24. In the *Dictionary of Middle English Musical Terms* compiled by Henry Holland Carter (Bloomington, Indiana U. Press, 1961; Kraus reprint New York 1980) we learn from the fifteenth-century *Polychronicon* of Ranulf Higden that 'Seynte Aldelme, bischop of Schirburn' had 'in habite and in use instrumentes off the arte of musike, as in harpes, pipes, recordres'. One must admire the imagination of the chronicler as St Aldhelm, Bishop of Sherborne, died in 709. However, he does not seem to regard playing the recorder as unsaintly, despite its connotations of worldly pleasures. This is one of the early references to the instrument; another – difficult to date precisely – is in a Cornish play, *Origo Mundi*. But (see Hunt, pp. 3–4) in the household accounts of Henry, Earl of Derby (later King Henry IV), for 1388 a payment is noted for a *fistula nomine Ricordo*; this is frustratingly ambiguous as '*Ricordo*' could mean 'keepsake' or it could be the first mention of 'recorder'.

25. Recorders, flutes and other instruments appear on the title pages of several sixteenth-century publications of psalm-settings and 'Geistlicher Lieder'. See Gottfried S. Fraenkel, *Decorative Music Title Pages* (New York, Dover, 1968), pls. 48, 51, 53, 55 and 56 and even 27 – a Mass.

26. The CD 'A Concorde of Sweete Sounde' (note 4) includes the Agnus Dei from Robert Carver's *Missa 'L'Homme armé'*.

27. 'One can play them on violins, spinets, transverse flutes, and flutes with nine holes, hautboys and all sorts of instruments. They can even be sung. But the tabor with its regular rhythm is an immense help in bringing the feet into the correct positions required by the movements of the dance.' (*Orchésography*, trans. Mary Stewart Evans (New York, Dover, 1967), p. 67.) Arbeau gives this unchanging and light regular rhythm as ♩♩♩ for pavans and ♩♩♩♩♩ for basse danses (also for galliards), although some renaissance dance groups prefer not to have percussion. For 'Playing for renaissance dance' see Shirley Baker in *The Recorder* (Melbourne) 16 (Dec. 1992), pp. 1–4.

28. Jacques Moderne's *Musique de Joye* (Lyons *c*1550) contains twenty-one four-part ricercars and twenty-nine French dances, all intended for instrumental performance ('espinetes, violons & fleustes') though they could also be sung ('tant à la voix humaine').

29. This remains true of baroque dance. Plate 27 shows a dance ensemble of pipe and tabor, recorder, violin, viola and bassoon.
30. A common group was three shawms and bombarde or slide trumpet, whose experienced professional players would improvise parts to the basse-danse tune.
31. Never more so than El Greco's angel musicians in his *The Annunciation* at the Prado in Madrid, a detail of which is reproduced in colour in *Early Music*'s first 'Iberian Discoveries' issue (20/4) of November 1992, p. 619, and on the cover of the September 1994 issue of *The Recorder Magazine*. But this painting may also approximate to actual performance practice with voice or voices (presumably), recorder – a lovely image (see the inset to pl. 15A) – virginal, lute, harp and gamba.
32. Pictures with three recorder-playing angels such as in Plate 7, and in the Vallmoll altarpiece by Jaume Huguet (1414–92) in the Museu Nacional d'Art de Catalunya at Barcelona, may relate to Trinity symbolism. But this is not the case with the depictions of recorders in the tapestry series *Le Triomphe des vertus sur les vices* (1519–24) in the Musées Royaux d'Art et d'Histoire at Brussels. A group of three courtly recorder players from these tapestries adorns the cover of Hans-Martin Linde's *The Recorder Player's Handbook* as well as that of Freda Dinn's *Early Music for Recorders* (London, Schott, 1974); but, from the same source, plate 13 shows three noblemen playing recorders with three ladies singing. A rather similar group appears in a Brussels tapestry in Saragossa Cathedral with long three- and four-holed pipes instead of recorders, and with one of the ladies both singing and playing the lute. Partly because of the way the performers are grouped, these two tapestries give the impression that the recorders are doubling the voices, though probably not all the time.
33. See Anthony Baines, *Woodwind Instruments and their History* (London, Faber, 1957), Ch. X: 'The sixteenth century and the consorts'. Virdung in 1511 still shows only three sizes of recorder (G, C and F bass); quartets required two tenors. Proliferation soon followed (see Hunt, pp. 17–25 and pl. V). The four-part consort shown in plate 14, however, does not have a bass recorder, and consorts without bass may have been common until well into the sixteenth century.
34. The repertoire, some of which may be found in the Fitzwilliam Museum, Cambridge, is considered in detail by David Lasocki in 'The recorder consort at the English court 1540–1643', *The American Recorder* 25/3–4 (August and Nov. 1984), pp. 91–100 and 131–5. Some of the *Royal Wind Music* is published by Nova, ed. Peter Holman. The fantasias are every bit as complex as those for viols, and this suggests that recorder players should not allow viol players to appropriate as their own this superb 'viol fancy' repertoire, but should rather follow Clifford Bartlett's advice (p. 202): master some unfamiliar clefs, and explore the Elizabethan and Jacobean consort repertoire in greater depth.
35. Following the fourth centenary of his birth in 1592, much more of John Jenkins's voluminous consort music has become available, including recorder editions by 'desk-top' publishers such as Marks's Music and the Chiltern Recorder Consort series.
36. Matthew Locke's Suite No. 5 in G minor is played by the Amsterdam Loeki Stardust Quartet on L'Oiseau-Lyre 414 277.
37. When the diarist John Evelyn wrote that the *flute douce* was 'now in much demand for accompanying the voice' (20 Nov. 1679) he would have been referring to the new 'baroque' recorders recently brought over from France, with their refined and less open tone than renaissance recorders. But at both periods it was the recorder's tonal contrast with the voice that would have been noticeable, as well as its articulatory capacity to imitate vocal music.
38. In a picture it is not always easy to tell whether a person is singing or not (see pls. 19 and 23A), but chansons on the water were presumably a feature of the boating parties illustrated by plate 4, of which there are many, including a beautiful example in Cambridge's Fitzwilliam Museum from a Flemish Book of Hours c1500 (MS 1058–1975).
39. Try Alfonso Ferrabosco II's 'Four-note Pavan' (no. 63 in Musica Britannica 9: *Jacobean Consort Music*) with (preferably) a boy's voice, and four recorders (Tr⁸ T

Plate 17 Although there are other versions of Titian's *Venus and Cupid with a Lute-Player* painted in the 1550s and 60s, for example in New York, only the one in the Fitzwilliam Museum, Cambridge, shows the music clearly. It also depicts the symbolic recorder accurately, complete with the paired little-finger holes (see p. 29 and pls. 29 and 42). Edgar Hunt writes about this and other Titian pictures with recorders in *The Recorder Magazine* (10/4 Dec. 1990), pp. 94–5. The music is a bassus part-book, presumably played on the bass viol standing by it in the corner. The closed tenor part-book lies beneath. Hunt refers to Alfred Einstein's belief that the music is from a set of madrigals – it is marked 'XVI'. Einstein's ingenious suggestion that the few words shown under the music, not at all legibly, begin 'O bella mano', and that this relates both to Venus's beautiful left hand and to the name of Titian's model (possibly one of two Venetian lutenists and madrigal singers Franceschina and Marieta Bellamano), unfortunately does not stand up to close scrutiny. Nevertheless, this elusive and still unidentified music has a madrigal appearance. It would then be of particular interest that the recorder, lute (playing two lines of four-part music) and bass viol are associated with an expressive and sophisticated madrigal, not a lighter chanson, frottola or canzonetta. WB 96

    T and B). The melody, a setting of Ben Jonson's 'Hear me, O God', is simplicity itself.
40. Recorder sound is very responsive to resonance. The gentleman in plate 31 plays his recorder by a lake the better to capture the echo effect. Pepys had a favourite echo by the lake in St James's Park where he played his flageolet.
41. 'Copies' of the Dordrecht recorder, and of early renaissance recorders in pictures, made by John Hanchet of Essen, respond best to high breath-pressures.
42. Large collections of recorders to provide different consort groupings were in the

property of town waits, although their normal daytime instruments were shawms and bombardes, and, later, cornetts and sackbuts. The recorders may have been used to provide the music of the night-watch (reminding us of Holborne's piece so titled) three or four times each night to reassure good citizens, and warn burglars, of their presence on the unlit streets – see p. 168 and Bowles, *Pratique*, p. 197. The waits were also employed for serenading and it is reasonable to conjecture that 'the am'rous flute' (p. 94) might have been a feature of such occasions.

43. See Hunt, *The Recorder and its Music*, pp. 47–9.
44. When he saw a revival of Massinger's *Virgin Martyr* at the King's Theatre on 27 February 1667 – see Hunt, *The Recorder and its Music*, p. 46.

3   The baroque recorder sonata*

ANTHONY ROWLAND-JONES

The baroque recorder sonata is something of a phenomenon. Almost all of those designated for solo recorder and basso continuo were written during the fifty years from about 1690 to 1740,[1] a period which saw the publication of several hundred recorder sonatas. Moreover, this was largely a north-European development, for most recorder sonatas, even those by Italian composers, were published in London (usually by Walsh), Amsterdam (by Roger, then Le Cène), Hamburg and Paris. The latter is included because of the similarity between the solo suite for dessus, i.e. any treble melody instrument, and the dance-based *sonata da camera*; for a time the words 'suite' and 'sonate' were almost synonymous.

Recorder players were by no means limited to sonatas specifying their own instrument. From 1700 onwards a substantial literature developed for the traversa, or German flute. Occasionally a sonata, for example by Handel[2] or Geminiani,[3] would be published in both flute and recorder versions. But recorder players were invited, by Telemann and others, to transpose flute or violin music a minor third up where suitable, as it often was, to accommodate it to the treble recorder in F. This was not difficult for players accustomed to reading from the French violin clef, a treble clef with g′ at the bottom line of the staff (see Ex. 6) and making the necessary modifications in accidentals. Those who played the voice flute, a 'tenor' recorder in D, did not need to transpose, and they could then play flute sonatas without having to master the difficulties of flute embouchure. This practice continued until late in the eighteenth century.[4]

Furthermore, although there were plenty of flute sonatas, especially

---

* Oxford University Press have kindly given permission for this chapter to draw upon Anthony Rowland-Jones's *Playing Recorder Sonatas: Interpretation and Technique* (1992), here referred to as '*PRS*'. The other in-text references are to his *Recorder Technique*, 2nd edn (Oxford 1986 – '*RT*'), to Edgar Hunt's *The Recorder and its Music*, rev. edn (London, Faber, 1977 – 'Hunt') and to Hans-Martin Linde's *The Recorder Player's Handbook*, trans. R. Deveson, 2nd edn (London 1991 – 'Linde').

by French composers, flautists often adapted compositions for violin, and composers such as Leclair indicated those which were suitable. In his *Pièces de Clavecin en concert* Rameau advises flautists exactly how to modify the violin part. A recorder player can profitably extend his repertoire to flute sonatas by J. S. and C. P. E. Bach (including the two unaccompanied ones), Leclair, Stanley, Boismortier, Locatelli and others. The possibility is then opened up of combining pleasure with instruction by playing Telemann's twelve *Sonate metodiche* (1728 and 1732) which include his suggestions for ornamenting the slow movements, as well as his twelve sonatas of 1734, also for violin or flute. Six of Corelli's Op. 5 violin sonatas, including No. 12, the 'Follia' variations (*PRS*, pp. 132–4), were pirated by Walsh in recorder versions within a year of their first publication in Rome in 1700, and more were available, all in improved recorder arrangements, by 1707, two 'with the proper Graces by an eminent Master'.

Out of the hundreds of sonatas and suites which specifically designate recorder during the 1690 to 1740 period, only a few score can be deemed to be any more than competent and pleasant. Most were published for an amateur market, and are not technically demanding. Unlike much twentieth-century music (especially the avant-garde), the difficulties are beneath the surface, interpretational; many will give pleasure simply by playing them through, though Telemann's Hamburg amateur recorder players seem to have been unusually skilled.

Some of the baroque sonata repertoire, however, is of a high musical standard. Four or perhaps five of Handel's six recorder sonatas are as musically rewarding as those for violin, and four of Telemann's nine, though very different (and harder to play), are of the same high quality. Henry Purcell wrote no recorder sonatas, and J. S. Bach unfortunately did not encounter recorder players who inspired him to write the equivalent of his flute sonatas, but he included the recorder in twenty-one cantatas (Hunt, pp. 77–81), two Brandenburg Concertos, and also perhaps two trio-sonatas.[5] On a lower plane of musical excellence, however, one can pick out a gratifying number of recorder sonatas which are of considerable merit. Although very much a matter of personal opinion, a selection might include J.-B. Loeillet's Op. 1 Nos. 1 and 2 (*PRS*, pp. 144–6) and Op. 3 No. 3 (*PRS*, pp. 8–10), No. 6 of the 'Il Pastor Fido' set formerly attributed to Vivaldi and now known to be by Chédeville, and Albinoni's 'Op. 4' No. 6 sonata in B minor,[6] together with some drawn from those composed by Finger, Veracini, Benedetto Marcello (especially Op. 2 No. 8 in D minor), Barsanti and Giuseppe Sammartini. Other contenders for a place in such a list would include Daniel Purcell, Paisible (*PRS*, pp. 134–9), Bononcini, and possibly Pepusch, van Wassenaer and the Swedish composer Roman. Then there are some excellent French suites by Hotteterre, Marin Marais,

Dieupart (those he arranged for recorders from his 1701 harpsichord suites which J. S. Bach copied), La Barre and de Caix d'Hervelois.[7] Couperin is in a category of his own; some of his *concerts* may be played by recorder and keyboard and have been so published. While there is no absolute evidence that Couperin's chamber music was played on the *flûte-à-bec*, he states it to be 'a l'usage de toutes les sortes d'instrumens de musique'. Marais in 1710 enlarges upon this type of statement by listing suitable instruments for his own suites, including both flute and recorder; he expects the performer to choose the one best suited to each piece of music.[8]

The majority of earlier sonatas are multi-part. For example, Gabrieli's *Sonata Pian & Forte* (1597) is in eight parts. Later in the seventeenth century, Schmelzer wrote a sonata for seven recorders and continuo, while Biber's *Sonata pro Tabula* has five recorder and five string parts (Hunt, pp. 34–6). Both Schmelzer and Biber wrote solo sonatas, but specifically for violin, exploiting technique of a virtuosity which even modern violinists find formidable (e.g. in Biber's 'Rosary' sonatas of 1678). By their time, sonatas were generally associated with the violin. The earliest seventeenth-century Italian canzonas and sonatas, however, for example those by Cima, Marini and Frescobaldi, were often published 'for any sort of instrument'; this designation had been dropped by the time Uccellini's set of solo violin sonatas was published in 1649. There are a few seventeenth-century sonatas for trumpet (e.g. by Fantini) and for bassoon (Bertoli). Riccio was one of the few composers to designate 'un Flautin', and recorder players have regarded this as evidence that other early Italian canzonas and sonatas 'per Soprano solo'[9] were also played on the descant recorder. Certainly to hear those by Dario Castello or Fontana on open-toned renaissance-type recorders is a beguiling and exciting experience.

Although the use of recorders may have declined as the seventeenth century progressed, it was by no means in abeyance. The recorder makes an appearance in Milton's *Paradise Lost* (1667),[10] and in many seventeenth-century paintings.[11] Mersenne discusses and illustrates recorders in his *Harmonie universelle* of 1636–7, and Blankenburgh's tutor for the *Hand-Fluyt* was published in Amsterdam in 1654. Recorders were used as 'special occasion' instruments in stage works as well as in sacred and courtly vocal music by composers such as Schütz, Biber, Lully and Charpentier with the same symbolic connotations (Hunt, pp. 47–9) as they had in later baroque operas by Alessandro Scarlatti, Handel and others. There is also a history of small recorders playing piccolo-type parts in dance-style music in operatic and other contexts, for example in Monteverdi's *Orfeo*, and Handel's *Water Music*. But in the middle of the seventeenth century, recorders were not generally considered to be serious solo-sonata instruments.

The whims of fashion play a large part in these processes. Pepys provides much evidence of the popularity of the six-holed French flageolet, and Thomas Greeting's tutor for that instrument (1661) went through new editions over three decades.[12] Pepys's famous diary entry for 27 February 1667/8 (Hunt, p. 46) suggests that the sound of a recorder consort was at that time for him a ravishing novelty; but by 1679 John Evelyn says that the *flute douce* is 'now in much demand for accompanying the voice'. John Hudgebut claimed that his 1679 tutor for the recorder (pl. 30) was 'the first Essay of this kind', and the publication of a series of further tutors for the instrument indicates that the recorder gradually ousted the flageolet from favour. As Hudgebut had pointed out,[13] the recorder had the greater potential, and, popularised by professional musicians such as James Paisible and John Banister II in the environment of London concert-giving, it soon acquired a status matching that of the oboe or violin. Perhaps a similar change in attitude towards the instrument in Holland may be inferred from, on the one hand, the publication in 1644/46 of Jacob van Eyck's *Der fluyten lust-hof*, a collection of about 150 tunes with variations as played to entertain the people strolling in the church precincts at Utrecht, and, on the other, the publication of serious recorder sonatas by Sybrand van Noordt and Servaas de Konink in 1690 and 1700 respectively. By 1700 the fashion for recorder sonatas was well established, and, to quote from Sir John Hawkins's *General History of Music* (1776), they were played 'by many who wished to be thought fine gentlemen ... and he that could play a solo of Schickhard of Hamburg, or Robert Valentine of Rome, was held a complete master of the instrument' (Hunt, p. 61). Perhaps Sir John's sarcasm misfires; for today it is the case that good performances of recorder sonatas, even Schickhardt's and Valentine's sometimes uninspiring ones, do require a mastery of the baroque approach to music, as well as sound technique, musicianship and imagination.

The approach to performing a baroque recorder sonata, or any music for that matter, may be seen as having two overlapping stages. The first objective is to be able to play the music accurately and competently, the second to achieve a good and persuasive performance.

The first stage initially involves the process of translating the written music into sound, in Pepys's phraseology 'taking out' the music from the written notes. In the baroque period the score was seen as the starting point towards the creation of music, bearing the same relationship as an architect's plans do to a completed building, or as a script does to a film. For this collaborative process to operate effectively, the player has to understand – in our case looking back three centuries – the significance of the musical conventions within which the composer worked, relating, for example, to the pitch and length of notes, their grouping into phrases, their dynamic level, and the speed and rhythmic character of the piece as a whole.[14]

The first stage also, most importantly of all, involves matters of musical competence, such as playing in tune, keeping time, maintaining good and well-balanced ensemble with other players, and articulating notes accurately and clearly. It also calls for an understanding of the qualities, strengths and weaknesses of the recorder generally, and of the instrument one is playing on the occasion – not just whether it is a descant or treble but what kind of sound its maker had in mind when designing it. Players possessing several instruments may choose one with a tone-quality that suits a particular style of music, the nature and pitch of the continuo instrument(s) (modern, or baroque low pitch?), and the conditions of performance. A player needs to acquire competence in production of a beautiful and persuasive tone-quality, otherwise there is little justification in playing a sonata on a recorder rather than another instrument; this is largely a function of good breathing, breath-pressure control and air-flow delivery. His fingering must be adept, and he should know how to use different fingerings not only for neatness in fast passages (including ornamentation) but also to give tonal variety, to support phrasing, and to maintain accuracy of intonation at different dynamic levels. He should be aware of the recorder's outstanding potentialities in variety of articulation (*RT*, pp. 38–52, and *PRS*, pp. 77–84) – this was probably the main reason why it was thought that the recorder more nearly approached the perfection of sung music than did other wind instruments.[15] He should practise synchronisation of fingering with breath-delivery and articulation in order to overcome the propensity of the recorder to produce 'clicks' which interfere with good phrasing in certain contexts in legato passages, especially across register breaks. All these matters of technique are dealt with in manuals such as *RT*, Alan Davis's *Treble Recorder Technique* (London, Novello, 1983), and the three volumes of Walter van Hauwe's *The Modern Recorder* (London, Schott, 1984, 1987 and 1992).

Having reached a point where an audience will not have their attention distracted by incompetent playing (they may well overlook a few 'fluffs' if the music is otherwise well played), the player needs to achieve a quality of performance that moves and entertains them, and, as far as it is possible or desirable to try to do so in our modern contexts, achieves the effect that the composer intended. It is here that the approach to a baroque and a twentieth-century sonata differs. If Lennox Berkeley's *Sonatina* (*PRS*, pp. 153–5) is played note-perfect with all the composer's dynamic and other markings respected, and if the ensemble with the keyboard is accurate, it will be well on its way towards becoming a good performance, except that qualities of passion and commitment, and an understanding of the composer's wit and style, may be missing. In a baroque sonata, choosing the right speeds (no metronome marks!), phrasings, dynamics and ornamentation, including slurs and occasional vibrato, all depended upon the musical imagination and creativity of the performer. Some composers, such as J. S. Bach, tried to mitigate the frequent ill effects of collaborative music-making by writing out their own ornamentation in full, and Couperin went to the extent of putting in phrasing commas and asking for no additions to the marked ornamentation explained in his table of ornaments. This, however, was felt by performers to be an unnecessary appropriation of their responsibilities and lack of faith in their good taste.

It is therefore necessary for the player of a baroque sonata, without becoming academic or inflexible in the process, to acquaint himself with the conventions and expectations of baroque performance practice ('baroque' in this chapter is used as applying to the recorder sonata period, not to the entire baroque era which spanned 150 years). Such an understanding will often considerably enhance both his own and his audience's enjoyment and appreciation of the music he plays. Because of their interpretational demands, it is advisable to select sonatas which, in relation to his technical abilities, look easy. Perhaps one or two more demanding pieces could be picked out as a challenge for future performance. A list of easier sonatas is provided in Appendix 2 of *PRS*.

Even if some recorder sonatas seem to have no greater intention than to supply entertainment for gentleman amateurs (to the profit of both composer and publisher), their main purpose was to affect an audience, and the sonata was regarded as a serious form of music. If there is any difference between the use of 'canzona' and 'sonata' in the early seventeenth-century Italian repertoire it is that the canzona is in a lighter, more tuneful vein; and in France the distinction between *suite* and *sonate* is that the latter is associated with wider-ranging and more emotional Italian violin music.[16] The function of entertaining and moving an audience applied equally to dance, theatre, poetry, painting, sculpture and architecture (see pls. 18 and 19). Baroque writers on music frequently drew parallels with other arts, such as comparing dynamics in music to light and shade, chiaroscuro, in painting.

The affect of vocal music upon its audience, in each of the three categories into which baroque music was divided – church, theatre, and court or chamber – was largely determined by the significance of the words. In a baroque opera the plot is advanced by recitative, but the flow of narrative frequently pauses in order to allow a character to express in a da-capo aria his or her emotions, state of mind or point of view. These arias form the musical substance of the opera, rather in the same way as a sonata is made up of a succession of movements. A sonata's integrity, the mood of the whole, may be expressed through a significant theme or other figure common to each movement (*PRS*, pp. 145–6).

Instrumental music, despite having its own non-vocal characteristics, suffers from the considerable disadvantage that it does not have words to convey its meaning, and, if it has no *Affekt*, as Mattheson put it, the music 'can be considered nothing, does nothing, and means nothing'.[17] Before performing a baroque sonata, the player therefore needs to attempt to discover what affect, or group of affects, the composer had

Plate 18   The east frontage of the Old Schools, Cambridge, between King's College Chapel and the Senate House (designed by Stephen Wright and built 1754–8). Parallels between architecture and music may be derived from this baroque façade, in its entity, good order, clearly defined sections and symmetry. The building is symmetrical both laterally with matching recessed bays and at different levels with two complementing balustrades. Its appearance is theatrical like a stage set, with mysterious dark central openings, and, above, swags festooned beneath the cornice draped at their ends like curtains. The firmness of the lower part of the building, with its 'rusticated' arcade and its middle opening faced as if the hewn rock had just come out of the ground, is similar in music to a *basso fundamento*, or a ground bass. The building's dominant design statements, like the melodic line of a baroque sonata with its development and resolution, are concentrated at an upper level. The appearance of a further round-arched window glimpsed through the climactic central window adds a touch of fancy and surprise. Above that, there are discreet, harmonious, well-balanced yet varied decorations of swags and symbolic faces of the four seasons, with stone vases ornamenting and punctuating the top line of the building, a model for baroque musical embellishment. (Author's photograph)

in mind to communicate. The language of music, though itself developing as composers maintained freshness and appeal by introducing new ideas, was in the baroque period well enough understood for the composer's intended affects to be recognised from, for example, the key of the music,[18] its title (particularly in French music), the tempo directive, for example *gayement* or *affettuoso*, and from the use of dance forms.[19] 'Every dance should convey some affection of the soul' (Mattheson). Quantz tells us that affects may also

> be discerned by whether the intervals between the notes are great or small, and whether the notes themselves ought to be slurred or articulated. Flattery, melancholy and tenderness are expressed by slurred and close intervals, gaiety and boldness by brief articulated notes, or those forming distant leaps. ... Dotted and sustained notes express the serious and the pathetic; long notes, such as semibreves or minims, intermingled with quick ones [as in a French overture] express the majestic and sublime.[20]

It is a valuable exercise to go through all of Handel's recorder sonatas and by using a series of appropriate adjectives or descriptive phrases to ascribe a mood or character to each movement, and, where it seems appropriate, to the sonata as a whole. Sometimes Handel does this for us: Walsh's edition marks the third movement of the D minor sonata 'Presto', but Handel's autograph states 'Furioso', and it uses the language of the operatic anger aria with its torrent of semiquavers between the bass and treble parts (Ex. 1).

Example 1 also shows the importance of working on treble and bass

Example 1   Handel, Recorder Sonata in D minor, third movement (Presto or Furioso): a copy of first section from Handel's autograph in the Fitzwilliam Museum, Cambridge (lines 1, 3 and 5 are the treble recorder part, lines 2, 4 and 6 the figured basso continuo). The treble part of the whole movement from Thurston Dart's edition is printed, with tonguing suggestions, in *PRS*, p. 83.

parts together in preparing a baroque sonata; many were conceived, and sometimes also published (e.g. J.-B. Loeillet's Op. 1 sonatas), in duet form. Handel's Op. 1 No. 2 recorder sonata is in G minor, a key which, according to Mattheson, expresses 'serene earnestness mixed with happy loveliness'. It avoids becoming too serious and grand by not using the customary fugato form in the second movement, which is more saraband-like in style – at least in the recorder line, for the bass part gruffly interrupts the recorder's lyricism (see Ex. 3). Handel's A minor recorder sonata, the first movement of which has an antecedent in a cantata aria which refers to 'weeping' and 'dejection',[21] may be treated as a complete operatic *scena* (*PRS*, pp. 5–6). This interpretational approach was still being employed by critics even in Mozart's time.[22]

Although the affect approach seems to yield little insight in performing some light-weight recorder sonatas by minor composers, it should never be lost sight of, and in some sonatas it profoundly influences one's interpretation. This is the case with Telemann's great D minor sonata from *Essercizii musici* of 1739/40. D minor is characterised in Charpentier's list as 'grave and pious'; it was later the key of Mozart's *Requiem*. *PRS* (pp. 46–59) provides a fully worked-out analysis of this sonata in terms of affects such as 'faith', 'doubt' and 'prayer'. Reverting to G minor, here is the opening of the first movement of J.-B. Loeillet's Op. 3 No. 3 sonata (the movement is considered in full in *PRS*, pp. 8–10). The effect is of contentment and naivety, like a story with a happy ending. The words of its imagined narrative are almost audible within the (unstated) siciliana dance-measure (Ex. 2).

Example 2   J.-B. Loeillet, Recorder Sonata, Op. 3 No. 3, in G minor: opening of the first movement (from the Walsh and Hare publication of Loeillet's twelve Op. 3 sonatas (*c*1718) in the Cambridge University Library, pirated from Roger's original Amsterdam edition of *c*1715).

First then, the performer needs to 'divine the intentions of the composer' and 'should seek to enter into the principal and related passions that he is to express' (Quantz),[23] for he 'cannot move others without himself being moved' (C. P. E. Bach).[24] He therefore takes on the role of an orator in gaining the attention of, moving and entertaining an audience. If there is no audience, the players should imagine one. Baroque music generally was not written for the self-indulgence of the composer or the performer. It was written, and thereafter often appropriately adapted, for particular musical occasions and purposes. The parallel between musical performance and rhetoric was a common theme among baroque writers, and was worked out with German thoroughness by Mattheson. For example, an oration, like a movement in music, has its *Exordium*, in which its character and intentions are set out to prepare the listener and arouse his attention and interest (this might be achieved by one opening chord), followed by the *Narratio* or exposition. In the Loeillet example above, the exposition does not begin until the quaver up-beat at the end of the third bar, for this is the start of a stanza consisting of four lines of two bars each. Much music is conceived in terms of four lines of verse, and/or of phrases of four notes or four beats. The opening two bars of Loeillet's movement are introductory, like drawing back the stage curtains to reveal the scene. They should be played with expectancy, but without the forward drive of the quatrain starting at bar 3.[25] On the recorder this is achieved by gradations of tonguing articulation, especially in the placing of the semiquavers within the siciliana pattern.

Each movement of a baroque sonata then, constantly keeping the parallel with the orator in mind, is made up of paragraphs, sentences and words. Words consist of strong and weak syllables, and the rhythms and metre of baroque music depend on the alternation of strong and weak notes. Violinists generally did not attempt to equalise the less strong up-bow and the stronger down-bow, but tried to ensure that down-bows fell on the stronger, more stressed notes. Keyboard playing was similarly based on weak and strong fingers, with awkward fingerings so placed that they preceded a note that required a fractional delay in its placing within the moulding of a phrase. Recorder players may also modify their fingerings to respond to the expressive needs of the music (*PRS*, pp. 120–1), and should give careful consideration to the placings of minute silences of articulation – Couperin's commas – and to the points at which to take smaller or longer breaths. Paragraphs should be kept well separated, with large breaths marking off the ends of sections, taking full advantage of the latitude which a listener tolerates in the placing of what seems to be a regular pulse. The audience should never be in doubt where, in the performer's inter-pretation, one phrase ends and another begins. Legato smoothness is not a feature of baroque performance practice, though slurs were used

Plate 19   *Sonata da chiesa?*
This is a detail of Egid
Quirin Asam's *The
Assumption of the Virgin* in
the Monastery Church, Rohr,
Bavaria, a sculpture in
painted stucco (1718–22).
There is a strong sense of
movement in the swirling
draperies and angels' wings,
but it is contained within the
structural framework of a
round arch, though itself
decorated. There is an
equally strong sense of form
in the relationship between
the three figures. But most
noticeable of all is the
rhetorical attitude of the
Virgin, gesturing like a
baroque singer.

for note-grouping and as ornaments. Generally, baroque and renaissance music was played in a more detached style than nineteenth- and
twentieth-century music,[26] with more unevenness in the weight and
length of the notes within a phrase. This makes it all the more
important to identify, mould and characterise each of the individual
phrases that make up the sentences of the music (*PRS*, pp. 8–10,
referring to the Loeillet example given as Ex. 2). Baroque music should
never sound desiccated or mechanical. It should be flexible and
persuasive, with, as Donington puts it, 'a transparent sonority and an
incisive articulation'.[27]

Baroque sonatas, with their need for as clear and significant a
phrasing as one would accord to a poem in reading it aloud (but
without losing sight of the underlying metre), provide in their nuances

Example 3   Handel, Recorder Sonata in G minor, Op. 1 No. 2 (Walsh, 1732): opening of the second movement.

Example 4   Handel, Recorder Sonata in G minor, Op. 1 No. 2 (Walsh, 1732): last nine bars of the first movement, Larghetto. 'Adagio' at the end of this movement here indicates a gradual rather than an abrupt slowing down, and is an invitation to the player to indulge in some graceful (but not excessive) cadential ornamentation.

Example 5   Handel, Recorder Sonata in F, Op. 1 No. 11 (Walsh, 1732): second movement, Allegro, bars 16–24.

of phrasing an element of personal choice by the performer. Paragraph and sentence ends are usually clear because of the frequent cadencing of baroque music, but the necessary identification of 'mini-phrases'[28] within these sentences may not always be obvious. Take for example the opening of the second movement of Handel's G minor recorder sonata – which of the two commas in bar 2 is correct? Listening to recorded performances shows that different players have different ideas – but consider what follows in Example 3 in order to arrive at a 'solution'.[29]

How should the thirteen consecutive quavers in bars 14–16 in the Larghetto of the same sonata be divided into three mini-phrases? In Example 4 neither studying the bass line or its chords, nor seeking to derive a solution from what follows, is of any help.[30] How does one phrase the semiquavers in the second movement (Allegro) of Handel's F major sonata, especially at bar 23 (Ex. 5)?[31] The challenge in phrasing much passage-work is to achieve a conversational effect between solo and bass, or, as in Example 5, within a solo part.[32] It is this dialogue that endows many baroque sonatas with a spirit of urbanity – 'conversations galantes et amusantes' to quote the title of Guillemain's 1743 *Sonates en quatuor.*

The recorder-sonata period coincided with the time when the differences between the Italian style and the French developed by Lully to epitomise the glory and refinement of the Versailles court were at their most marked. There were, of course, other national styles such as 'the English singularity' which Purcell combined with the 'beauty of the Italian way' and 'the graces and gaiety of the French',[33] but, largely through the influence of Corelli and later of Vivaldi, most recorder sonatas are written in the Italian manner. Composers such as Telemann and Bach wrote in both styles, and the former was instrumental in finally drawing together the two in the *galant* style of the mid-eighteenth century, although Telemann's solo sonatas and trios with recorders are mostly Italian in character. Nevertheless, French *sonates* and *suites* form an important part of the recorder player's baroque repertoire, and it is well worth the effort to cultivate both styles.

The table (*PRS*, pp. 62–3), taken with the two illustrations (pls. 20A and B, from *PRS*, pp. 42 and 64), outlines the differences between the French and Italian styles.

French style	Italian style
delicacy, 'soft, easy, flowing'	vivacity, briskness, fire
moderation and constraint	extremes of expression, unrestrained
'caress the ear', 'perpetual sweetness'	energy, violence, strangeness
taste, 'goût'	passion, gusto

French style	Italian style
formality and propriety (with risk of dullness)	novelty and display (with risk of emptiness)
'natural melody, easy smooth tone'	'superfluous artifices, extravagant ornamentation, frequent and harsh leaps'
poise and refinement	urgency, drive and swagger
clarity and elegance	chiaroscuro, dramatic light and shade
'serious, tender, and sustained passions'	'excess of imagination'
mainly dance-based, and character or descriptive ('genre') pieces	more academic pieces (e.g. fugues) and movements indicating strong affects
restrained harmony and prepared dissonances, except for special effects (e.g. discords in Rebel's 'chaos')	dramatic and sometimes surprising discords; frequent dissonant suspensions
rhythmic variety more within the pulse (e.g. by inequality of pairs of notes)	rhythmic variety on a broader scale
accents marked by ornamentation (called 'accens')	accents marked by stress (bow- or breath-pressure)
specified ornamentation integrated into the composition as a form of expression	free extemporisation left to the performer, especially in slow movements (Adagios)
French tempo indications and other directions	Italian tempo indications and affect words
less wide-ranging dynamics and tempi	louder–softer, quicker–slower
flute-sound	violin-sound
objective and dispassionate first approach during which the player becomes enticed, charmed and moved by the music, though his playing attitude never oversteps 'délicatesse' (see pl. 20A).	immediate identification with and total immersion by the player in the affect of the piece. Demonstrative playing attitude (see pl. 20B). Italian music, said Aubert, 'is not to the taste of the ladies'.

Plates 20A and 20B   French and Italian Styles

Plate 20A (top opposite)   The elegant spirit of French music pervades *La Gamme d'amour* (*Love's Gamut*) by Antoine Watteau (1684–1721) in the National Gallery, London. In his book on the National Gallery, Michael Wilson talks of 'the poised, over-refined characters' in their silken fancy dress 'inhabiting an undefined region some-where between reality and fantasy'.

Plate 20B (bottom opposite)   Italian style is illustrated by a detail from Tiepolo's *Europa* (1753) in the Residenz at Würzburg, showing a group of musicians (including a recorder player) probably playing Vivaldi. In comparison with the Watteau, note the players' energy and fire, in almost shameless enjoyment in the communication of their music. Note, too, the opulent splendour of light and shade and the deliberate dramatic discord created by the angles of the bows.

The differences set out in the table in no way modify what has been said earlier in this chapter about baroque performance generally. Affects are as important in French music as in Italian, though French composers also cultivated genre pieces descriptive of people, animals, birds (e.g. Couperin's 'Le Rossignol en amour')[34] and inanimate objects (e.g. his alarm clock).[35] Moreover, French-style suites and sonatas, though constrained within one key when their instrumentation includes the musette (small bagpipes) or vielle (hurdy-gurdy), are less unified in conception. The player may substitute or omit pieces from them, and decide about repeats to suit the circumstances of performance. An Italian-style sonata was seen so much as an entity that Roger North (1728) says 'during the whole sonnata, the *basso continuo* should not cease for one moment'.[36] It is certainly wrong to make substantial pauses between the movements of baroque sonatas, unless the continuo cello has gone badly out of tune.

The dependence of a composer upon a performer, then as now, is greatest in choice of speeds, both for the most potent expression of the affect of a particular movement and its relation to the rest of the sonata. Speed also depends on room resonance. While baroque music should never drag (unless deliberately so under a marking such as 'mesto'), playing music fast – again, unless its mood or character requires impetuousness or extreme virtuosity – makes it impossible to express nuances of sentence-structure and phrasing, and flexibility within the pulse. Time-signatures[37] and time-words[38] may to some extent indicate the composer's intentions, but it is surprising how many movements are marked just 'Allegro' or 'Gracieusement'. Furthermore, one has to become familiar with the different and varied significance of terminology in the baroque period. Purcell's 'Largo' is not slow; he calls it 'a middle movement'. 'Vivace' means 'lively', and was often seen as slower than 'Allegro'. Baroque evidence suggests that the speed of a minuet was at least $\downarrow$ =160.

While the established pulse of a piece should remain fairly steady, particularly in the bass line, for the music to maintain its coherence and its impetus, the value and rhythm of the notes within that pulse were open to considerable flexibility. Frescobaldi and other seventeenth-century musicians describe how varied the rhythm of four quavers within a minim beat can be.[39] This inequality is particularly important in French music as French words have little or no tonic emphasis, and the metre of French poetry and the rhythm of its delivery derive more from the varying length of syllables than their stress. So close is recorder playing to actual speech that this affects the way tonguing consonants are used in playing French music – the slow-speaking 'r' carries more weight than the quick-speaking 't', and 'r' therefore comes on the down-beat.[40] Once articulated, the down-beat establishes itself by its length, occupying a greater proportion of the time between pulses than the following note, so setting up a lilting inequality. Inequality ratios in French music are subject to considerable variety in expressing the mood of the music. They may be *piqué* or sharply dotted, or *louré* (lilted), or the inequality may be reversed, rather like a 'Scotch snap'. The performer has to decide from an infinite variety of inequality possibilities within a steady ongoing pulse how best to communicate the music's character, its subtlety and its liveliness. He is constrained only by what might be regarded as a series of rules or conventions governing when and when not to employ inequality (set out in *PRS*, pp. 65–7),[41] and by his good taste.

In French-style music, where it is inappropriate to rely upon stress to bring out the pattern of the notes within a phrase, ornamentation may be used by the composer, often marked just with a cross above or below a note (see Ex. 6), in order to delineate the shape of a melodic line. Additional ornamentation is liable to stand in the way of the subtle effects of variation of inequality. In Italian music, however, robust stress and dynamic variation can mould phrases without the assistance of ornamentation, but added mordents and half-trills may enhance the effect. In both styles, cadences require ornamentation, which can be florid and extended in Italian style. In French music, descending thirds from a stronger to a weaker note, especially at phrase-ends, can be infilled with a *coulé*. In Example 6 the *coulé* forms part of the theme itself, raising an interesting question of inequality.[42]

Free ornamentation, i.e. the addition of notes or figures outside conventional 'graces' marked or assumed by the composer, is a feature of Italian-style sonatas, especially in Adagios. Where a section is repeated, additional ornamentation – but without slowing down to

Example 6 De la Vigne, Sonate, Op. 2 No. 5, 'La Persan' (Paris, Boivin, 1739): first section of the third movement. Note the use of the 'French violin clef' (g′ on bottom line).

cope with it – is usually required, for example, in the repeat of a minuet (even, discreetly, in French sonatas).

Baroque ornamentation is a subject too vast to be treated in any detail here, but it is worth making four fundamental points:

(1) Ornamentation should be well prepared and under complete control, but should sound spontaneous. It is best to start learning it by mastering regular eight-semiquaver turned trills on different notes, from which can be derived the mordent and the half-trill.[43]

(2) Much effective ornamentation can be achieved by the appropriate addition of only one note to what is written,[44] for example, an appoggiatura or a *coulé* (Ex. 6), a process which rarely involves problems of technique.

(3) Vibrato,[45] however produced, and slurs are ornaments. They should be used sparingly, and always with a definite musical purpose in mind.

(4) The prime purpose of ornamentation is to intensify the perceived affect of the music, and to make one's communication of a sonata more moving, pleasurable and exciting. It is only incidental if this happens to show off the performer's skill or virtuosity.

Many composers of baroque sonatas did not use dynamic markings, except for echo effects, and not always then. And some people say that as the recorder has little or no potential for dynamics, it is as well that baroque recorder-sonata composers did not seem to want them. This is a double fallacy. The recorder is not as loud as a baroque oboe or violin, but it can play forcibly and with penetration, and it can also produce beautiful notes very quietly indeed. Dynamic variation is mentioned in the earliest recorder tutor, Ganassi's *Fontegara* of 1535.[46] The redesign of the recorder by Hotteterre and his contemporaries in the late seventeenth century increased the flexibility of the instrument as well as its range. The recorder player's greatest problem is that, unlike the flute or the violin, it is very difficult to maintain accurate intonation at different dynamic levels, but every sonata player should practise and master the required techniques of shading, refingering and partial venting (*RT*, pp. 56–62 and 94–6). For it is beyond doubt that recorder-sonata composers expected wide dynamic variety,[47] otherwise Telemann, for example, would not have written double echoes in his D minor recorder sonata (Ex. 7).[48] Baroque composers regarded dynamics generally to be part of the performer's responsibilities, a further resource towards fulfilling his role as the composer's orator, especially in declaiming the drama of an Italian-style sonata. Two types of dynamics should be recognised. The first is structural dynamics where an *f* or *p* general level is assigned to a section, a repeat, or even a movement as a whole, such as the prayer-like Grave of Telemann's

Example 7 Telemann, Recorder Sonata in D minor from *Essercizii musici* (Hamburg 1739–40): the recorder part (in French violin clef) of the first movement from the print in the Library of Congress, Washington. After four chords in the continuo, the recorder enters dramatically on a seventh chord; the opening phrase should therefore be played *f*, contrasting with the double echo that follows.

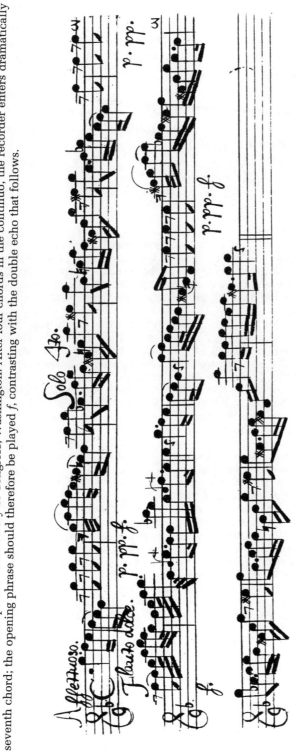

D minor recorder sonata. The second is expressive dynamics, which, within the 'terrace' of a section, rise and fall to express the contours and undulations of phrases and groups of phrases. This calls for crescendos and diminuendos, including upon a single note, such as the *messa di voce*[49] in which a long note swells and dies away. No singer would fail to exploit the resources of dynamic rise and fall, and recorder-sonata players should be equally bold, imaginative and dramatic. 'If ... you play everything with the same colour or volume, the listeners will remain completely unmoved.'[50] The sonata will then lose all its significance and purpose.

Notes

1. A few recorder sonatas were written after 1740 in the new *galant* style, for example three for 'Flauto solo e Basso' by Antonio Michele di Lucca (1749, 1750 and 1752). There was a vogue for the 'Flûte douce' in Vienna and elsewhere during the period 1810–40 (or thereabouts) in the guise of the 'czakan', a small keyed recorder of Hungarian origin for which composers such as Heberle and Krähmer contributed a repertoire of some hundreds of engagingly sentimental pieces, including a few sonatas (see pl. 33).
2. D minor recorder/B minor flute sonata. 'Clearly the sonata was written for the recorder and later transposed for the flute, either by Handel or by Walsh' (Lasocki–Holman Faber edition of Handel's flute sonatas, p. 59. This is a companion to the excellent Lasocki–Bergmann edition of Handel's six recorder sonatas).
3. Walsh published 'Six Sonatas or Solos compos'd by Mr Geminiani & Castrucci', four by Castrucci and two by Geminiani, taken from a collection of twelve – six by each composer – 'a Flauto Traversie, o Violino, o Hautbois e Basso Continuo', *c*1720. Those selected were 'contriv'd & fitted' as recorder sonatas.
4. See *PRS*, p. 198, note 45. Sonatas from this period are discussed in *PRS*, pp. 146–50.
5. Trio-sonata in G for two flutes and continuo BWV 1039, which can be played on recorders (in B flat as published by Peters–Hinrichsen). See also Michael Marissen, 'A trio in C major for recorder, violin and continuo by J. S. Bach?' *Early Music*, 13/3 (August 1985), pp. 384–90, referring to BWV 1032. This reconstruction of BWV 1032 is published by Hänssler (HE 11.227).
6. Michael Talbot, in his *Tomaso Albinoni* (Oxford 1990), pp. 151 and 153, suggests that both 'Op. 4' No. 6 and Op. 6 No. 6 might have originated as recorder sonatas. Other Albinoni violin sonatas, and other baroque violin sonatas generally, can, in accordance with practice of the time, often be successfully adapted as recorder sonatas. Choose those that require little or no modification in regard to their range, that do not depend on double-stopping for their effect, and which provide enough rests or phrase-points at which to take breath.
7. All the composers mentioned in these lists, and many more besides, are considered in William S. Newman, *The Sonata in the Baroque Era* (New York, Norton, 1959; paperback 1983).
8. *Avertissement* to Marin Marais's *Troisième Livre*. Couperin, moreover, states that he quite understands that those who play his pieces will want to play them on their own instruments.
9. Dario Castello's designation; meaning, like 'Canto solo' (Frescobaldi), a high instrument with continuo accompaniment, for example organ or theorbo. Sonatas of this period are considered in *PRS*, pp. 100–12 (Fontana), and 130–2 (Riccio).
10. They add to the splendour of Satan's army as it moves
     In perfect *Phalanx* to the *Dorian* mood
     Of Flutes and soft Recorders   (*PL* Bk 1 550–1).

The continuation of this passage, like Dryden's poem 'Alexander's Feast', well illustrates the baroque belief in the power of music to 'move the affections'.

11. For example in Baglione's *Euterpe* (1620), the frontispiece of *PRS*, where three tenor recorders are depicted.

12. Greeting's *The Pleasant Companion*, probably first published in 1661, appeared in later editions in 1668, 1672, 1675, 1680, 1682, 1683 and 1688.

13. The passage from the preface to Hudgebut's *Vade Mecum* is quoted in Hunt, pp. 54–5.

14. It is a prime task of editors to clarify notational matters, for example whether ♩♩ should be assimilated to a prevailing ♩♩♩ or be played ♩♩ . It is better for a person beginning to play baroque sonatas not to use facsimiles – see end of note 29 on errors in bar 6 of Example 3.

15. Sylvestro Ganassi in his recorder tutor *Fontegara* (Venice 1535), ed. Hildemarie Peter, trans. Dorothy Swainson (Berlin-Lichterfelde 1959), says 'it is possible with some players to perceive, as it were, words to their music ... the aim of the recorder player is to imitate as closely as possible all the capabilities of the human voice. For that it is able to do' (p. 9). And Hudgebut (1679 – note 13 above) says, 'Of instruments ... there is none which comes nearer in Imitation to the Voice...'.

16. Dornel's wording of 'Sonates à violon seul et Suites pour la Flute traversière' (1711) is significant. Characteristics of Italian style gradually became fused into French music from 1695, the time of Couperin's first 'Sonades', for example Elizabeth Jacquet de la Guerre's 'Sonates pour le violon et le clavecin' of 1707. Among several by lesser-known composers, for example Duval, Francœur, Mascitti and Senaillé, writing in this fascinating mixed genre, is a fine sonata by Anne Danican-Philidor, unusually specifying recorder (1711, *PRS*, pp. 142–4). Philibert de la Vigne's 1739 Sonates for a variety of instruments, including recorder but excluding violin, are, however, in the prevailing courtly style of French suites (*PRS*, pp. 67–71).

17. This and the other Mattheson references in this chapter are commented on in *PRS* (pp. 4, 5, 6, 10, 12, etc. and 176, note 29).

18. Charpentier (1692), Mattheson (1713) and Rameau (1722) all deal with the affects of keys – see *PRS*, pp. 4–5 and 174, note 16.

19. Many sonatas contain dance-style movements (see Exx. 2, 3 and 6; and could Ex. 5 be seen as an allemande?). The *sonata da camera*, like the suite, consists mainly of a series of dances, but, named or not, dance-style movements often occur in the *sonata da chiesa*, which quickly lost its church affiliations and became the standard baroque slow–fast–slow–fast four-movement sonata form.

20. J. J. Quantz, *On Playing the Flute*, trans. Edward J. Reilly, 2nd edn (London 1985), pp. 125–6.

21. See the first of three articles by David Lasocki and Eva Legêne, 'Learning to ornament Handel's sonatas through the composer's ears', *The American Recorder* 30/1, 3–4 (Feb., August and Nov. 1989), pp. 9–14, 102–6 and 137–41. The authors quote the whole aria with its words, which suggest not only the affect of the movement but also its nuances of phrasing and style of ornamentation.

22. See Peter le Huray, *Authenticity in Performance* (Cambridge 1990), Chap. 8.

23. The references to Quantz, *On Playing the Flute*, are from pp. 90 and 124–5.

24. C. P. E. Bach, *Essay on the True Art of Playing Keyboard Instruments* (1753), vol. III, p. 13; trans. and ed. W. J. Mitchell (London 1949).

25. Loeillet uses the same device at the beginning of the last movement of this elegantly crafted sonata, with identical opening bass notes.

26. In his *Essay*, C. P. E. Bach says, 'Notes that are neither detached, connected nor fully held are sounded for *half* their value. ... Crotchets and quavers in moderate and slow speeds are usually performed in this semi-detached manner' – see le Huray, *Authenticity*, pp. 16–18.

27. Robert Donington, *Baroque Music: Style and Performance* (London 1982), p. 167.

28. See Theron McClure, 'Making the music speak: silences of articulation', *The American Recorder* 29/2 (May 1988), pp. 53–5, quoted in *PRS*, p. 176, note 33.

29. I would favour the second comma. The phrasing in bars 5–9 (and beyond) is in six-

beat modules, constituting a sequence. Moreover, the saraband rhythm is displaced one crotchet forward at bar 5, which makes it especially important to substantiate the six-beat saraband theme within bars 1–2 and bars 3–4. This interpretation could be strengthened at the repeat by playing a trill at $f\sharp''$ in bar 2. Readers may like to identify the one error and two omissions made by Walsh's engraver in bar 6.

30. There are several ways of phrasing this passage. The rising-fourths figure which Handel embarks upon at the last two notes of bar 13 does not give as much help as one would have hoped as there are no rising fourths in treble or bass within bar 15. In fact, that bar smothers the effect of the rising-fourths figure, preparing the way for a new decorative figure in bar 16. The thirteen quavers could be played with completely neutral phrasing after the first two in a long line as if the music were losing its way, i.e. without mini-phrases. Otherwise they may be grouped 4+4+5, or 5+4+4. One's choice from these and other possibilities in this meandering passage should not be conveyed by stresses upon notes, but simply by imagining commas between notes to mark off the groupings. Well-placed ornamentation will clarify and enhance one's chosen interpretation.

31. The semiquavers start (at the end of bar 18 and again at the end of bar 20) as conversational groups of four. But at bar 23 do these groups of four semiquavers continue, as might be suggested by the continuation of the bass rhythm in this bar? Or, despite the bass, should one, for variety, here change to a down-beat pattern for the semiquavers in bars 23–4? Other possible alternatives are (1) starting with the second semiquaver in bar 23, to group the remaining notes up to the quaver d'' in bar 24 as 6, 7, 6; or (2) starting with the last three semiquavers in bar 24, to group 6, 4, 4, 4 (or 6). All these interpretations can be sustained within the logic of the music. What happens at the end of bar 19 into bar 20? Passage-work never speaks for itself; you have to make it talk.

32. See *PRS*, pp. 136–7, for an example from a Paisible sonata.

33. The full quotation, from the *Gentleman's Journal* (January 1691) (see Dorothy Hartley and Margaret M. Elliott, *The Life and Work of the People of England – The Seventeenth Century* (London 1928), p. 19), is 'Mr Purcell, who joins to the delicacy and beauty of the Italian way the graces and gaiety of the French, composes the music' (of 'a new opera' – *King Arthur*). It is surprising that 'delicacy' is associated with Italian rather than French style. The phrase 'the English singularity' is Roger North's (*Roger North on Music*, ed. John Wilson (London 1959), p. 25, and see also *PRS*, pp. 134–5).

34. A copy of Couperin's 'Le Rossignol en amour' in the Museum at Carpentras, Vaucluse, France, has this note: 'This "Rossignol" is successful on the flute – one can't do better (when it is well played)'. And it contributes to our knowledge of French performance practice by adding, 'One shouldn't keep too strictly to the beat in the *Double*' i.e. the variation, which Couperin marks 'Plus lentement et très doux'. 'Everything must be sacrificed to good taste, to neatness in the flow of the phrases, and to playing the ornaments I have marked in with great tenderness.' Although Couperin says 'Flûte Traversiere', Carl Dolmetsch, following good precedents, has very effectively appropriated this piece from Couperin's Book III, *Ordre* 14, for the sopranino recorder.

35. 'Le Réveil-matin', Book I, *Ordre* 4.

36. *Roger North on Music*, p. 260. See *PRS*, pp. 115–16 and 193, note 3.

37. See Robert Donington, *The Interpretation of Early Music*, rev. paperback edn (London 1989), Chap. XXXVIII.

38. *Ibid.*, 'Time-words' Chap. XXXVI and 'Dance tempos' Chap. XXXVII. The reference to Purcell's 'Largo' is on p. 388, and to the minuet on pp. 398–9 and 403–4 (Quantz).

39. *Ibid.*, pp. 455–6, quoting Caccini and Frescobaldi.

40. See David Lasocki, 'The tonguing syllables of the French Baroque', *The American Recorder* 8/3 (Summer 1967), pp. 81–2. He explains the position of the 't', articulated lightly but sharply at the top of the front upper teeth, alternating with 'r' as a single articulation on the palatal teethridge, almost like 'd'. This sets up a forward-and-back tongue movement in playing French music (*PRS*, pp. 65 and 79).

David Lasocki's translation of Jacques Hotteterre le Romain's *Principes* of 1707 (*Principles of the Flute, Recorder and Oboe* (London 1968)) has a long and useful introduction including a section on articulation (pp. 19–23). This has now been superseded by Patricia Ranum's brilliant article, '*Tu-Ru-Tu* and *Tu-Ru-Tu-Ru*: Toward an Understanding of Hotteterre's Tonguing Syllables', in David Lasocki (ed.), *The Recorder in the 17th Century: Proceedings of the International Recorder Symposium Utrecht 1993* (Utrecht 1995).

41. The conventions of inequality are described by Lasocki (trans.), *Principles*, and in editions of Hotteterre's music; le Huray, *Authenticity in Performance*, pp. 46–53; George Houle, *Meter in Music 1600–1800: Performance, Perception and Notation* (Bloomington 1987); and by David Fuller in *The New Grove*, under 'Notes inégales'.

42. The time-signature 3 and the word 'Gracieusement' indicate that the quavers are unequal. In bar 1 and its restatement in bar 9, the *coulé* (shown with the small note *a'*, slurred to the crotchet *g'*) is, as usual, played before the beat. The temptation is to play it exactly as written, turning the opening minim *b'* into a dotted crotchet. But as the general inequality of this opening section of the movement is a 2:1 *Louré* (variations in inequality come later, even slightly in bars 13 and 14), the value of the small quaver is only that of the last note of a triplet, as if the time-signature were $\frac{9}{8}$ – though that is too rigid a device for editing this music.

   Bar 8 is a sub-section end, and a breath, or at least a phrasing comma, needs to be taken there. No breathing problem arises at the less important phrase-ends at bars 4 and 12 because the dotted minims there can be slightly shortened, but if the last quaver *c''* of bar 8 is only equivalent to the last note of a triplet, this leaves no time for the implied breath to be taken after it. The inequality of the descending quavers in bar 8 should therefore be smoothed out so that the last of them becomes an equal quaver, giving a little more time to take the breath, and, with a slight decrescendo, slackening the phrase-end. A similar situation arises in bar 24 of the first movement of this sonata; *PRS* (p. 68) quotes the whole of the recorder part of that movement from a modern edition, and offers tonguing and inequality suggestions.

43. *RT*, Chap. IX, and *PRS*, Appendix 1.

44. See Frederick Neumann, *Ornamentation in Baroque and Post-Baroque Music* (Princeton 1978), pp. 47–199, 'One-note graces'.

45. *Ibid.*, pp. 511–22.

46. *Fontegara* (see note 15), p. 89: 'Remember that you can sound every note softly by slightly uncovering a finger-hole and using less breath. ... You should half-close the holes somewhat more or less as your ear requires and as you feel to be right.' See Rowland-Jones, 'A Short History of Partial Venting', *The Recorder Magazine* 15/2 (June 1995), pp. 48–50.

47. Donington, *Interpretation*, pp. 482–90, and le Huray, *Authenticity*, pp. 38–41.

48. See *PRS*, pp. 51–3, for advice on playing these double echoes. The opening of this sonata is the subject of David Coomber's 'Rhetoric and affect in baroque music', *The Recorder* (Melbourne) 3 (Nov. 1985), pp. 23–7.

49. See *PRS*, p. 188, note 4.

50. Quantz, *On Playing the Flute*, pp. 276–7.

4   The baroque chamber-music repertoire

A commentary on the recorder's seventeenth- and eighteenth-century repertoire, actual and potential, other than solo sonatas, concertos and orchestral usage

ANTHONY ROWLAND-JONES

Iconography suggests that, as the sixteenth century progressed, the recorder became less widely employed,[1] although, as a famous passage in *Hamlet* and references in other plays confirm,[2] it continued to be used in the theatre and probably in court masques, as well as by the waits (see p. 168). Early seventeenth-century consorts were usually of viols or violins,[3] and if wind instruments are referred to they are rather more likely to be cornetts and sackbuts than recorders. Except in England, the sixteenth-century tradition of consorts of like instruments was going out of vogue even by the time Praetorius published *De organographia* in 1618–19. Vincenzo Giustiniani, in his *Discorso sopra la musica* (after 1628), refers to the difficulty of keeping 'viols or flutes … in tune (for not being played frequently they became absolutely useless)'. The opulence of instrumentation of the Florentine *intermedii* or of Monteverdi's *Orfeo* (1607), both involving the recorder, also passed out of fashion, and the growing dominance of the versatile and expressive violins eventually caused even the glorious cornetts to join the recorders in relative obscurity. Recorders remained among the properties of civic and court establishments, but when the fourteen-year-old Purcell was appointed in 1673 to assist John Hingeston in repairing the royal wind instruments, including recorders, that part of his responsibilities must have been a sinecure, as well as originally 'without fee'.

Strong traditions of wind-instrument playing persisted in Venice, where the virtuoso cornettist Girolamo Dalla Casa had been head of the official wind band, as well as in the musical centres of the Austrian Empire. But the *Sonatella a 5 Flauti et Organo* by the Venetian Antonio Bertali (1605–69), Kapellmeister at Vienna, and the pieces by Schmelzer[4] and Biber referred to on p. 53 (see also Hunt (cited p. 51, footnote), pp. 33–6) can only be regarded as occasional compositions, however much their existence is valued by recorder players. Similarly, the use of recorders in German cantatas and opera (see Linde (cited p. 51, footnote), pp. 87–8) is for special occasions. Schütz in *Jubilate*

Deo, omnis terra (1629, SWV 262) uses the extremes of bass voice and 'duoi Flautini' to encompass 'the whole world', a magnificent effect. It is typical of changes in seventeenth-century scoring that Schütz's second and third sets of *Symphoniae sacrae* with German texts (1647 and 1650) call for 'two violins or the like' instead of his earlier more varied range of accompanying instruments, although two descant recorders are 'ad lib' in *Meine Seele erhebt den Herren* (SWV 344). In his *Weihnachtshistorie* (1660) he uses recorders to accompany the shepherds. In some of his music, Schütz simply leaves parts as instrumental without a definite specification. This, together with 'or the like', and statements by other composers such as Schein or Peuerl (Linde, pp. 84–5), reminds us how fluid scoring was in the baroque period – Schein even suggests that the second soprano part of his *Waldliederlein* might be played by violin or recorder. Schütz was perfectly prepared for his *Jubilate* to be performed with violins if recorders were not available. Playing the music well, in a lively, committed and persuasive manner, was more important than what instrument it was played on, provided that the range and sound were right, even when a special effect was intended. Especially for the earlier baroque period, it is therefore quite reasonable to conjecture that recorders were used to play a variety of parts in German music from this time, probably more often in mixed ensembles, although the collection of the Liechtenstein band at Kroměříž in Moravia contains music specifying a recorder consort. Intradas, other dance-style pieces, and dance suites by Peuerl, Schein,[5] Scheidt, Hassler, Orologio and others may be regarded as 'probable repertoire'. This music has the unusual merit of being both interesting and easy to play. Nor must we overlook the contributions to the German repertoire of English *émigrés* such as Brade and Simpson.[6] Just to give one example from another German composer of the time, Altenburg's 1620 *Intrada XII* (LPM EML 117) sounds splendid on five recorders with a voice or contrasting instrument doing the 'Ein feste Burg' cantus firmus. The opening, appropriately, sounds like a festive peal of bells.

Linde (p. 88) mentions that Capricornus (1628–65) prescribes five recorders to accompany his bass aria *Ich bin schwarz*. This, with the Bertali, Biber and Schmelzer examples previously mentioned, and the even later evidence of the Liechtenstein collection, leads one to suppose that the recorder consort remained in existence in Germany until well into the seventeenth century, as also in Venice where Massimiliano Neri's *Sonata 10 à 8* of 1651 is for three recorders, three violins, two theorbos and organ continuo. And the players involved must presumably have performed other music. Bearing in mind the fluidity of early baroque instrumentation, and the similarity in sound of a recorder consort to a baroque pipe-organ (see p. 27), it is tempting to regard German organ music of the late renaissance and baroque periods as potential recorder repertoire, both in contemporary and modern arrangements. The Altenburg *Intrada* mentioned above is in effect a chorale prelude, and many such organ pieces transfer well to recorders – much better, for example, than the florid keyboard writing of, say, *The Fitzwilliam Virginal Book.*[7] Many German organ pieces are conceived in terms of clear four-part writing, often within a compass suited to recorder arrangements. The list of renaissance and baroque organist composers is enticing – Paumann (a recorder player – see p. 45, note 8), Hofhaimer (who played organ arrangements of Lieder also played on recorders), Hassler, Scheidt, Praetorius, Froberger, Buxtehude, Pachelbel, Walther and J. S. Bach, and one can look further afield to Sweelinck in Amsterdam, and to Cabezón, Merulo and Frescobaldi in Spain and Italy as sources for arrangements. Some of Bach's keyboard music works surprisingly well on recorders, including pieces from *The Art of Fugue* such as *Contrapunctus IV* and the long but incomplete *Contrapunctus XVIII*, both profoundly moving.

A return to Venice brings us to the centre of development of the purely instrumental canzona, of which three types need to be recognised. The first and earliest, derived from the French chanson and retaining its light-heartedness, is usually for four voices 'to be played by all sorts of musical instruments' (Frescobaldi, *Primo Libro delle Canzoni*, 1628), though some composers specified, for instance, violin, cornett and two trombones (Viadana, for a 'Canzona d'aria francese a 4' published in 1602). The second is the spectacular and sonorous multi-choir canzona typified by Giovanni Gabrieli's *Sacrae symphoniae* of 1597, of which recorders can only produce a pale imitation, however enjoyable the attempt may be. The third is the canzona (or sonata)[8] for one, two or more instruments with a mainly supporting bass. The first and the third are of considerable consequence to recorder players.

The equal interest of all the parts, and the light-heartedness of the polyphonic *canzona francese* makes it very suitable for performance by recorders.[9] The repertoire is well represented in London Pro Musica editions, including Merulo, Maschera, Guami, Banchieri, the Neapolitan Trabaci, and Gabrieli himself, who wrote lively quartet canzonas as well as others in up to seven parts. The second of Gabrieli's 1608 four-part canzonas catches the idiom perfectly, and Canali's *La Stella* (1600) is ingeniously succinct. The *canzona francese* continued until well into the seventeenth century with compositions by Cima, Riccio, Frescobaldi and others, though provided with a supporting bass. Even as late as 1634 Frescobaldi still does not specify particular instrumentation.

The third type of canzona emulates for three or four players the emotional intensity of Gabrieli's large-scale works, with antiphonal alternations of treble parts against a slower-moving bass, sudden dramatic changes of tempo, rhythm and dynamic, and outbursts of florid written-out decorations. Some composers, for instance Cima who wrote the first 'trio-sonatas' in 1610, also exploited contrasts of timbre by specifying instruments such as cornett, bassoon or trombone, and several others associated with Venice[10] occasionally specified recorders, as in Biagio Marini's *Sonata per doi Flautini* of 1626.[11] Riccio's 1612 and 1620 canzonas for recorders and bass have passages of dialogue recalling Monteverdi's vocal models, and the second, *La Rizza*, is derived from Gabrieli's 1597 *Canzon in echo*.[12] But alternative instruments are often suggested, and many canzona and sonata composers use phrases such as 'per ogni sorte di stromenti' or mark the upper parts simply 'soprano' or 'canto'.[13] This, and the status of the recorder as a suitable canzona instrument (even if only in Venice), will encourage its players to tackle the more difficult trio-sonatas of Colista, Turini and Dario Castello (who was head of the wind instruments at St Mark's), and the slightly easier ones of Rossi and other composers working before the genre became suited to violins only. We may be inspired by a dedication to an amateur recorder player, Adriana van den Bergh, of an anthology published in Amsterdam in 1644 by Paulus Matthysz:

If G. B. Buonamente, T. Merula, and M. Uccellini and other phoenixes of this noble art could hear your Honour, they would express wonder and would appreciate that their efforts to compose difficult music has been accepted so graciously and has resulted in performance by such a lady.[14]

During Holland's 'Golden Age' in the mid-seventeenth century, Dutch players such as Jacob van Eyck became virtuosi on the small recorder in C known as the *hand-fluit* (see pls. 21 and 39). This and its treble equivalent are frequently seen in Dutch pictures, for example by Molenaer (pl. 37), Metsu and, especially, Edwaert Collier. The recorder appears in domestic (pl. 23A) and social scenes, even in a tavern (pls. 22 and 23B). Rembrandt was painted with a *hand-fluit* (pl. 21). No musicians of such high quality emerged in Holland, though some pleasant duets for *Fluit* were published by Matthysz in 1644 (ed. Thiemo Wind, Earlham Press 1993), and his two volumes of *'t Uitnement Kabinet* (1646 and 1649) contain some trio-sonatas, several of Italian origin (Merula and Barlasca), for two 'above' instruments and bass, probably recorders or violins.[15] Exercising caution and taste, recorder players may doubtless find further 'probable repertoire' among mid-seventeenth-century string music,[16] or even wind music such as Pezel's *Fünff-stimmigte blasende Musik* of 1685. Some of the 1653 sonatas for three violins and continuo by William Young, an Englishman working at Innsbruck, are perfectly adaptable to recorders. Moreover, designated repertoire continues on an occasional basis throughout the century; as David Lasocki says, 'it is abundantly clear that the recorder featured in a great many seventeenth-century

Plate 21 Govert Flinck, *Portrait of Rembrandt as a Shepherd* (Rijksmuseum, Amsterdam), dated 1639. Even as a 'left-hand-down' player, the excellent finger-positions suggest that Rembrandt, here painted by a pupil, actually played the recorder. Perhaps this is the same instrument that is visible being played in the shadows in the left background of his great *Belshazzar's Feast* in the National Gallery, London – the player goes on unconcerned as he is out of sight of the momentous writing on the wall and the disembodied hand. The recorder is there associated with a supernatural event; here the association is with the pastoral and shepherds (see p. 93). Rembrandt plays a typical Dutch *hand-fluit*-type recorder with its choke-bore design which makes high notes more secure (see pl. 15A). An extant example of a *hand-fluit*, in ivory, is illustrated on page 19 of *Playing Recorder Sonatas*.

compositions, especially vocal ones, that have not yet been catalogued or made available to the public'.[17]

The recorder's own baroque Golden Age in England is gloriously ushered in by a piece probably for three recorders in F and continuo, though it has come down to us transposed to D for violins – a fine *Chaconne* by Henry Purcell, '3 parts upon a Ground' interestingly discussed in Peter Holman's book *Henry Purcell* (Oxford 1994, pp. 69–73). Despite Purcell's advocacy of the Italian trio-sonata, however, such works with recorders did not appear until after his death in 1695, although the violin virtuoso Nicola Matteis published airs with recorder, violin and continuo in 1685. Purcell's own trio-sonatas do not sound very convincing on recorders, or even with recorder and violin, although some lie within the range of the tenor instrument. But on the strength of the three-part chaconne and the canonic 'Two in one upon a Ground' in *Dioclesian* (see p. 94), recorder players may appropriate the string *Chacony* in G minor, which with limpid high notes and a firm bass can sound beautiful in a recorder arrangement. Purcell's considerable contribution to the recorder literature is dispersed throughout his theatre and vocal music,[18] including pastoral cantatas such as *How pleasant is this flow'ry plain* in Playford's *Banquet of Music* of 1688, a genre later developed by Croft, Pepusch and Arne.[19] Excepting the six recorder sonatas, the same is true of Handel who wrote one youthful trio-sonata (in F) with two recorders when he was in Italy, although two others (in ·F major and C minor), not original recorder works, remain in the recorder canon.[20] Handel wrote several Italian cantatas with obbligato recorder parts, of which the best known, *Nel dolce dell'oblio*, describes 'the night thoughts of Phyllis' (soprano); it was published by Schott in 1952 in their 'Voice and Recorder' series but sadly – and this can only be because recorder players are not creating a sufficient demand for music of this kind – it is now out of print.

The use of two recorders and continuo in theatre and other airs, the instrument's growing fashion among amateur gentleman players inspired by the example of professional performances by James Paisible and others at the newly established London concerts (which after 1688 became more important than music at court), and then, around 1700, the impact of Corelli's music, led to an outburst of trio-sonata activity over the first two decades of the eighteenth century. Lasocki has traced numerous recorder arrangements of trio-sonatas from Corelli's oeuvre.[21] Other composers, generally inspired by Corelli though never attaining his quality and craftsmanship, sought to meet this fashionable demand. They include Finger, Corbett, William Williams, Daniel Purcell, Keller, Bononcini, Loeillet and Sammartini (the London ones). Finger, Keller and Pepusch (six 'concerti', Op. 8) paired the lines of a trio-sonata, creating quintets of two treble recorders, two other instru-

Plate 22   *A Musical Party* by Theodoor Rombouts, signed and dated 1627. This shows a treble recorder with what appears to be a perforated fontanelle protecting the keywork for the bottom little finger, usually a feature of renaissance-style tenor and especially bass recorders, as in those illustrated by Virdung (1511), Agricola (1528) and Praetorius (1620) – see Hunt, *The Recorder and its Music*, pp. 17, 21 and 30. But many renaissance recorders managed without keys, partly by oblique cutting of the differently sized (though generally large) holes through the instrument's thick walls (see pl. 36). The recorder played here appears to be near-cylindrical throughout its length, probably with a wide bore. Iconographical evidence suggests that this type of design, which would have had strong low notes but a generally limited compass, co-existed from about mid-fifteenth century to mid-seventeenth on a more or less equal footing with recorders of a mainly cylindrical or slightly tapering shape but with a marked flare at the bell end; these were capable, according to both Ganassi and Praetorius, of producing a 'falsett' range of up to two and a half octaves. El Greco (see pl. 15A inset 1) painted both types – one of each kind appears in two different Immaculate Conception pictures from 1607–10. Dutch 'Utrecht School' paintings by followers of Caravaggio such as Jan van Bijlert and Honthorst frequently included recorders, of the near-cylindrical design – compare plate 39 (Honthorst) with plate 37 (Molenaer).

This painting again illustrates the long-standing combination of voice, recorder (or flute), and a plucked instrument, here an archlute (see pls. 4 and 15B). For the highly emotional music of this period an instrument of the lute family was generally preferred to virginals or harpsichord as it was more capable of expressive nuances of tone and dynamics, supporting the more limited expressivity of the recorder. Unfortunately, the music itself is not shown legibly. Note how the recorder player's left little finger is used to give lateral support to the instrument. Picture from Graham Wells, 'London Salerooms', *Early Music* 5/2 (April 1977), p. 251.

ments such as oboes, flutes or violins – or even unauthentic tenor recorders rather than leave the music unplayed – with continuo bass. One quintet dating from about 1690 is for four treble recorders and continuo.[22] But most of this English repertoire is for two recorders, with or without bass, though the trio-sonatas involving another instrument, such as those with recorder and oboe by John Loeillet, are particularly attractive.

Telemann's recorder music deserves a book by itself, for it is far and away the recorder player's most important source of baroque chamber music, both in amount and quality. Such a book might identify and describe the trio-sonatas, quartets, chamber cantatas, duos, etc. originally designated for recorders; those (where the recorder writing is less idiomatic) for flute but indicated as for recorders by playing a minor third higher, and those with flute, oboe or another instrument which nevertheless 'work well' on recorders.[23] Although instrumental music is a relatively small part of Telemann's immense and mainly vocal output, and music with flute a small part of that, and with recorder even less, some of his most inspired music is written with flute or recorder. This applies especially to the quartet form – for example, flute, violin, cello and keyboard, or recorder, two violins and continuo. Beneath its *galant* charm, lightness and gaiety, and a craftsmanship exceeded only by Handel and Bach, there is sometimes in the slow movements a deep beauty which transcends facile sentiment and in the fast movements an exhilarating driving force that goes beyond mere tunefulness and vigour. These elusive qualities are not to be found in the trio-sonatas with two recorders,[24] attractive as they are, but are more likely to be discovered in the quartets and in the trio-sonatas with recorder and violin,[25] or recorder and oboe, especially the one in C minor. Telemann wrote a 'paired' trio with two recorders, two oboes, two violins, and continuo, and his Hamburg contemporary Prowo paired recorders, oboes and bassoons in a similar sonorous mix. Telemann somehow omitted to write trios for three recorders, so we must be particularly grateful for Mattheson's rewarding, if slightly ponderous, contribution to this genre; and, like Telemann, he also wrote duets. Nor did Telemann compose 'concertos' for four recorders and continuo, a gap filled by Schickhardt. On page 95 there is a reference to recorders at Dresden in the court orchestra (pl. 26) – the enthusiastic amateurs of mercantile Hamburg and Amsterdam for whom Telemann, Mattheson, Prowo, Schickhardt, de Konink and others composed trio-sonatas were not the only recorder players in countries where wind instruments were much cultivated. The Darmstadt library among much else contains *XII Divertissements Melodieux sur la Flutte à bec ou Travers, avec leurs Basse chiffrée* by Count Friedrich Karl of Erbach (1680–1731) and there may well be more

Plates 23A and 23B   The recorder – virtuous and unvirtuous

Plate 23A Recorders feature frequently in Dutch seventeenth-century pictures extolling the virtues of family life, its order and harmony symbolised by music. In this picture of *Family Music* painted at Delft about 1665, Pieter de Hooch (1629–83) shows mother – a formidable lady – controlling the family by keeping time and perhaps also singing the top line, father accompanying on the violin, daughter (or daughter-in-law) strumming a cittern, and son (or son-in-law) playing the *hand-fluit*, while the faithful dog watches, and a happy continuation of this good order of things is promised in the recorder chamber music waiting to be discovered in collections in north and east Europe.[26]

Telemann seems to have enjoyed his self-imposed 'musical exercises' in writing trio-sonatas for different combinations of instruments. He even wrote for recorder and natural horn, and to great effect for recorder and viola da gamba in the trio-sonata in F and in two concertos. Vivaldi, although he too was a great experimenter, wrote only one trio-sonata with recorder, but its partner is the bassoon (RV 86).[27] This is an effervescent virtuoso piece, but Vivaldi is generally much less demanding in his chamber music with recorder. He wrote eight typically lively, urbane and finely balanced chamber concertos including recorder (see p. 115), four of them with oboe, violin, bassoon and continuo: RV 94, 95 (*La Pastorella* (alternatively violins on the top two parts, which spoils the bucolic effect)), 101 and 105. RV 87 has recorder, oboe, two violins and continuo, RV 92 recorder, violin and bassoon or cello, and RV 108 is a delightful work where the recorder engages in discussion with two violins. Unusually, RV 103 in G minor seems to have no continuo bass and is then a trio with recorder, oboe and bassoon; its chromatic last movement is Vivaldi at his best, full of passion and drive. Vivaldi wrote five concertos with recorder, and the instrument has an orchestral role in seven large-scale works, including representation on both sides in a double-orchestra concerto (RV 585).

Like Vivaldi (see p. 99), Alessandro Scarlatti uses the recorder in operas and other vocal works. Of special significance are his chamber cantatas, which inspired Handel. Recorders feature in eleven of them, though one is unfinished.[28] Eight are for soprano voice, three for contralto. Although Scarlatti wrote comparatively little instrumental music, the recorder features in his twelve concerti grossi (p. 113), seven sonatas for *flauto* (probably recorder) and strings,[29] two quartet sonatas, and a serene quintet in A for two recorders (or flutes?), two violins and continuo. The quartet sonatas are splendid works. Both are in F; one is for recorder, two violins and continuo, and the other for three treble recorders, in close harmony, and continuo. Mention should

background. (Cleveland Museum of Art) WB 84. Another domestic painting by de Hooch, *The Duet*, shows a lady and a gentleman playing a lute and a handsome tenor recorder with a strongly flared bell and (?) ivory mouthpiece.

Plate 23B Dir(c)k Hals, a younger brother and pupil of Frans, often painted scenes of merrymaking, generally in taverns, possibly as a warning against licentiousness. To us they may have the opposite effect, so happily are his characters indulging in profligate activities such as playing the recorder, violin, lute and archlute. The picture is signed and dated 1625 and is reproduced by kind permission of the Noortman Gallery, London and Maastricht. WB 85

also be made of Alessandro Marcello's unique *Concerto di Flauti* for an ensemble of recorders doubling with muted strings,[30] as well as the twelve *Balletti a quattro* 'sonatas' (*c*1700) arranged for three recorders and bass which are rather dubiously attributed to Albinoni or Corelli.[31]

Chamber-music occasions at Versailles, Paris and some other French cities involved an even greater freedom of instrumentation than elsewhere. Sonatas might be played as 'ensemble sonatas' doubling parts, and it was often accepted that a player would make his own choice of instrument for a piece, one he preferred to play, or on which he felt the music sounded best, even changing between movements of a suite. Composers would have their own instrument chiefly in mind, so when the Chédevilles, La Vigne and many others wrote *musique champêtre* for the fashionable vielle or musette, their duos and other compositions are usually so narrow in range as to suit recorders in either C or F. Hotteterre's trio-sonatas are for 'Flûtes traversières, Flûtes à bec, Violons, Hautbois, etc.', and he recommends transposing a minor third up for recorders, turning G minor into an awkward B flat minor. La Barre, Blavet and others, through the quality of their flute playing, caused the transverse flute to become fashionable earlier in France than in England or Germany. The outcome is an immense repertoire of 'designated' recorder music but hardly any where the recorder is listed first. This should not put us off, because the music itself is often well suited to the recorder, as experience of playing the *pièces en trio* by composers such as Marais, Lalande, La Barre and even Couperin[32] will show. Later French composers such as Boismortier and Michel Corrette write in a more Italianate manner, but this does not greatly reduce the accessibility of their music to recorder players.

Jacques Loeillet, who had settled at Lyons, wrote an enticing B minor quintet for two transverse flutes, two voice flutes (recorders in D) and continuo.[33] This is one of several gratifying compositions which bring together recorder and flute. Quantz's trio-sonata in C for this combination, full of *galant* curlicues and sentiment, is more imaginative than some of his later flute music. Quantz also composed, in the same key, an equally idiomatic trio-sonata with recorder and violin. Johann Christoph Schultze has left us, apart from his lively *Ouvertüren* (suites) for two recorders and continuo, a trio-sonata for recorder and flute, with a catchy second movement.[34] Fasch wrote for the combination of two recorders and one flute with continuo (see pl. 24),[35] as well as a quartet for recorder, oboe, violin and continuo, and a suite for double orchestra with three recorders taking part on one side, and one recorder and three flutes on the other. Lully, Charpentier and Heinichen mix the two instruments; J. S. Bach does so within a cantata, but flute and recorder do not appear together in the same item.[36] Again it is Telemann who is the supreme master of the mixed media – a fine concerto (p. 112) and, perhaps the best piece in the recorder's entire

baroque instrumental chamber-music repertoire, the quartet for recorder, two flutes and continuo in D minor from the *Musique de table*
(1733); the last movement combines the depth of feeling of Telemann's
best slow movements with outbursts of controlled frenzy inspired by
eastern European dance music.[37]

Walter Bergmann's wishful thinking that a Haydn trio in F, probably
with baryton, might also have been intended for the treble recorder

Plate 24 Two recorders, flute and harpsichord. Detail from an engraving by Bernard
Picart (1673–1738), dated 1709, though Walter Salmen ascribes it to Karl Reusshard of
Augsburg (1678–1735). This is the instrumentation of an undated Sonata in G by J. F.
Fasch (1688–1758), but the explanatory poem beneath the print refers nostalgically to
'the charms of beautiful music (either of Baptiste [i.e. Lully] or Lambert)'. As in so
many pictures of recorder playing, the music is played out of doors, in a château
garden – 'In the shade of a thicket on a beautiful summer day, This agreeable company
tastes the sweet pleasure harmony gives, Since all is well orchestrated' (translation
from Laurence Libin, 'An 18th-century view of the harpsichord', *Early Music* 4/1 (Jan.
1976), p. 18, where the engraving is illustrated). It is interesting that Hermann Moeck
in his 1955 edition (Ed. 1040) of the Fasch sonata suggests that it may have been
written for a garden concert.

because it sounds so good on that instrument reminds us that the recorder's 'probable repertoire' extended until well into the eighteenth century. If, at the composers' own suggestions, flute music could be played on treble recorders a minor third up from D to F, that same music could certainly be played by voice flute in D without transposition. And, remembering the proposal by Stanesby and Merci in 1732 (Hunt, pp. 66–7) to make the tenor recorder the main, non-transposing, instrument of the recorder family, surely its players must occasionally

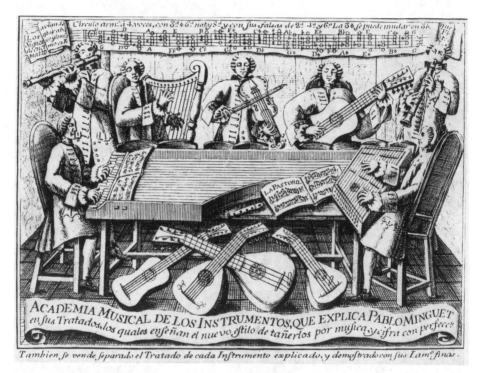

Plate 25 Recorder and flute remain in amicable conjunction. This is the frontispiece of *Reglas y Advertencias generales* in Pablo Minguet e Irol's *Academia Musicál de los Instrumentos* published as late (for a recorder) as 1752–4 (Salmen, *Kammermusik*, pp. 122–3). In his book Minguet describes 'the best and most usual instruments', and, as well as an inevitable range of types of guitar, they include 'Flauta traversa, Flauta dulce y la Flautilla' (the latter, a flageolet with two thumb-holes underneath, lies beside the music, *La Pastoril*). As in the frontispiece to Peter Prelleur's 1731 compendium of largely pirated tutors *The Modern Musick-Master*, where flute and recorder also play together, the instruments are shown, improbably though not impossibly, performing in concert – 'instruments giving various sounds playing and discoursing as one concord' according to the descriptive poem beneath the mixed baroque ensemble illustrated on p. 93 of Linde's *The Recorder Player's Handbook* (also Salmen, *Kammermusik*, p. 83). Two interesting points of detail – there is no cello or gamba bass in the ensemble depicted; and admire how each player has his music conveniently placed in front of him, except for the long-sighted flautist (compare with pl. 41 and several others).

have borrowed traversa music if it was not too idiomatically written for the flute. By this means, chamber music with flute, including obbligatos in cantatas and arias, becomes available to recorder players. This includes ensemble pieces by composers such as Boismortier,[38] Leclair,[39] Stamitz,[40] J. C. Bach and C. P. E. Bach. The latter has even given us a 'designated' piece in his 1755 trio-sonata for viola and *flauto basso*, an unusual role for the bass recorder, also used in a trio-sonata by Graun.

Some present-day professional recorder players give programmes in which many pieces are arrangements, on the grounds that the recorder's baroque repertoire is too limited and rather dull. Perhaps it sometimes does look dull on the written page, but it should never be so in its communication to an audience. Presentation is the performer's task, and to divine and interpret to a modern audience the intentions of composers such as Couperin, Vivaldi, Telemann, Bach and Handel requires a lifetime of ever-growing understanding, and, with it, a deepening appreciation and enjoyment. If such music ever sounds uninspired, this may well reflect upon the inadequacies of its performers. The very limitations of the recorder's baroque repertoire create a self-renewing challenge.

Notes

Many articles on the music of the eighty or so composers mentioned in this repertoire section have appeared at various times in recorder and other journals. For reasons of space these are not referred to in these Notes except in acknowledgement. For full references to 'recorder composers' see Richard Griscom and David Lasocki, *The Recorder: A Guide for Players and Researchers* (New York, Garland, 1994). *The New Grove* contains bibliographical references at the end of each article on a composer – for example, there are 135 such references for Telemann.

1. Iconographical books on music in daily life in the fifteenth century have considerably more representations of the recorder than do similar sixteenth-century volumes. These books do not set out to show frequency of use of any particular instrument.
2. *Hamlet* (1600–1) Act III scene 2, ll. 336–63. Fletcher's *The Two Noble Kinsmen* (1634) has a stage direction 'Stil music of records'. See David Lasocki, 'The recorder in the Elizabethan, Jacobean and Caroline theater', *The American Recorder* 25/1 (Feb. 1984), pp. 3–10.
3. Of different sizes, the word 'violins' then including what we now call violas and cellos. Some consorts, however, were intended for recorders (see Peter Holman's prefaces to his editions of *The Royal Wind Music*, Nova 1981–2).
4. Alex Ayre's 'Chiltern' edition of this piece brings out its subtlety of phrasing.
5. In 1993, London Pro Musica ('LPM') published all twenty of Schein's 1617 *Banchetto musicale* dance suites for five instruments of any kind, but especially viols. They sound 'lieblich und lustig' (to quote Schein) on recorders.
6. LPM have also published much of Brade's music suitable for recorders (Brade's 1617 volume title page says 'suitable for all sorts of instruments especially for violins'), including the five-part *Pavans, Galliards and Canzonas* of 1609 as a boxed set. Similarly presented is Simpson's four-part *Taffel-Consort* collection of

1621 which includes some Dowland pavans in German style with two closely related and lightly embellished descant parts. The same style is evident in Simpson's own excellent Ricercar on 'Bonny Sweet Robin'.

7. Like other keyboard music, organ tabulations, in Germany as elsewhere, were often in ornamented form. But ornamentation was just as often left to a performer. Möseler edition publish a series of such (unornamented) arrangements of chorale preludes, ricercars, fugues, etc. from this period, of considerable interest for recorder quartet. There is no shortage of recorder arrangements (Moeck, Schott, Oriel Library, Polyphonic Publications, etc.) from Bach's chorale preludes, the '48' and *The Art of Fugue*.

8. In his book *The Italian 'Trio' Sonata* (Oxford 1992), pp. 49–52, Peter Allsop discusses what little difference of significance there was at the time in the use of these two terms.

9. The Amsterdam Loeki Stardust Quartet perform canzonas by Merula, Guami, Frescobaldi, Trabaci and others on L'Oiseau-Lyre 430 246.

10. At the August 1993 Utrecht Recorder Symposium (see note 17) Peter van Heyghen said he had 'identified only ten early seventeenth-century *symphonie, canzoni* and *sonate* that specify recorders, all of which were written by organists of a Scuola Grande or of a monastic church in one area of Venice' (report by D. Lasocki, *The American Recorder* 34/4 (Nov. 1993), p. 3). Allsop, *The Italian 'Trio' Sonata*, says that, apart from Riccio, 'Picchi also requires the *flauto* in several sonatas of 1625, and it is listed among the ten melody instruments suggested on the title-page of Neri's *Sonate* (1651)' (p. 32).

11. Included in LPM's Dolce edition *Easy Music of Monteverdi's Time*, nine pieces for two descant recorders and keyboard; this is the best introduction to this repertoire as it eschews the dazzling displays of composers such as Dario Castello – see Allsop, *The Italian 'Trio' Sonata*, pp. 262–3. The other main publisher of early Italian trio-sonatas is Nova.

12. See Allsop, *The Italian 'Trio' Sonata*, pp. 260–1.

13. But see Eleanor Selfridge-Field, 'Instrumentation and genre in Italian music, 1600–1670', *Early Music* 19/1 (Feb. 1991), pp. 61–7 – 'The blanket freedom thought to be conferred by the designation *per ogni sorte di stromento* to the whole repertory of early instrumental music is, for Italy after 1600, largely illusory...'. See also her *Venetian Instrumental Music from Gabrieli to Vivaldi* (Oxford 1975); she mentions Francesco Usper's *Sinfonia prima à 8* of 1619 for strings, recorder, lute and organ continuo, which has an episode with recorder and lute concertato.

14. Quoted by Allsop, *The Italian 'Trio' Sonata*, p. 32.

15. Published by Saul B. Groen, Amsterdam, in ten playing-edition books.

16. For example by Hammerschmidt, Rosenmüller and G. B. Vitali.

17. *The Recorder in the 17th Century*, Proceedings of a Symposium held at Utrecht, August 1993, ed. D. Lasocki (Utrecht, STIMU, 1995).

18. Listed in Walter Bergmann, 'Henry Purcell's use of the recorder' (1965), reprinted in *Recorder and Music Magazine* 7/12 (Dec. 1983), pp. 310–13. This list, however, requires updating in the light of recent research.

19. Schott have published several of these delightful cantatas. The Purcell cantata referred to is in the Bärenreiter catalogue (HM 164). From Purcell's time, Schott include Philip Hart's *Proceed sweet charmer of the ear* for two sopranos, two treble recorders and continuo.

20. See Terence Best, 'Handel's chamber music', *Early Music* 13/4 (Nov. 1985), pp. 476–99, especially pp. 488–90 and 492. The beautiful C minor trio-sonata, probably written about 1717–18, is for flute and violin, and the flute part (there was a B minor version as well) is frustratingly low for the recorder. The slightly later F major trio-sonata is most likely to be for flute and violin, but fits the recorder well.

21. Introduction to the Trio-Sonata in D by Corelli, arranged for recorders by Schickhardt – rather well – and published by Nova in 1979, along with pieces by some of the other composers listed in this paragraph, such as Finger.

22. Edited Layton Ring (Schott). No name is given in the MS. It was originally thought to be by Paisible but is now attributed to Finger.

23. It would cover well over a hundred compositions, a substantial element being vocal music such as cantatas 'for private and home use as well as for public devotions in a church' as Telemann himself says. Eight of these, for soprano, recorder and continuo, are published along with many other Telemann compositions by Hänssler (Stuttgart), and others by Bärenreiter in their 'Concerto Vocale' series.

24. This remark is in no way intended to denigrate Telemann's three trio-sonatas for two recorders, especially that in C with *soli* and *tutti* recorders, affectionately known as 'Telemann's girl-friends' (Bärenreiter HM 10) – the lyrical Corinna and Celia swimming the Tiber are great fun, and one has to be sorry for Lucretia (in C minor) and for Dido 'Triste' and 'Disperato'.

25. For example, in the first and last movements of the trio-sonata in G minor. Telemann's trio-sonatas may be found in Schott, Hinrichsen–Peters, Moeck, Hänssler and other editions. There is an excellent synopsis of Telemann's chamber music by Martin Ruhnke in vol. II of his thematic catalogue ('Instrumental Music') published by Bärenreiter (Cassel, etc., 1992). This lists fifteen trio-sonatas with recorder: three for two recorders, six with violin (including the three *Diskantgambe* ones), four with oboe, one with viola da gamba and one with harpsichord concertante – a beautiful work in B flat (Bärenreiter HM 36) with sounds like water splashing in a fountain. Ruhnke lists three quartets with recorder: in D minor with two flutes (from *Musique de table*); in G with oboe and violin (also published by Schott in F); and in G minor with two violins (published by Schott as 'Concerto di camera', emphasising the concerto element which occasionally appears in Telemann's recorder chamber music and more frequently in Vivaldi's – see p. 116).

26. Apart from Dresden with Zelenka and Heinichen (see p. 95), there were composers of music with recorders, and presumably musicians to play it, at Frankfurt, where Telemann worked from 1712 to 1721, Cöthen (J. S. Bach 1717–23), Vienna (Fux), Darmstadt (Graupner), Stuttgart (Pez), and Nuremberg, which was of course a renowned centre of wind-instrument making. No chamber music with recorder by Bach survives, but see p. 70, note 5. Although Fux wrote little for the recorder, as he preferred the louder wind instruments such as trombones, he has left us within the *Nürnberger Partita* (1701) a fascinating *Sinfonia* (Nagel edition), which is in effect a trio-sonata for recorder and oboe; it includes an Andante where the recorder plays a $\frac{6}{8}$ *Aria italiana* and the oboe a $\frac{4}{4}$ *Aire française* simultaneously, followed by a finale called *Les enemis confus, maestoso e deciso*.

27. 'RV' refers to Peter Ryom's catalogue (Leipzig 1974). He lists 585 instrumental pieces by Vivaldi, not counting operas and other vocal works. As with Telemann, the transverse flute is used far more frequently than the recorder.

28. Two of these cantatas use two recorders. Moeck publish one (Ed. 2554), *Clori mia, Clori bella*, and some others are published by Kunzelmann (GM 376), Zimmermann (ZM 1028) and the Società Italiana del Flauto Dolce (two in *Musica da Suonare* 5). The Moeck catalogue, beautifully presented, contains an excellent range of baroque chamber music with recorder.

29. See Edwin H. Alton, 'The recorder music of Alessandro Scarlatti (1660–1725)', *Recorder and Music Magazine* 4/6 (June 1973), pp. 199–200. These sonatas sound well with recorder, two violins and cello – there is no viola part.

30. The piece is in four parts: two descant recorders doubled by two muted violins, two treble recorders and muted viola ('violetta'), one tenor recorder and muted viola, and bass recorder with cello, unmuted, and keyboard. Other examples of bass recorder as part of a continuo group may be found in Lully, the 1692 Purcell *Ode for St Cecilia's Day* (no. 3 – 'Hark, each tree') and in Telemann's Concerto (grosso) in B flat with two treble recorders and strings. See plates 26 and 40.

31. See Michael Talbot, *Tomaso Albinoni* (Oxford 1990), p. 79.

32. The Musica Rara editions of Couperin's chamber music are excellent.

33. Bärenreiter HM 133.

34. There are surviving manuscripts of this trio-sonata under the names of Schultze and Prowo. They are probably the same person, for German *Schultze* and French *Provôt* both mean 'provost'.

35. Bärenreiter HM 26. For 'Johann Friedrich Fasch' see Brian Clark, *The Recorder Magazine* 13/3 (Dec. 1993), pp. 64–5.
36. Cantata 180; and *The St Matthew Passion* with flutes in many items, but not No. 25 where two recorders and oboe da caccia accompany the tenor aria 'O Schmerz'.
37. What he called the 'barbaric beauty' of the music he collected in Poland and adapted into some of his fast movements is as special to Telemann as Rameau's wild Tambourins (with 'petites flutes' – the new piccolos or descant recorders?) are characteristic of that remarkable composer.
38. For example, his music for flute, two violins and bass, of which Moeck have published a version for recorders (Ed. 2811).
39. A trio-sonata for 'une Flûte allemande, une Viole et Clavecin' arranged by Höffer-von Winterfeld (Hamburg, Sikorski).
40. Two of Carl Stamitz's quartets for flute, two violins and cello are published in recorder editions by Schott (Antiqua series).

5 The orchestral recorder

ADRIENNE SIMPSON

When Claudio Monteverdi composed the music for *Orfeo*, a new opera to be presented at the Mantuan court as part of the 1607 Carnival celebrations, he made use of some forty-five different instruments.[1] Many appeared only briefly, to add colour to a particular number. Typical of these was the sopranino recorder that, with strings, lutes, harpsichord and harp, imparted a glittering sound to the Act I pastoral chorus 'Lasciate i monti'. *Orfeo* was simultaneously a progressive and an old-fashioned work. The relatively specific nature of its instrumentation exemplified a new trend, but its diversity of instrumental timbres belonged to renaissance tradition. By 1643, when Monteverdi wrote *L'incoronazione di Poppea* for a Venetian opera house, the more restricted orchestral palette he employed reflected one of the fundamental developments of the baroque era: the transition from a plethora of instrumental sonorities to a more standardised ensemble, based on the homogeneous sound of strings and continuo.

Ten years after the première of *L'incoronazione di Poppea*, the young musician Jean-Baptiste Lully entered the service of Louis XIV of France as an instrumental composer and director. Under his influence, strings and continuo were consolidated as the basis of the baroque orchestra. His elite creation, the 'petite bande' (also known as the 'violons du cabinet'), and the larger 'vingt-quatre violons du roy' which he controlled from 1664, revolutionised the concept of orchestral music and set new standards of player competence and musical discipline. At much the same time, and possibly spurred by the growing dominance of the strings, professional wind players at the French court began a process of instrument modification. Structural changes, made by members of the Hotteterre, Philidor and Chédeville families, transformed the woodwind instruments of the renaissance band into the new baroque oboes, bassoons, flutes and recorders. These were quickly adopted throughout Europe. French orchestras of the late seventeenth century routinely included oboes and bassoons. As other centres emulated the musical institutions of the French court, both instruments became accepted as core members of the orchestra.

The recorder never attained the same status. Like the flute, it hovered on the periphery of orchestral developments. Unlike the flute, it remained there. Nevertheless, for over half a century, the enhanced intonation and compass of the baroque recorder made it a valuable addition to the palette of orchestral colours. Cross-fingerings enabled it to be fully chromatic, and initially it was the only member of the woodwind family that could be played in tune in all keys. During a period spanned approximately by the careers of Lully (1632–87) and Handel (1685–1759), the recorder was often specified for orchestral use. It was also deployed, to beautiful and telling effect, in numerous obbligato passages found in large-scale sacred and secular vocal works. Until well into the eighteenth century, the appearance of the word 'flauto' or 'flute' in a score meant 'recorder'. The instrument that eventually ousted it from orchestral favour was indicated by names such as 'flauto traverso', 'flûte traversière', 'German flute' or just 'traversa'. While a comprehensive account of the recorder in an orchestral context is not possible here, a survey of the way it was used by some major composers will illustrate the richness of the repertoire in which it participated.

Recorders appeared in a number of French works from the late seventeenth century onwards. They were found particularly in operatic scores and in the accompaniments to those spectacular examples of French religious music, the *grandes motets*. In the French opera orchestra recorder and flute coexisted – a point well illustrated by the 'Prélude pour l'amour' from Lully's ballet *Le triomphe de l'amour* (1681), where the scoring carefully indicates both flutes ('flûtes d'Allemagne') and three sizes of recorders: tenor, bass and great bass ('quinte de flûtes', 'petite basse de flûtes' and 'grande basse de flûtes').

A late seventeenth-century French composer who made considerable use of the recorder was Marc-Antoine Charpentier (1634–1704). He had an excellent ear for orchestral colour, frequently deploying his instruments concerto-style, in contrasting combinations. His scoring indications are very precise and recorders are specified in many of his operatic scores, dramatic works and religious works. In his Christmas motets they are used to emphasise the pastoral aspects of the nativity story. His early pastoral opera *Actéon* (1683–5) features recorders in a similar context. Other passages worth noting are the delicately chromatic prelude to Act IV of his dramatic opera *Médée* (1693), and the *De Profundis* he wrote to mark the death of Queen Marie-Thérèse (30 July 1683), which contains a wonderful bass solo with two obbligato recorders, 'A custodia matutina...' ('Israel hopes for the coming of the Lord as a watchman does for the morning').

Perhaps the finest of all Charpentier's religious works to include recorders is his *Magnificat à 8 voix et 8 instruments*, which dates from the early 1680s. Conceived on a grand scale, it calls for six vocal soloists, double chorus and two orchestras, each made up of strings, recorders, oboes, bassoons and a continuo group. The full forces are deployed in the first, middle and last of the work's seven symmetrically arranged movements. The third and sixth movements are trios, while the second and fifth are scored for solo voices with different pairs of obbligato instruments. In the second, the soprano soloist is accompanied by two recorders and continuo.

French influence was very apparent in English music of the late seventeenth century. The country's cultural life had been disrupted during the Civil War and Commonwealth. When the monarchy was restored in 1660, the revived court musical institutions were modelled on those to which Charles II had become accustomed during his long exile in France. French composers and instrumentalists were brought to London to help establish the new musical style. Among them were players of the baroque recorder, including at least one notable virtuoso, James Paisible, who arrived in London in 1673. English composers adopted the instrument with enthusiasm, and parts for the 'flûte douce' or 'flute', as it became commonly known, soon appeared in contemporary scores. John Blow (1649–1708), for example, used recorders in the accompaniments to his anthems, *Lord who shall dwell* (c1681) and *Sing unto the Lord, O ye saints* (c1682), to accompany the love scene in the masque *Venus and Adonis* (c1684) and, with exquisite poignancy, in his 1696 *Ode on the Death of Henry Purcell* ('Mark how the lark and linnet sing').

The latter is a chamber, not an orchestral, work, but it demonstrates one of the contexts in which recorders were often used. According to conventions that had grown up in the renaissance theatre, and that continued to be observed by composers as different as Purcell, Bach and Handel, recorders were considered particularly appropriate for music accompanying funerals, or associated in some way with sorrow. As an extension of this, they were also found frequently in music depicting otherworldly and supernatural events. Other common uses were in pastoral scenes, in passages expressing love or other tender emotions, for the imitation of birdsong, and for obvious illustrative effect when composers set texts referring to woodwind instruments.

Many examples of these orchestral uses of the recorder can be found in the occasional odes, welcome songs and incidental music of Henry Purcell (1659–95).[2] In the birthday ode *Come, Ye Sons of Art* (1694), the countertenor aria which begins 'Strike the viol, touch the lute; Wake the harp, inspire the flute', evokes suitably pictorial scoring. The recorder dissonances in the lament 'But ah, I see Eusebia drowned in tears' from *Arise, my Muse* (1690), the second of his six odes for Queen Mary's birthday celebrations, are no less affecting because Eusebia turns out to be a personification of the Anglican Church bewailing William III's need to champion her cause in Ireland.

Purcell's recorder parts are not difficult. He generally uses pairs of instruments, sometimes to provide obbligatos in duets and arias, sometimes to give colour to the ritornello sections before falling silent when the voice enters – as in the orchestral ritornello to the duet 'Sing ye Druids' from *Bonduca* (1695), which is an instance of the recorder's association with the supernatural. His obbligatos, with their fusion of voice and instrument, are inevitably more interesting. In the light-hearted love song 'One charming night', from the incidental music to *The Fairy Queen* (1692), an alto soloist declares that 'One charming night is worth a hundred lucky days' and his words are given point by two recorders entwining deliciously in the ritornello, and playing pairs of notes punctuated by rests to create an almost staccato effect during the aria itself. A rare example of a purely instrumental movement featuring recorders is the Chaconne in *Dioclesian* (1690), known as 'Two in one upon a Ground'. In this, two recorders play in canon over an inexorably downward-moving ground bass, creating a plangent expression of grief.

Some of Purcell's most brilliant scoring can be found in the *Ode for St Cecilia's Day* (1692). Recorders are used only in two numbers. For the duet 'In vain the am'rous flute' they occur with conventionally illustrative effect in the ritornello section. The duet 'Hark each tree' is far more ambitious. The words present a delightful analogy of the fir and box trees giving tongue when fashioned into instruments. The music takes the form of a vocal contest between a countertenor and a bass, the former extolling the affecting elegance of the recorder, the latter representing 'the spritely violin'. Two trebles and a bass recorder similarly contest with two violins and a bass viol until eventually the contending forces unite in flowing and consonant passage-work.

French composers utilised many of the same conventions as the English. Examples of recorders used in association with death, and with pastoral themes, have already been cited. Until about 1730, when overtaken by the baroque piccolo, birdsong was often represented by recorders in French operatic scores, as were passages expressing tenderness and love, particularly where the singer was a woman. In Act III scene 2 of Charpentier's *Médée*, for instance, Medea sees Jason, the man she loves, approaching. 'My heart is moved to tenderness', she says. 'Let me speak to him' – and as she advances to do so, she is accompanied by a short instrumental ritornello featuring recorders.

A convention which became particularly associated with French composers was the *sommeil*, or sleep scene. This involved a character being lulled to sleep, often under the influence of a god or magician. It was frequently the signal for a dream sequence. Lully introduced the *sommeil* to the French stage in *Les amants magnifiques* (1670), a *comédie-ballet* in which the third *intermède* begins with a 'ritornelle pour les flûtes'. However, the model for subsequent composers was the elaborate *sommeil* (Act III scene 4) in his opera *Atys* of 1676. The passage is a device by which the goddess Cybèle tells Atys of her love for him. Following a lengthy prelude, the spirits of sleep sing to the slumbering Atys, first separately and then in trio. 'Songes agréables' point out his good fortune. Contrasting 'songes funestes' warn of the consequences should he prove unfaithful. The opening prelude, which is reprised later in the scene, features recorders, moving stepwise in slurred pairs of notes, in alternation to the strings.

After *Atys*, the *sommeil* became a set piece in many French operas, and in nearly all cases recorders featured prominently. A typical example, also from a Lully opera, occurs in Act III scene 2 of *Persée* (1682), when Mercury is ushered in to the sounds of 'deux flûtes douces et deux violons' in order to render the Gorgons harmless by sending them to sleep. The *sommeil* is also found in other types of music. Charpentier included one in his oratorio *Judicium Salamonis* (1702). The richly harmonised prelude to the second part of this work creates an almost mystical effect with its gentle mix of recorders and muted strings.

The transition from recorder to flute occurred relatively quickly in France. From the early eighteenth century it was clear that the transverse flute had grown enormously in fashionable esteem, thanks in part to a succession of small improvements that gave it greater range and flexibility than its rival, and in part to the persuasive advocacy of flute virtuosi such as La Barre and, later, Michel Blavet. Two 'flûtes allemandes' were particularly specified among the orchestral personnel at the Paris Opéra (or l'Académie Royale de la Musique) for the 1712–13 season.[3] Although recorders are found in a French operatic score as late as Montéclair's *Jepthe* (1732), they occur there in the context of a *sommeil* closely modelled on that in Lully's *Atys*. In France the recorder had effectively yielded its orchestral place to the transverse flute well before 1740, the year in which Blavet became a specialist flautist in the orchestra of the Paris Opéra.

Musical developments in France were centred upon Paris, those in England largely upon London, but the German lands had a host of little princedoms and dukedoms, most of which boasted musical establishments. Some were very large. The Dresden court orchestra (pl. 26) had both flutes and recorders in its complement, and the latter were used to excellent effect in several concerted works by Johann David Heinichen (1683–1729) who was Kapellmeister there from 1717 until his death. However, the resources available to composers did vary markedly from court to court and German writing for the recorder in an orchestral context is therefore hard to categorise. In general, it tends to be more technically demanding than its French and English

Plate 26   This is a greatly enlarged small detail of a copperplate engraving of the first performance of Antonio Lotti's *Teofane* in the new Dresden opera house in 1719, part of the marriage festivities for Frederick August II and Maria Josepha. It shows half of the splendid Dresden orchestra around the harpsichord (just seen on the lower right of the plate), and includes at the bottom left three (?treble) recorders, two playing and one resting. In front of and beyond the two prominent theorboes are what may be bass recorders, and beyond them, before the start of a large section of violins, there are two transverse flutes. These are roughly the forces required for Heinichen's concertos (see p. 113). One of the flautists on this occasion may have been Pierre-Gabriel Buffardin, Quantz's teacher, and one of the violinists Francesco Maria Veracini, who wrote excellent solo sonatas for violin or *flauto*. The recorders would presumably have been played by Dresden oboists of the time such as François La Riche, Johann Christian Richter and Peter Glösch. From Douglas Alton Smith, 'Sylvius Leopold Weiss' (lutenist and theorbo player), *Early Music* 8/1 (Jan. 1980), p. 49.

equivalents. The decentralisation of music in the German lands meant that the trend towards standardised ensembles advanced more slowly, and composers seem often to have written for individual, highly skilled, performers.

Undoubtedly the most famous German composer of his day was Georg Philipp Telemann (1681–1767). A man of prodigious energy and skill, his flair for orchestral colour was born of practical knowledge. He apparently played nine different instruments, including both the flute and the recorder, and in his orchestral works he often contrasts the two. Telemann included important recorder parts in some of his highly individual concertos for three or more solo instruments (*Gruppenkonzerte*), and in several of his nearly 140 surviving orchestral overtures and suites. Some of these, such as the well-known Suite in A minor for solo recorder and strings, are concertos in all but name. More interesting, from the point of view of orchestral usage, are works such as his Overture in C major, *Hamburger Ebb und Fluht* ('Hamburg Ebb and Flow'), a delightfully pictorial 'water-music' suite first performed in Hamburg on 6 April 1723. It is scored for two recorders, *flauto piccolo*, two oboes, strings and continuo. A particularly effective use of recorders occurs in the sarabande entitled 'The Sleeping Thetis', where the duple time of the other instruments contrasts with rocking triplet figures in the recorders. It is a good example of Telemann's penchant for combining different rhythmic structures.

Part of Telemann's musical appeal lies in his skilful scoring and easy combination of French and Italian musical influences. His orchestral suites derive from Lullian models, although expanded in scale, yet sometimes include Italian elements. His concertos are based on Italian principles, but also occasionally contain echoes of French style. The same absorption of techniques from both major sources of baroque musical influence can be found in the works of J. S. Bach (1685–1750).

Like all composers of his day, Bach wrote for the forces he had at hand. Sometimes a wider variety of instruments than usual could be available for special occasions. An example is his cantata for the election of the Mühlhausen town council, *Gott ist mein König* (BWV 71, 1708), which uses 'choirs' of trumpets and timpani, oboes and bassoon, recorders and violoncello, plus strings and continuo, as well as choir and soloists.

Usually, however, he wrote for a specific body of performers. When he worked at Weimar, he had available some proficient solo singers, a mediocre small choir, about half-a-dozen good string players, a skilled bassoonist, a couple of competent oboists who could double on recorder, and himself on keyboards. On festive occasions the local military could provide trumpets and drums. He therefore wrote for these forces throughout his time at Weimar. When he moved to the more sophisticated court of Cöthen in 1717 he had greater resources to call on, and could write orchestral suites and concertos with the considerable technical demands found in the Brandenburg Concertos (BWV 1046–51).

Bach was as practical as any of his baroque contemporaries in his attitude to the music he wrote. The original (1723) and revised (1730) versions of the *Magnificat* exemplify this. That of 1723 is in E flat (BWV 243a) and the aria 'Esurientes implevit bonis' features an obbligato for a pair of recorders, in the key of F which is ideal for the instrument. The text runs 'He has filled the hungry with good things and the rich he has sent empty away'. There is a wonderful touch at the end of the aria, when the recorder ritornello finishes unresolved (perhaps illustrative of those sent empty away) and the continuo is left to supply the cadence.

In the 1730 revision (BWV 243) the overall key of the work is lowered a semitone. The 'Esurientes' obbligato no longer fits the recorder, and is assigned to transverse flute instead. In all Bach's works an increased usage of the flute is apparent from the mid-1720s onward; indeed, he seems to have virtually stopped scoring for recorders after 1726. Among the many reasons why the *Magnificat* could have been revised, a lack of proficient recorder players must be a possibility. It would be typical of baroque practicality to alter a work for such a reason. Today we are finicky about substituting instruments. Baroque tradition was far more elastic, as the frequent designation of solo sonatas as appropriate for violin, oboe, recorder or flute suggests.

Many of the same conventions of recorder usage common to French and English composers can be found in Bach's works and those of his German contemporaries. His cantatas provide a particularly rich source of examples. The association with death and the supernatural is most aptly illustrated in the funeral cantata *Gottes Zeit ist die allerbeste Zeit* (BWV 106, c1708) where recorders and gambas create an atmosphere of poignant resignation, or in *Komm, du süsse Todesstunde* (BWV 161, 1715), in which the singer longs for death to the heavenly sound of two recorders. The use of the instrument in a pastoral context can be found in works such as the Christmas cantata *Das neugeborne Kindelein* (BWV 122, 1724), and in the aria for Pales, the god of shepherds, from the secular cantata *Was mir behagt* (BWV 208, 1713). This is known to millions as 'Sheep may safely graze'. The expression of tender feelings appears in *Meine Seufzer, meine Tränen* (BWV 13, 1726) and *Schmücke dich, o liebe Seele* (BWV 180, 1724).[4]

Most of Bach's orchestral music seems to have been lost. Among the surviving works are the six Brandenburg Concertos, which were written over a period of several years, and brought together in a beautiful fair copy, dated 24 March 1721, which Bach presented to the Margrave of Brandenburg, presumably in hope of gaining preferment or a lucrative commission. Few details are omitted from the score. The second of the six concertos calls for treble recorder, oboe, trumpet and violin as the solo instruments: a seemingly unlikely combination which works beautifully when played on instruments of the appropriate period (particularly the small F trumpet). It represents a genre in which German composers excelled: the concerto grosso with a concertino group composed of widely disparate instruments. The trumpet dominates the outer movements, but the other instruments are heard to great advantage, in constantly changing groupings, in the central Andante.

In the fourth Brandenburg Concerto, the solo instruments are a violin and two *fiauti d'echo*. Exactly what type of recorder Bach meant by that designation has puzzled scholars for years, and although the consensus of opinion tends to favour trebles in G, many other possible solutions have been put forward. The work is a fascinating mixture. The violin is sufficiently prominent in the outer movements for them to take on the flavour of a violin concerto. The recorders attain parity in the middle movement, where the first recorder has two little solo cadenzas, and the three instruments function like the concertino group of a concerto grosso. Perhaps it is not altogether fanciful to think that the recorders' echoing role in this movement led Bach to describe them as *fiauti d'echo* in the score.[5]

In writing his Brandenburg Concertos, Bach was influenced by what he knew of Italian music, particularly the works of Antonio Vivaldi (1678–1741), some of whose compositions he transcribed for harpsichord or organ. Our current concentration on Vivaldi's concertos has obscured his vast array of other works, some of which feature the recorder. Arias in which an obbligato wind soloist plays in the ritornello and then accompanies the singer in the first section of vocal music were common in Italian vocal writing of the period. Vivaldi regularly uses horns, trumpets, recorders and oboes as obbligato instruments in his operas. He often calls on recorders for pastoral scenes, as in 'Bel riposo de' mortali' from Act I scene 4 of *Giustino* (RV 717, 1724). Unusually, he employs the *flauto grosso* (tenor recorder) in two operas, *Tito Manlio* (RV 738, 1719) and *La verità in cimento* (RV 739), first produced in 1720.

He also uses recorders in the score of his only surviving oratorio, the monumental *Juditha Triumphans* (RV 644, 1716). This was written for the Pietà in Venice, the girls' orphanage with which he was connected between 1703 and 1740. The score requires two recorders, two oboes, chalumeau, two clarinets, two trumpets, timpani, mandolin, four theorboes, obbligato organ, four viols and viola d'amore, as well as strings and continuo. Needless to say, these are not all used at the same time. The basic baroque orchestra of strings and continuo, supplemented by oboes and bassoon, is joined by particular instruments to characterise specific passages in the work. So, recorders at their most insinuating lend colour to an aria in which Vagans sings a curious lullaby – 'Umbrae carae' – to his drunken master, Holofernes.

During the early eighteenth century the rivalry between recorder and flute was as apparent in Italy as elsewhere in Europe. Until approximately 1725 the designation 'flauto' in a Vivaldi score always refers to recorder. Thereafter, he shows more interest in the increasingly popular transverse flute. Some of the concertos in his Op. 10 collection began life as recorder works. By the time they reached publication in 1729/30 they had been reassigned to the flute, in an obvious concession to changing taste (see p. 108).

The later baroque period was dominated by the new instrumental and vocal developments in Italy, and particularly by the widespread fashion for Italian opera. One of the finest exponents of that genre was George Frideric Handel. In the operas he wrote for London audiences, he used both transverse flutes and recorders, although he gives the latter relatively little to do. During his early career in Italy he had tended to use the instrument conservatively, mainly doubling the violin. In England, where he had some excellent players available to him, he employed it with greater flair. His recorder parts often parallel the vocal line, moving in unison or in consonant thirds and sixths. At other times voice and recorder imitate each other, or exchange melodic fragments. As in all Italianate vocal music with obbligato, the sense of competition between singer and instrument is frequently present.

Of the seventeen operas Handel wrote between 1704 and 1726, recorders feature in eleven.[6] In his first London opera, *Rinaldo*, performed in 1711, sopranino and trebles play off stage, imitating birdsong, in the aria 'Augelletti che cantate' from Act I scene 4. According to the 1711 libretto this was set in 'A delightful Grove in which the Birds are heard to sing, and are seen flying up and down'. The scene caused a furore at the première when live birds were released on to the stage. *Rinaldo* is an opera full of stage effect and superficial brilliance. A more imaginative use of recorders can be found in 'Senza procello ancora' from Act II scene 4 of *Poro* (1731), where they are combined with horns against a background of pedal notes in the strings. The trio for two trebles and bass that introduces the alto aria 'Può ben nascer' in Act I scene 4 of *Giustino* (1736) is an Italianate version of the French *sommeil*. Giustino is ploughing when he is overcome by drowsiness. In the ensuing dream sequence his elevation to Roman emperor is symbolically revealed. The recorders play, characteristically, in the passage where Giustino is lulled to sleep.

Handel's non-operatic works also contain delightful examples of the orchestral use of recorders, as in the slow movement of his Op. 3 No. 1 Concerto Grosso. Piping *flauti piccoli* add brilliance to the air and first Gigue from the G major *Water Music* suite. *Acis and Galatea* (1718) has three arias that use recorders, not for their solo properties but for the colour they impart when doubling the violin line. The most famous of the three is the grotesque love song for the giant Polyphemus, 'O ruddier than the cherry'. Here the recorder not only illustrates the pipe that Polyphemus intends to make and play for his beloved Galatea, but continues the convention of using the instrument in love scenes. It has become usual to employ the sopranino in this aria, and although the original scoring was undoubtedly for treble, there is certainly something irresistibly comic in the contrast between a lumbering giant and the stratospheric sound of the pipe he makes for his 'capacious throat'.

Although the number of works featuring the recorder as an orchestral instrument may seem impressive, it is essential to realise that they represent a very small part of each composer's output. Purcell, for example, used recorders more often than many of his contemporaries, yet they appear only in seven of his fifty operatic and theatrical scores, three of his nine Welcome Odes, and three out of seven Birthday Odes. Of Bach's 200 surviving sacred cantatas, only nineteen have recorder parts. Such statistics confirm that the recorder, like the flute, was used sparingly in an orchestral context during the baroque era. Oboes and bassoons were the only woodwind instruments regularly added to the basic baroque orchestra of strings and continuo. It seems certain that most of the musicians who played the recorder orchestrally, at least in France and England, were primarily employed for their expertise on other instruments.

Since oboes and recorders rarely play simultaneously in a score, it is likely that many of the oboe players listed in inventories of the period doubled on recorder, in the same way that an oboist in a modern orchestra does on cor anglais.[7] Several English practitioners were primarily string players, including John Banister the Younger and Robert King who are assumed to have taken the recorder parts in two of Purcell's Birthday Odes, *Arise my Muse* (1691) and *Celebrate this Festival* (1693).[8] The ability to double on other instruments appears to have been a common skill among musicians of the baroque period. Despite the fine array of woodwind required for Vivaldi's oratorio *Juditha Triumphans*, for example, only one kind is heard at a time in the score, and it is almost certain that some of the performers played more than one instrument.

If further confirmation is needed, it can be found by examining the membership lists for Handel's London opera orchestra.[9] No specialist recorder players are listed in these, although the instrument was clearly required in most of his operas. The situation for Handel was the same as that which obtained in Purcell's day. Other instrumentalists, generally oboists, doubled on recorder. Peter La Tour, Jean Christian Kytch, Francesco Barsanti, John Loeillet and Giuseppe Sammartini were among the foreign virtuosi who made their living in England, primarily as oboists. All are known to have also played the recorder, and all were in the opera orchestra available to Handel at various times between 1721 and 1738. Virtually every opera Handel wrote during that period makes use of the instrument. After 1738, recorders abruptly vanish from his scores – apart from an isolated and much later example in *Judas Maccabeus* (1747). Sammartini left the opera orchestra around 1738. Kytch died that year, and La Tour is presumed to have done so as well. The inference is clear. It did not merit a place in the orchestra on its own account, but was a useful extra which some players were able to offer. Today, when the recorder is more widely played than any other instrument of the baroque period, it is salutary to be reminded that it was not nearly as important in its own day as the twentieth-century recorder revival would lead us to believe.

The developments that led, gradually, to the relatively fixed combination of instruments we describe as an orchestra today, were pioneered in the opera theatres of Italy and at the French court. By about 1740 the recorder had virtually ceased to have any part in these. Some writers consider that its disappearance from the orchestral palette was due to its quiet sound.[10] This cannot be wholly true. When matched with instruments of its own period the recorder carries rather better than the baroque flute. The major cause of its demise was the lack of nuance and dynamic flexibility that made it less suitable for the more overtly expressive style of writing introduced into European music in the mid-eighteenth century.

Changes rarely happen overnight. Recorders did not fall out of use immediately. There were still being made and played towards the end of the eighteenth century. Burney, for example, reports hearing a recorder player in Florence in 1770.[11] Edgar Hunt has made out a persuasive case for the 'flauti' that played the 'Dance of the Blessed Spirits' in the original score of Gluck's *Orfeo ed Euridice* (1762) being recorders, and examples of the recorder as an orchestral obbligato instrument with the voice are occasionally found after that date.[12] Paisiello used it briefly in his opera *Il barbiere di Siviglia* (1782), and it is possible that the 'small flute' and '8th flute' specifications in Shield's *The Farmer* (1787) referred to recorders. There was even some awareness of the instrument among composers of the early nineteenth century. Rossini once owned an elegant Italian treble recorder, veneered in tortoise-shell and inlaid with gold and mother-of-pearl, although he probably regarded it as a historical curiosity rather than as a practical means of music-making.[13]

Since the recorder revival of the twentieth century, the instrument has again appeared very occasionally in orchestral scores. An example is the small stage-band of recorders in Britten's opera *A Midsummer Night's Dream* (1960). It makes a more notable contribution to the same composer's opera, *Noye's Fludde* (1958), which was written for children and scored – in true baroque fashion – for a small concertino section of professional players and a large ripieno group of young amateurs (pl. 28). Two easy parts for descant recorders and one for

Plate 27 Like Plate 15A this is another well-known picture from the Wallace Collection, London, reproduced by their kind permission. Nicolas Lancret's *Mademoiselle de Camargo Dancing* in her own open-air theatre, was painted about 1730 when this famous dancer was twenty. There are similar pictures in the Hermitage at St Petersburg (where she is shown in a red dress), Nantes and Potsdam. What is often overlooked is the participation of the treble recorder in the dance band in the bushes, along with violin, viola and bassoon, as well as the pipe and tabor on the left. Small recorders may have remained part of the orchestral forces for ballet until well into the eighteenth century. WB 32

trebles are assigned to the ripieno. The concertino features a solo treble. Britten played the recorder himself, and his writing for the soloist is idiomatic and inventive, particularly in the effective flutter-tongued passage that illustrates the questing dove dispatched by Noah to seek out dry land as the flood waters abate.

Works such as *Noye's Fludde* and *A Midsummer Night's Dream* are rarities, not harbingers of an orchestral revival. The use of the recorder in an orchestral context remains a short-lived baroque phenomenon. Although the wealth of sonatas, chamber music and concertos written for the instrument during that period has, rightly, monopolised the attention of today's recorder players, it would be a pity if its brief but often beautiful and effective contribution to the orchestral repertoire was overlooked.

Plate 28   Rehearsal in Orford Church for the first performance, which took place on 18 June 1958, of Benjamin Britten's *Noye's Fludde*. The photograph shows some of the recorders – there were about thirty in all – including the professional Stanley Taylor (upper left) who played the treble recorder solo part, with flutter-tonguing for the cooing of the dove. The timpanist is James Blades. As everybody is playing, this may be the storm section – 'The waves roll and crash, the wind (recorders) howls through the rigging. At the height of the storm the ark rocks wildly and the animals panic. The monkeys try to climb the rigging, a squirrel almost falls overboard, but finally Noye and his family calm the frightened animals. Above the hubbub of the storm rises the hymn *Eternal Father, strong to save*, sung by Noye and all the others in the ark. The congregation joins in the second verse, and slowly the storm begins to abate' (from libretto). Photograph by Kurt Hutton, Britten-Pears Library, Aldeburgh.

Notes

1. See Neal Zaslaw, 'Three notes on the early history of the orchestra', *Historical Performance* 1/2 (1988), p. 63.
2. A list of Purcell scores which include the recorder can be found in Walter Bergmann, 'Henry Purcell's use of the recorder', *Recorder and Music Magazine* 1/11 (1965), pp. 333–5. (See also p. 88, note 18).
3. *Privilège* for the Académie, see Jürgen Eppelsheim, *Das Orchester in den Werken Jean-Baptiste Lullys* (Tutzing 1961), pp. 150, 215.
4. For some further examples of Bach's orchestral use of the recorder see Edgar Hunt, *The Recorder and its Music*, rev. edn (London 1977), pp. 77–81.
5. See David Lasocki's article on echo flutes in the *Galpin Society Journal* 45 (1992), pp. 59–66; also the discussion, by John Martin and others, in *The Recorder* (Melbourne) 9 and 10 (1989), pp. 1–3 and 19–24 respectively, and David Lasocki, 'More on echo flutes' in the same journal, 13 (1991), pp. 14–16. See also p. 117, note 18.

6. See the table in Winton Dean and John Merrill Knapp, *Handel's Operas: 1704–1726* (Oxford 1987), p. 636.
7. Occasional exceptions do occur; for example, in the duet 'Shepherds, shepherds leave decoying' from Purcell's incidental music to *King Arthur* (1691) where both oboes and recorders are employed in the introduction.
8. See Lasocki, 'Professional recorder playing in England: Part II – 1640–1740', *Early Music* 10/2 (1982), pp. 184–7, for a more extensive discussion about specialists on other instruments doubling recorder when required.
9. See Donald Burrows, 'Handel's London theatre orchestra', *Early Music* 13/3 (1985), particularly p. 355.
10. For instance C. F. D. Schubart, *Ideen zu einer Ästhetik der Tonkunst* (Vienna 1806), p. 209.
11. Charles Burney, *Music, Men, and Manners in France and Italy, 1770*, mod. edn (London 1969), p. 116.
12. Hunt, *The Recorder and its Music*, p. 88.
13. The recorder is in London's Victoria and Albert Museum, item no. 1124–1869.

Select bibliography

Books

James R. Anthony, *French Baroque Music from Beaujoyeaulx to Rameau*, rev. edn (New York 1978)
Malcolm Boyd, *Bach* (London 1983)
Winton Dean and John Merrill Knapp, *Handel's Operas: 1704–1726* (Oxford 1987)
H. Wiley Hitchcock, *Marc-Antoine Charpentier* (Oxford 1990)
Edgar Hunt, *The Recorder and its Music*, rev. edn (London 1977)
John Manifold, *The Amorous Flute* (London 1948)
Richard Petzoldt, *Georg Philipp Telemann* (London 1974)
Michael Talbot, *Vivaldi* (London 1978)
Sir Jack Westrup, *Purcell*, rev. edn (London 1960)

Articles

Nicholas Anderson, 'Georg Philipp Telemann: a tercentenary reassessment', *Early Music* 9/4 (1981), pp. 499–505
    'Vivaldi – the priest impresario', *Recorder and Music Magazine* 3/10 (1971), pp. 360–2
Denis Arnold, 'Monteverdi the instrumentalist', *Recorder and Music Magazine* 2/5 (1967), pp. 130–2
Janet E. Beat, 'Monteverdi and the opera orchestra of his time', *The Monteverdi Companion*, ed. Denis Arnold and Nigel Fortune (London 1968), pp. 277–301
Walter Bergmann, 'Henry Purcell's use of the recorder', *Recorder and Music Magazine* 1/11 (1965), pp. 333–5; reprinted, *ibid.* 7/12 (1983), pp. 310–13
Donald Burrows, 'Handel's London theatre orchestra', *Early Music* 13/3 (1985), pp. 349–87
David Lasocki, 'Professional recorder playing in England: Part II – 1640–1740', *Early Music* 10/2 (1982), pp. 183–91
    'Vivaldi and the recorder', *The American Recorder* 9 (1968), pp. 103–7

Douglas Macmillan, 'The recorder in the late eighteenth and early nineteenth centuries', *The Consort* 39 (1983), pp. 489–97

Hans Joachim Marx, 'The instrumentation of Handel's early Italian works', *Early Music* 16/4 (1988), pp. 496–505

Joel Newman, 'Handel's use of the recorder', *The American Recorder* 5/4 (1964), pp. 4–9

Philippe Oboussier, 'The chapel of the Sun King', *Music and Musicians* 20/3 (November 1971), pp. 30–2

Hans-Joachim Schulze, 'Johann Sebastian Bach's orchestra: some unanswered questions', *Early Music* 13/1 (1989), pp. 3–15

Eleanor Selfridge-Field, 'Vivaldi's esoteric instruments', *Early Music* 16/3 (1988), pp. 332–8

'Italian oratorio and the baroque orchestra', *Early Music* 16/4 (1988), pp. 506–13

Caroline Wood, 'Orchestra and spectacle in the *tragédie en musique* 1673–1715: oracle, *sommeil* and *tempête*', *Proceedings of the Royal Musical Association* 108 (1981–2), pp. 25–46

Neal Zaslaw, 'When is an orchestra not an orchestra?', *Early Music* 16/4 (1988), pp. 483–95

6 The eighteenth-century recorder concerto

DAVID LASOCKI AND ANTHONY ROWLAND-JONES

Baroque concertos with recorders came in four kinds. The three types of 'orchestral' concertos were: those for solo instrument and orchestra, those for two or more dominating solo instruments (double concertos, etc.) and the 'concerto grosso' type. A fourth kind, sometimes not recognised as such even in the eighteenth century because of the scoring, was the chamber concerto, written for a chamber ensemble without orchestra (see also Chap. 4).[1]

Antonio Vivaldi's solo recorder concertos were probably written for the celebrated Venetian girls' orphanage called Pio Ospedale della Pietà. The composer taught there from 1703 to 1718, and afterwards continued to supply concertos for its musicians for the rest of his life. Many of the Pietà girls developed into performers of the highest technical accomplishment. The players for whom Vivaldi wrote the C minor recorder concerto (RV 441), the trio-sonata in A minor for recorder, bassoon and continuo (RV 86), and the three 'flautino' concertos (RV 443–5) deserve recognition as the greatest virtuosi of the baroque era.

'Flautino' means, literally, 'small recorder'. Although the keys of these concertos (C major, C major and A minor) and their highest notes, tessitura and degree of difficulty all suggest the sopranino recorder, one of the Vivaldi flautino concertos goes below the range of that instrument. Because in one of these concertos he also included a few notes for the violin that go outside its range, it is likely that he was merely careless and did have the sopranino recorder in mind for the solo part. Other possible solo instruments that have been suggested by modern scholars – the piccolo transverse flute and a small flageolet – are far less plausible.

Vivaldi's well-known flautino concerto in C major (RV 444) is a virtuoso work from beginning to end. The ritornello parts of the fast movements are cut to a minimum, allowing the solo instrument full scope in the relatively extended solo sections for rapid scales, arpeggios, trills, triplets and leaps comparable to those in the composer's violin concertos. The slow movement is in A minor. Between short opening and closing phrases in which the upper four parts are in unison, the soloist is given an elaborately ornamented melody line containing some of the same devices as the fast movements (trills, rapid scales and triplets) over pizzicato semiquavers in the strings. The other two flautino concertos do not have as strong a melodic profile, but the passage-work is at least as brilliant.

The six flute concertos, Op. 10, by Vivaldi were published in Amsterdam by Le Cène around 1728.[2] Only the fourth seems to have been specially written for the publication, the other five being reworkings of counterparts that survive in Vivaldi's manuscripts. One is a solo recorder concerto (No. 5 in F major), in which the middle movement was originally in F minor rather than G minor (RV 442). The remaining four are chamber concertos, which Vivaldi converted for publication as solo works by giving all the parts except the top one to violins or violoncello. According to modern Vivaldi scholarship, the top parts of three of the chamber concertos were written for the flute, one of them for the recorder. Yet the keys, range and tessitura of all four top parts suggest that they were originally meant for the recorder.

Concerto No. 3 in D major, subtitled *Il gardellino* (the goldfinch), is a good case in point. Its chamber concerto version (RV 90) survives in one copy with autograph inscriptions and another copy from Vivaldi's circle. On the first one, the instruments are marked, in Vivaldi's hand, 'flauto o viol[in]o p[ri]mo', 'hautbois o viol[in]o [secondo]', 'viol[in]o 3zo', 'violoncello o fagotto' and 'basso cont[inuo]' (treble recorder or first violin, oboe or second violin, third violin, cello or bassoon, and basso continuo). In the other copy the top part is marked, not in Vivaldi's hand, 'flauto trav[erso]' (i.e. flute) for the first movement, but 'flauto' (i.e. treble recorder) for the second. Although D major is the home key of the flute, Vivaldi called for the recorder in three other chamber concertos in that key (RV 92, 94 and 95). Moreover, the recorder, not the flute, was traditionally associated with birdsong. Taken together, this evidence points to the treble recorder rather than the flute as having been Vivaldi's original choice for *Il gardellino*. Moreover, the range of the solo part (*f♯'–e'''*) in the Op. 10 version fits the treble recorder exactly.

Vivaldi's great C minor concerto (RV 441) is probably the most virtuoso recorder composition of the entire baroque era, surpassing even the A minor flautino concerto in that respect because of the key (which requires many cross-fingerings) and the large leaps in the rapid passage-work.[3] The opening Allegro non molto, for example, begins deceptively calmly, but the first episode launches the soloist into semiquaver triplets, leading back to the second ritornello with a little cadenza of demisemiquavers.

In France, the flute had already eclipsed the recorder among professional musicians by around 1700, and by the time solo concertos began to be written in that country twenty or thirty years later, the recorder had ceased to be even a popular amateur instrument. It comes as no surprise to discover that French composers do not seem to have written any recorder concertos. The Op. 17 of the Parisian music-seller Jacques-Christophe Naudot (*c*1690–1762), however, is a collection of concertos for vielle (hurdy-gurdy), musette (bagpipe), flute, recorder or oboe with two violins and basso continuo. The common French practice of listing several possible instruments on the title page was presumably designed to increase the publisher's market. The keys, melodic range and harmonic scope of such works show that they were primarily intended for the musette or vielle, both of which possessed drones and could not, therefore, move far from the home key. These 'pastoral' instruments were all the rage at Versailles, where courtiers dressed up as shepherds and shepherdesses and acted out bucolic scenes. The dedication of Naudot's collection to the vielle virtuoso Danguy *l'aîné* implies that his instrument was the one the composer really had in mind. Nevertheless, the concertos are well suited to the recorder – another instrument that baroque composers used to represent the pastoral element – and Naudot achieves an unusual amalgam of Italian concerto form and French pastoral charm.[4]

In England, the recorder concerto – particularly for the small sizes of recorder known as the 'fifth flute' (descant in C) and 'sixth flute' (descant in D) – enjoyed an extraordinary vogue for about twenty-five years, featuring prominently in public concerts and in the mini-concerts given in the intervals of plays at the theatres. The first known performance (1709) of a recorder concerto was by John Baston (whose own concertos were later published by Walsh); the first known performance (1715) of a concerto for a small recorder was by the French expatriate virtuoso James Paisible. (Curiously, both Baston and Paisible made their living primarily as cellists, although recorder concertos would have given them their greatest public exposure.) Then concertos were taken up by virtually all professional recorder players whose performances were advertised: Lewis Granom, John Jones, Jean Christian Kytch, Jacob Price, Giuseppe Sammartini and Johann Christian Schickhardt.

William Babell (*c*1680–1723) was a violinist and harpsichordist in the theatre and opera orchestras as well as a church organist. His posthumous recorder concertos, Op. 3 (*c*1726), four for one sixth flute, one for two sixth flutes and one for two trebles, seem to have been the first solo concertos ever published for the instrument. They are scored for an orchestra of violins and cellos (no violas), including a solo violin part, suggesting that they were written for the recorder players John Baston and his brother Thomas, also a violinist. The title page proclaims that the concertos were 'performed at the theatre with great applause'. Most of Babell's concertos are fully Vivaldian in conception and design. In No. 3, however, the predominant influence is that of Handel, whose musical style Babell would have absorbed while playing in the London opera orchestra. The binary third movement has the melodic style of a Handel sonata over an accompaniment of unison violins in the Vivaldian manner. Although Babell's concertos were published as being 'in 7 Parts', in fact the *tutti* passages contain a lot of doubling, and the solo episodes with their largely stepwise passage-work are very lightly scored. They therefore sound quite adequate in reduced keyboard editions, transposed to suit the descant recorder.[5]

Baston's own guileless concertos (1729) are also published today for nimble fingers to play on descant or treble recorder with keyboard.[6] They are Vivaldian in their four-square themes and spun-out passage-work, although not in their inspiration or their tendency to remain in or close to the home key. But they were designed to entertain through their verve and virtuosity, and in this they succeed, even if the passage-work is sometimes tedious, as in No. 3. Baston resorts in Concertos 3 and 6 to repeating the Allegro after the slow movement, with no other finale. Perhaps the original audience welcomed the encore, but the listener of today feels short-changed.

Robert Woodcock, a civil servant, marine painter and amateur woodwind player, was a more interesting composer than the professional Baston. Of his twelve woodwind concertos, published by Walsh in 1727, six are for recorders (three for one sixth flute, three for two).[7] Five of these have first movements based on the ritornello principle (like Vivaldi's concertos) or incorporating the *Devise*, in which the soloist interrupts the first ritornello (like Albinoni's), although the melodic material is again generally much more stepwise than that of the Venetians. Concerto No. 5, on the other hand, owes more to Handel in construction and melodic material, and violas are added to the orchestra. The three solo concertos are again amenable to keyboard reduction.

Although the descant recorder balances better with strings than does the treble, there is only one original[8] solo descant concerto of real substance in the repertoire: that in F major by Sammartini, which is deservedly popular both in its original form and in keyboard reduction. It was probably written in the late 1720s or 30s, after the composer moved to England, presumably for his own use. Despite its generally Vivaldian outlines, the themes, the syncopations and the simplicity of the bass are all quite *galant*, and there are many chromatic touches, verging on the *empfindsam*, especially in the heartfelt Siciliano. Despite the virtuosity of the imaginative passage-work, the whole concerto is suffused with a wistful air.

Apart from the celebrated A minor Suite, in which the recorder plays a concertante role, Georg Philipp Telemann wrote only two solo recorder concertos. That in F major survives in a manuscript score and parts in Darmstadt, the latter in Johann Christoph Graupner's hand.[9] The work combines spectacular show, including third-octave G sharps and A's, with imaginative compositional touches, such as the quiet chromatic episode at bars 18–22 of the Allegro and the treatment of the ostinato bass in the Adagio. (It also exists as a flute concerto in D major, which may have been the original version.) The second concerto, in C major, which also survives in a Darmstadt manuscript in Graupner's hand, again has a high tessitura, allowing the recorder to stand out from the strings.[10] Its ravishing Andante in A minor is reminiscent of the *Air à l'italien* from the Suite in the same key. The witty and effective written-out ornamentation includes syncopated figures and some surprising chromaticism. The binary finale, marked 'Tempo di Minuet', is really a *polacca*, with plenty of the unusual rhythmic stresses and repeated notes of the Polish folk music Telemann had heard in the early years of the century. Both concertos were probably written for the flute, recorder and oboe virtuoso Johann Michael Böhm (*fl.*1685–1753), who was concertmaster of the Darmstadt orchestra from 1711 to 1729.[11]

Although an edition of Graupner's own recorder concerto in F major was published as long ago as 1939, this significant work has been strangely neglected by modern performers.[12] The composer worked for most of his life at the Darmstadt court, so it is probable that this concerto was written for its orchestra. Christa Sokoll remarks, however, that the manuscript score dates from 1735 to 1737, so that it is unlikely to have been written for Böhm, who left Darmstadt for Ludwigsburg in 1729. The most probable dedicatees are the court's two oboists, J. Corseneck and J. F. Stolz. The first movement is in an abbreviated ritornello form. For most of it the soloist holds sway, opening with a strikingly held high C, then playing a variety of passage-work, including a section of triplets that forms an effective contrast to the basic duple rhythms. The slow movement features the soloist throughout over pizzicato strings, the *galant* melody, frequently punctuated by short rests, containing some effective arpeggio figures. The final movement is a five-voice fugue, in which the recorder enters as the fifth voice in the exposition. Graupner also wrote an imaginative 'Ouverture' (suite) in the same key for concertante recorder and strings.[13]

The most ambitious baroque recorder concerto – at least, in length and orchestration – has also been ignored. Johann Christian Schickhardt's concerto in G minor is preserved in an autograph manuscript presented to Queen Ulrika Eleonore of Sweden, dating from the 1720s, the period when the woodwind player and composer worked in Scandinavia.[14] The piece is in no fewer than six movements. The first, fifth and sixth use the full orchestration of two oboes and strings with concertino violin and violoncello; the second features the oboes and concertino strings; the third and fourth drop back to using only the concertino violoncello. Although the passage-work is generally rather aimless, the concerto contains many felicitous touches of orchestration and surprising turns of event.

The double (etc.) concerto differs from the concerto grosso in that the string parts play a mainly supporting role to two or more prominent soloists, who may have substantial episodes on their own with only a lightly sketched accompaniment. Woodcock's concerto No. 4 in A minor adds a concertante solo violin to the descant recorder soloists, and occasionally uses the second violin(s) of the ripieno as the support line (there are no violas), with the continuo bass resting – a trick picked up from Vivaldi.[15] Vivaldi's own double concerto (RV 533), although marked for the transverse flute, fits the range of the treble recorder ($g'-d'''$) and may have originally been written for it. Unfortunately, the result is rather pedestrian.

Such concertos were a stock-in-trade of the Kapellmeisters and directors of music of Germany's numerous courts and cities.[16] None has the vitality and variety of Bach's Brandenburg Concertos, the second of which uses four concertante instruments (trumpet, recorder, oboe and violin).[17] Michael Marissen writes that 'The soloists are treated so equally that, unusually for Bach, there is no essential differentiation in the style of writing ... despite the fact that they represent a wide repertory of different ways of producing sound in the early eighteenth century (brass-woodwind-reed-string). ... The ripieno section of the ensemble performs only a doubling or an orchestral basso-continuo function whenever it appears.' The fourth Brandenburg Concerto makes great play with the identity of the soloist(s): does it have one (the solo violin) or three (the violin plus the pair of recorders?)[18] Marissen points out that 'the recorders frequently carry the greater musical weight ... while the solo violin often attracts the greater share of immediate attention by means of technical virtuosity'.

Johann Gottlieb Graun pairs recorder and violin.[19] Telemann, who seems to have been inspired by unusual instrumentation,[20] wrote four excellent double concertos with recorder, two of them with viola da gamba, one with bassoon and one with flute.[21] This last, a splendid work in E minor, has a beautiful *arioso* slow movement in the major key with pizzicato strings, and it ends with a Presto that epitomises Telemann's unique Polish style, full of 'barbaric beauty' and controlled abandon.[22] This movement starts with the recorder and flute in unison over a drone bass, as shown in the music example opposite, and the excitement mounts to a sustained third-octave G on the recorder.

Johann David Heinichen wrote a concerto for *Flaut[o] Conc[ertante]*, three *Flaut[i] Ripien[i]* and strings – an apparently early work

preserved in a manuscript at Darmstadt in the hand of Graupner.[23] In the first and fourth movements the first recorder does indeed play a solo role, while the other three act as accompaniment, sometimes without the orchestra. The second movement is a *Pastorell* in folk style for unison recorder and violin over a drone in the viola and bass, and in the third movement the first recorder is paired with violin and violoncello. The uniqueness of the scoring makes up for the routine passage-work. (Reinhard Goebel has reconstructed what he believes to be the original Dresden version of this concerto, for three recorders and an orchestra containing flutes and oboes.[24])

In the early 1700s the word 'concerto' could imply any instrumental ensemble larger than that of a 'sonata'. Witness, for example, Alessandro Marcello's *Concerto di flauti*, scored in four parts: two descant recorders doubling two muted violins, two treble recorders doubling muted viola, two tenor recorders doubling muted viola, and bass recorder doubling violoncello/continuo.[25] This unique piece begins with an overture, full of dotted notes, suspensions and trills, continues with a short fugal Allegro and ends with a fugal giga of some contrapuntal ingenuity.

'Sinfonia' was more often than not an instrumental piece before or within a primarily vocal composition, although Alessandro Scarlatti's twelve pieces for what we would now call a chamber orchestra are confusingly termed 'Sinfonie di concerto grosso' (autograph manuscript dated 1715). All twelve have *flauto* parts. These well-crafted works are surprisingly neglected, though not for want of editions.[26] Despite their unpretentiousness, they are full of variety, not to mention good tunes, such as that in the last movement of *Sinfonia prima*, with two recorders (also the layout of No. 5). No. 4 pairs a recorder with oboe, and No. 2, like the second Brandenburg Concerto of J. S. Bach, has a recorder and trumpet, although, unlike Bach's, the writing is never florid. Scarlatti uses the recorder almost orchestrally but with a more prominent role in the slow movements. The remaining eight are for one *flauto* in conjunction with strings. No. 12 in C minor, *La geniale*, does indeed have a beautifully genial manner: two Adagios and two Andantes with no Allegros. The second movement is fugal – most of Scarlatti's concertos have such movements – and the last is a minuet.

We should not leave Scarlatti without mentioning the manuscript of no fewer than twenty-four concertos for recorder and strings by Francesco Mancini (twelve), Scarlatti (seven), Francesco Barbello, Giovan Battista Mele, Domenico Sarri, Robert Valentine and an anonymous composer (one apiece) preserved in the library of the Naples Conservatory and presumably once played at the Naples court. It contains some little-known minor masterpieces. The expensive facsimile[27] is now out of print, and the only modern editions are disguised as flute sonatas,[28] although five of the concertos were recorded by Gudrun Heyens and Musica Antiqua Köln in 1977.[29] The Scarlatti works are true concerti grossi. While the recorder occasionally has a more prominent part in the slow movements, the voices are generally equal; there is constant interplay with the violins, and each concerto has at least one long fugal movement. The writing is weighty, surprising, and full of character. This repertoire begs to be explored further.

The only other recorder concerti grossi of a comparable standard are by Telemann. Two are for two recorders and strings, one of them in B flat major,[30] the other in A minor,[31] preserved in manuscripts in Darmstadt and Dresden. Although apparently early works, they display the richness of Telemann's mature orchestral style. The same is true of his fine six-part Chaconne for two recorders and strings in F minor,[32] which comes out of the blue as the eighth movement of a nine-movement 'Ouverture' (suite) for strings, probably written for the Collegium Musicum in Frankfurt (1712–21).[33] Johann Christoph Pez wrote for the same combination, including a Christmas *Pastorale*.[34] Occasionally in his writing for two descant recorders and strings Woodcock achieved the elegance and balance of the concerto-grosso style – for example, in his concerto No. 5.[35] Telemann also wrote concerti grossi for two recorders, two oboes, bassoon, strings and continuo (ideally with two harpsichords), with three enchanting and skilful concertos in B flat major, F major and A minor.[36] In the concerti grossi of Heinichen, which are just beginning to be explored, recorders are found both among the soloists (the concerto in G major for two recorders, two oboes, violin and orchestra (Seibel 215)) and among the orchestra.

The descant recorder concerto in A minor by Francis Dieupart is a curious hybrid of concerto grosso and solo concerto.[37] The Corellian first movement is unusual in its dogged examination of one rhythmic motif, shared between the recorder and the violins and oboes in unison. The slow movement is a showpiece for the recorder, featuring two unaccompanied flourishes. The finale is a giga containing much interplay between the recorder and the first violin/oboe. One of Babell's concertos, No. 2, is also a hybrid. Its short opening Adagio is scored for the violins without accompaniment. The second movement, Allegro, is in ritornello form, but the soloists are the violins. It leads directly into an Adagio section where the recorder enters for the first time, on a high G held for eight bars, moving to an unaccompanied cadenza and other passages of rather birdlike warbling. Only the binary finale is at all conventional in its treatment of recorder and orchestra.

Unfortunately, this repertoire of concerti grossi by Scarlatti, Telemann and others does not suit the demands of today's virtuoso professional soloists, and string ensembles with their vast repertoire of great music are not usually given to inviting recorder players to join them to play a few obscure baroque pieces. Nevertheless, it is to be hoped that further editions will be published and that more players will come to experience the music's considerable delights.

In the chamber concerto, at least one fast movement is in ritornello form. The instruments take turns to play the solo sections (sometimes one plays all of them), while all the instruments generally take part in the ritornellos. Some concertos for that attractive grouping of recorder, two violins and continuo may also have been performed by a chamber group – no doubled strings, no violas. The chamber concerto seems to have been invented by Vivaldi; then it spread to Germany, where it was taken up by Telemann and composers working in Dresden and it had a considerable influence on J. S. Bach's sonatas, which intermix elements of the sonata and concerto.[38]

Vivaldi's chamber concertos (for a listing, see p. 83) are among the most delightful works in the entire repertoire of the recorder. *La pastorella* (RV 95), at least, seems to have been composed not for Venice but for members of Cardinal Pietro Ottoboni's orchestra in Rome in the 1720s, and perhaps others were too.[39] The high incidence of D major among these concertos may eventually be explained by a difference of pitch between the recorder and the other instruments.[40] On the other hand, once again the range and keys (C major, D minor, F major, G minor) of most of Vivaldi's chamber concertos involving the flute strongly suggest that they were originally intended for the treble recorder.

Chamber concertos by other composers are much less visible as such in the recorder repertoire, although a number of good examples exist. Telemann wrote four. The quartet in G minor for recorder, violin, viola and continuo (TWV 43: g 4) is an early work (*c*1708–1715), combining elements of the Vivaldian concerto with sonata procedures. In the first movement of his 'Concerto à 3' in F major for recorder, horn and continuo (TWV 42: F 14), the recorder takes the orchestra role, the horn that of the soloist. But in the second movement, Vivace, of the famous 'Quatuor' in D minor (TWV 43: d 1) from *Musique de table*

(1733) for recorder, two flutes and continuo, the recorder is the virtuoso soloist. Telemann's quartet in G major for recorder, oboe, violin and continuo (TWV 43: G 6) survives in two copyists' manuscripts, one labelled 'concerto', the other 'sonata'. Yet the first movement is in clear ritornello form, the recorder and oboe pairing as the soloists and the violin taking the orchestral role.

Schickhardt published a set of six chamber concertos for four recorders and continuo (*c*1713–1715) – really concerti grossi in which the recorders take the place of strings.[41] Some of the sections of the fast movements are even marked 'Trio' and 'Tutti'. The style is at times reminiscent of Corelli, albeit without his contrapuntal interest, at others of early Vivaldi. (Schickhardt also arranged some of Corelli's concerti grossi for two recorders and continuo.[42]) At the other end of the chamber scale, an apparently authentic 'Concerto di camera' by Tomaso Albinoni has just been discovered that is scored for descant recorder and continuo.[43] The bass participates fully, and the melodic writing in both lines is attractively angular and full of chromatic twists. This piece should have a promising future in recorder recitals.

In all, almost 100 concertos involving the recorder have come down to us from the early eighteenth century, mostly in manuscript. Because few amateurs had the technical ability to play the solo parts or the musical resources to provide the necessary accompanists, such concertos were unsuitable for sale by publishers, who had a largely amateur market. It is notable that only thirteen were published – the solo concertos by Babell, Baston and Woodcock, in England where the large numbers of both amateurs and professionals could have justified the risk of publication – and even these concertos came out ten to twenty years after they were written. For any recorder player today, however, concertos are a highly significant part of the repertoire, offering some of its greatest technical challenges and musical rewards.

Notes

1. Ingo Gronefeld has been cataloguing all baroque and classical concertos for the 'flute' (including recorder) in *Die Flötenkonzerte bis 1850: Ein thematisches Verzeichnis*, 2 vols. to date (Tutzing 1992–3). He plans to include 'double concertos, group concertos, sinfonie concertante, overtures/suites, early concerto forms, variations, and single movements', although it is not clear whether he will include chamber concertos. As well as well-known concertos, the catalogue draws our attention to a number of 'lost' works listed in eighteenth-century catalogues and some by Peter Johann Fick, Nicola Fiorenza, Graun and Anton Heberle not yet published in modern editions.
2. They have often been claimed as the first flute concertos ever published, although Robert Woodcock's, which came out in London a year earlier, seem to deserve that distinction. In any case, it is evident that Vivaldi and/or Le Cène wanted to capitalise on the growing interest in both the flute and the solo concerto genre all over Europe.

3. Musica Rara.
4. French flute concertos such as those of Blavet are not suited to the recorder, but Corrette's six pastoral concertos (Op. 8), his three *Concertos de Noëls* for three treble instruments and continuo, and his *Concertos comiques* for various instrumental combinations may be classed as 'extended' or even 'probable' repertoire (see James R. Anthony, *French Baroque Music*, rev. edn (New York 1978), p. 314).
5. Hargail, Universal, etc.
6. Hänssler, Schott, Zen-On.
7. The remaining concertos are for flute and oboe (three apiece). For an in-depth appraisal see David Lasocki and Helen Neate, 'The life and works of Robert Woodcock, 1690–1728', *The American Recorder* 29/3 (1988), pp. 92–104.
8. Although some players pirate oboe concertos by Albinoni, Alessandro Marcello and Handel, the descant recorder is generally a poor substitute for the tonal richness and variety of the baroque oboe.
9. Bärenreiter Hortus Musicus.
10. Moeck.
11. While Telemann worked in Frankfurt am Main (1712–21), as city director of music and Kapellmeister at the Barfüsserkirche, he often asked Böhm and other members of the Darmstadt orchestra to play with him there.
12. Curiously, the first edition was incomplete: twenty-seven bars are missing from the last movement. A complete edition has now been edited by Christa Sokoll (Carus 1986).
13. Nagels Musik Archiv.
14. The autograph dedication is reproduced in David Lasocki, 'Johann Christian Schickhardt', *Tibia* 3/3 (1977), pp. 337–43. For more on Schickhardt's relationship with the Swedish royal family, see David Lasocki, 'Johann Christian Schickhardt (*c*1682–1762): a contribution to his biography and a catalogue of his works', *Tijdschrift van de Vereniging voor Nederlandse Muziekgeschiedenis* 27/1 (1977), pp. 28–55.
15. Schott.
16. A. J. B. Hutchings, in *The Baroque Concerto* (London 1961), p. 219, calls this 'Kapellmeistermusik', but not disparagingly, for it is competent and elegant. For example, Christoph Graupner (1683–1760) wrote fifty surviving concertos, twenty-eight of which are for two or more solo instruments. The autograph manuscripts (along with Telemann's concertos copied by Graupner and others) are in the library of the former Hesse court at Darmstadt. A number involve flute and in earlier examples this may mean recorders – see Pippa Drummond, *The German Concerto* (Oxford 1980), pp. 233–4, who quotes from a Graupner six-part concerto in B flat major, a 'recorder key' more than a 'flute key'.
17. The most up-to-date surveys of these concertos are Malcolm Boyd, *Bach: The Brandenburg Concertos* (Cambridge 1993), and Michael Marissen, 'J. S. Bach's Brandenburg Concertos as a meaningful set', *Musical Quarterly* 77/2 (1993), pp. 193–235.
18. For a brilliant exploration of this point, see Michael Marissen, 'Organological questions and their significance in J. S. Bach's Fourth Brandenburg Concerto', *Journal of the American Musical Instrument Society* 17 (1991), pp. 5–52. Marissen also seems to have settled the question of the identity of Bach's *fiauti d'echo* as well as it can be on the basis of surviving evidence: they were treble recorders.
19. Moeck. The manuscript is marked only 'Graun' and the attribution to J. G. is not certain.
20. Perhaps Telemann's greatest concerto is that for transverse flute, oboe d'amore and viola d'amore. Its last movement has a moment of genius, the plaintive oboe entry at bar 25.
21. The A minor concerto with recorder and gamba, with its beautiful *dolce* third movement, is published by Moeck. The F major work, labelled 'Sinfonia', is in three movements (Schott) with recorder and gamba solos; the strings are magnificently supplemented by a cornett and three trombones. The recorder and bassoon concerto has been published in no fewer than three modern editions (Breitkopf &

118   David Lasocki and Anthony Rowland-Jones

Härtel, Möseler, Pegasus). Its spirited last movement is in ritornello form, with the soloists beginning each episode with a contrapuntal statement of the main ritornello phrase. The recorder and flute concerto (Bärenreiter Hortus Musicus) has been recorded many times.

22. Drummond, *The German Concerto*, pp. 200–1. Occasionally in performances of this piece a sopranino recorder is substituted for treble at the Presto finale, and even a light percussion added. This is taking liberties, but the effect is electrifying and inevitably leads to an encore. Gordon Jacob used the same device for the Tarantella finale of his Suite for recorder and strings, recorded by Michala Petri (Philips 7337–310). Jacob's work is one of a very English group of twentieth-century pieces for recorder and strings by composers such as Edmund Rubbra, Lennox Berkeley, Arnold Cooke, Alan Ridout (1979), Malcolm Arnold (1988) and Gordon Crosse (*Watermusic* 1989).

23. Moeck; Das Erbe Deutscher Musik, vol. 11.

24. See his programme notes for the Musica Antiqua Köln recording of Heinichen's *Dresden Concerti* (Deutsche Grammophon Archiv 437 549–2, 1993).

25. Nova Music. Recorded, along with other concertos involving several recorders, by the Amsterdam Loeki Stardust Quartet and the Academy of Ancient Music (conducted by Christopher Hogwood) on L'Oiseau-Lyre 436 905, 'Concerti di Flauti'.

26. Five published by Bärenreiter Hortus Musicus and two by Schott.

27. Rome, Vivarelli, 1977.

28. Domenico Sarri, *Sonata, A-moll, für Flöte, Streicher und Cembalo* (Munich, Leuckart, 1968); Alessandro Scarlatti, *Sette sonate per flauto, archi e basso continuo* (Milan, Nazionalmusic, 1969). The title page of the collection describes the works as 'Concerti', the individual captions as 'Sonata'.

29. By Mancini (two), Barbella, Sarri and Valentine (Deutsche Grammophon Archiv 2533–380).

30. Möseler.

31. Nagels Musik Archiv.

32. Schott.

33. Frans Brüggen suggests that this movement was modelled on Purcell's chaconnes.

34. Schott.

35. Schott.

36. Recorded by Musica Antiqua Köln (dir. Reinhard Goebel) on Deutsche Grammophon 413 788, with the *Water Music* (see p. 97). The manuscripts of these concertos are in the Darmstadt library, the one in F major being in the hand of Quantz. There is also a concerto grosso for recorder, oboe, two horns and bassoon (ed. F. Schroeder, Adliswil, 1972).

37. Piano reduction published by Zen-On.

38. For more on this intriguing subject, see Jeanne Swack, 'On the origins of the *Sonate auf Concertenart*', *Journal of the American Musicological Society* 46/3 (1993), pp. 369–414.

39. Such as *Il gardellino* (RV 90), ostensibly for flute (but see p. 108). Michael Talbot, 'Vivaldi and Rome: observations and hypotheses', *Journal of the Royal Musical Association* 113/1 (1988), pp. 28–46.

40. As has already been suggested by Bruce Haynes, 'Johann Sebastian Bach's pitch standards: the woodwind perspective', *Journal of the American Musical Instrument Society* 11 (1985), pp. 55–114.

41. Bärenreiter Hortus Musicus.

42. Jeanne Roger, Amsterdam, c1718–19; Walsh, London, 1720. The six pieces are made up of movements drawn freely from ten of Corelli's twelve Concerti Grossi, Op. 6 (published 1715). For an edition of the only piece taken from a single concerto (Nova Music) the third movement, omitted by Schickhardt, has been reinstated by the editor.

43. Schott, Amadeus.

7 Instruction books and methods for the recorder from around 1500 to the present day

DAVID LASOCKI

Three classes of musicians have always played the recorder: professionals, adult amateurs and children. With the possible exception of Ganassi's *Fontegara*, no extant early manuals could have provided adequate instruction for professionals. This is hardly surprising, because those musicians were taught orally. In the renaissance and baroque periods they served as apprentices, receiving their training from masters with little or no written assistance. In the twentieth century, would-be professionals generally begin with private teachers then go on to music schools or conservatories, instruction books serving primarily as a source of exercises, studies and progressive repertoire.[1]

By the sixteenth century there were enough amateurs in France and Germany to warrant the publication of general instruction books that included material on the recorder. The rise of the middle class in the seventeenth and eighteenth centuries and the accompanying interest in self-instruction brought with it a spate of recorder 'tutors' (or methods, to use a more modern term), particularly in England. Yet, despite the extravagant claims of some publishers, none of these instructions was ever intended to bring amateurs to anything like a professional standard of performance.

In all periods, whether the pupils have been professional or amateur, the finer points of performance, such as breath-control, intonation, ornamentation and musical interpretation, have been learnt with the aid of a teacher; they can hardly be imparted by a book. All instruction books are written for people who can hear contemporaneous music-making and absorb its style by ear. In the absence of the sound, even the most comprehensive instructions fail, the reader seeking in vain to develop that *bon goût*, or good taste, that early writers considered so essential. Recorder instructions of the past can give us therefore only a small idea of what recorder playing was like in a few scattered places at arbitrary times.[2]

Instructions for the renaissance recorder

The first published instructions for the recorder appeared in two similar German publications of the early sixteenth century (on a set of manuscript instructions written around the same time, see p. 11). Sebastian Virdung served as a chaplain and singer in Heidelberg and other cities, including Basel, where his *Musica getutscht und auszgezogen* (Music, translated into German and excerpted) was published in 1511.[3] In writing for the first time in the vernacular and seeking to present 'everything ... made simple', Virdung was clearly aiming at the amateur musician. His instructions for the recorder consist largely of descriptions of how to finger the instrument. His only other technical information is that you must blow into the instrument as well as 'learn how to coordinate the articulations ... along with the fingers'.[4]

Virdung reports that the recorder, which nominally had eight finger-holes, in practice had nine: the lowest hole was doubled to allow for both left-handed and right-handed playing, the unused hole being stopped with wax. He discusses (and depicts in woodcuts) recorders of three sizes: discant in *c'*, tenor in *c'* and Baßcontra or Bassus in *f°*, all of which were notated an octave lower than they sounded. The discant and tenor had a range of an octave and a minor seventh; the bass, an octave and a sixth.

Martin Agricola was the Cantor of the Protestant Latin school in Magdeburg. His *Musica instrumentalis deudsch* (Wittenberg 1529)[5] was written in 'German rhythm and meter for a special reason, so that youth and others who want to study this art might all the more easily understand it and retain it longer'. The information on the recorder is similar to Virdung's. The middle size is called both tenor and altus, the latter mistakenly being depicted a little smaller in the woodcut. Rather than describing each fingering Agricola refers readers to his fingering charts – one for each size of instrument – which contain some differences, giving the impression, as William E. Hettrick remarks, 'that he had experimented with three individual instruments, rather than using just one size and duplicating its fingerings for the other two'.[6] Agricola says that graces (*Mordanten*), which make the melody *subtil*, must be learnt from a professional (*Pfeiffer*).

The substantially rewritten text of Agricola's second edition of 1545 – aimed at 'our schoolchildren and other beginning singers' – includes some significant differences and additions. He mentions, approvingly, the use of vibrato (*mit zitterndem Wind*) for woodwind instruments, and he includes the earliest account of woodwind articulation. Maxima, longs, breves, semibreves, minims and semiminims take the syllable *de*; semiminims can also take *di ri*, the articulation for the shorter note-values (fusas and semifusas). Finally, he remarks that in the very small note-values of *passaggi* (*Colorirn*), some musicians use the articulation *tell ell ell ell ell elle*, calling it the 'flutter-tongue' (*flitter zunge*).

Sylvestro Ganassi, the author of the first book devoted entirely to recorder playing, *Opera intitulata Fontegara* (Venice 1535) (pl. 29),[7] was a notable professional player employed by the Doge of Venice and the Basilica of San Marco.[8] Ganassi's is at once the most revealing and the most frustrating of all recorder tutors. He declares that 'the aim of the recorder player is to imitate as closely as possible all the capabilities of the human voice',[9] and that the instrument was indeed capable of doing so. He then describes an astonishingly well-devel-

Plate 29 The frontispiece of Sylvestro di Ganassi's *Fontegara* (Venice 1535) is probably as familiar to recorder players interested in renaissance music as is its important and revealing (but sometimes tantalising) text. For references earlier in this book see pp. 14 and 16. Some significant points are: (1) The picture shows an all-male group (compare with pl. 14, dated 1531). (2) It includes a singer (see p. 40). (3) Moreover, it is the singer, not the unoccupied descant-recorder player standing on the right of the table, who beats the tactus (with his left hand). (4) The consort has no bass recorder. The recorders being played are presumably two tenors and a treble. The paired alternative holes for left- or right-hand little finger are clearly visible in the treble. Two players are 'right-hand down', one is 'left-hand down'. (5) The recorders are of a wide-bore, almost cylindrical design, rather similar to those illustrated by Virdung in 1511 and Agricola in 1528 (see p. 120), not of the flared-bell design seen in the Flemish painting of 1547 shown as plate 15A, and in its insets. Ganassi's high-note fingerings are not likely to have worked on the unflared recorders in his frontispiece. But he says 'recorders made by different craftsmen vary one from another, not only in their measurements, but also in the bore itself and in the shape and position of the finger-holes'. He therefore gives 'several different fingerings used by different players' (Chap. 4). (6) Three viols and a lute hang on the wall behind, and there are treble and tenor cornetts on a ledge in the foreground. The recorder players almost certainly used these instruments to lend variety to their performances. There is much to be learnt from Ganassi.

oped, expressive style of playing, achieved by good breath-control, alternative fingerings, a wide variety of articulations and extensive use of graces and divisions. Yet he fails to specify the musical contexts in which these techniques were used, and we cannot hear the 'practised and experienced' sixteenth-century singer he holds up as a model.

Ganassi gives the interval of a thirteenth as the basic range of the three sizes of recorder (sopran, tenore and basso). In addition, he describes his discovery of a further interval of a seventh, including the accidentals of ♯1, ♭3, ♯4 and ♯5 in the third octave, making a total compass of two octaves and a sixth.

According to Ganassi, imitation of the voice has three interdependent 'indispensable peculiarities'. The first is 'a certain artistic proficiency', part of which seems to be the ability to perceive the nature of the music. The second is *prontezza* (dexterity or fluency), achieved 'by varying the pressure of the breath and shading the tone by means of suitable fingering'. The third is *galanteria* (elegance or grace), achieved by articulation, for which Ganassi uses three basic kinds of syllables – *te che*, *te re* and *le re* – and by the use of ornaments, the 'simplest ingredient' of them being the trill, which varies according to the expression. The majority of Ganassi's treatise is taken up with a series of tables of the divisions or *passaggi* that may be applied to a melodic line. As Howard Mayer Brown has suggested, the complex rhythms of some of Ganassi's *passaggi* seem to be an 'attempt to capture in print the essentially free rhythmic style of some improvisations'.[10]

Jerome Cardan, the great Italian renaissance philosopher, mathematician and physician, was a keen amateur recorder player, who learnt the instrument as a child in Milan from a professional teacher, Leo Oglonus. Cardan's treatise *De Musica* (*c*1546) both confirms Ganassi's account and gives glimpses into aspects of recorder playing otherwise undocumented before the twentieth century.[11] He is the first to mention an unnamed higher size of recorder (in d^2). He is interested in the partial closing of the bell hole to produce a tone or semitone below the natural lowest note. After stressing the importance of breath-control to follow the expression of the music, he makes the crucial distinction between the amount and the force of the breath. One of his ways of controlling intonation is by closing the bell hole, by means of which 'all tones can be turned into semitones and dieses'.[12]

Besides giving articulation syllables, Cardan notes that the tongue can be used either extended or turned up towards the palate, improving, varying and colouring the notes. He describes a trill or vibrato called a *vox tremula* in which 'a tremulous quality in the breath' is combined with a trilling of the fingers to vary the interval from anything between a major third and a diesis. He is especially enthusiastic about the use of the interval of a diesis – 'a sound than which nothing finer, nothing sweeter, nothing more pleasant can be imagined' – which can also be produced by repercussively bending back the tongue.

The only French author of the sixteenth century to write about the recorder was Philibert Jambe de Fer, a composer and singer whose *Epitome musical* was published in Lyons in 1556.[13] His fingering chart has been taken as the earliest evidence of buttress- or supporting-finger technique – the keeping down of the third finger of the lower hand whenever possible – although it is used for only three notes (the tenor's *b♭'*, *c"* and *d"*). For the rest of recorder playing he refers readers to 'good teachers'.

The relatively modest amount of material on the recorder that the German composer Michael Praetorius included in his encyclopaedic *Syntagma musicum* (Wolfenbüttel 1619) has received a large amount of attention because of his scale drawings of no fewer than eight sizes (klein Flötlein or exilent in *g"*, discant in *c"* or *d"*, alt in *g'*, tenor in *c'*, basset in *f°*, bass in *B♭°* and grossbass in *F°*) as well as the four-holed *gar kleine Plockflötlein*.[14] He gives the range of the instrument as a thirteenth (largest sizes) or fourteenth (smaller sizes), although a skilled player could sometimes ascend four or even seven degrees higher. Praetorius seems to have been the first to explain that recorders can confuse the ear into believing that they sound an octave lower than pitch – which is presumably why they were commonly notated an octave lower. His charts show that recorders could be used in at least three ranges of consort: 2' (discant, alt and tenor), 4' (alt, tenor and basset) and 8' (tenor, basset and bass).

Instructions for the transitional recorder

In his great encyclopaedic *Harmonie universelle* (Paris 1636–7),[15] Father Marin Mersenne devotes a section to recorders, which he calls 'Flustes d'Angleterre, que l'on appelle douces, & à neuf trous' (English flutes,[16] which are called sweet[17] and nine-holed).[18] Mersenne's engraving shows a dessus (treble) recorder still made in one piece with a slight inverse conical bore. The range of the taille (tenor) in his fingering chart is two octaves, *c'* to *c'''*, with completely baroque fingering including the supporting-finger technique. The dessus, taille or haute-contre, and basse 'make the small register [*petit jeu*], as those that follow make the large register; but they can be tuned together, like the large and small registers of organs'. The large register consists of the basse in *f°* together with two lower sizes which are never specified, although the lowest is said to be from seven to eight feet in length.

Two tutors are closely associated with Jacob van Eyck's celebrated collection of solo recorder music, *Der fluyten lust-hof* (Amsterdam 1644–c1655), as they have survived in copies of that collection:

Vertoninge en Onderwyzinge op de Hand-fluit by P. M. (Paulus Matthysz, the publisher of the collection and the tutors) and *Onderwyzinge hoemen alle de Toonen en halve Toonen, die meest gebruyckelyck zyn, op de Handt-fluyt zal konnen t'eenemael zuyver Blaezen* by the Gouda organist Gerbrand van Blanckenburgh. Yet they were conceived, and the latter also survives, independently, having apparently been designed for the first and second editions respectively of another collection of instrumental music, *'t Uitnemend Kabinet II* (1649, *c*1655).[19] Both give prose fingering instructions for a C instrument.[20] Those in *Vertoninge* are similar to baroque fingerings (see below) without supporting-finger technique. Blanckenburgh gives separate fingerings for enharmonically equivalent notes as well as one or two trill fingerings for each note. As Ruth van Baak Griffioen has written, however, 'His fingerings are so nuanced (his instructions frequently call for covering a hole "a little more than half open", or trilling "against the rim of the [finger]hole") that one suspects that they fit his own recorder but not necessarily anyone else's'.[21] (But see p. 73, note 46).

Instructions for the baroque recorder

The earliest instructions for the baroque recorder are ostensibly in an anonymous Venetian manuscript tutor, 'Tutto il bisognevole per sonar il flauto da 8 fori con pratica et orecchia', which its scribe dated 1630.[22] It seems to be addressed to the amateur who knew something of singing, or at least the well-known tunes of the day. The author depicts a recorder in three joints with baroque turnery at each tenon, although the bore still appears to be cylindrical. For the first time the fingering chart is for a recorder in *f'*, showing fingerings up to *g'''* (including *f♯'''*, although curiously not *f'''*) with supporting-fingering technique.

More to be expected from seventeenth-century Italy, the manuscript *Compendio musicale* (1677, rev. 1694) by Father Bartolomeo Bismantova, a wind player in Ferrara, has an extensive section about a recorder in *g'* 'of three joints such as those used today' (he also gives a scale beginning on *d'*).[23] His instructions are full of the wisdom of an experienced professional. To lower the pitch, pull out the head joint 'then also lengthen [the recorder] just a bit at the foot joint, so that all the pitches will be in tune'. If the recorder is more than a semitone away from the right pitch and cannot be adjusted by elongating the tube, carefully place a little bit of wax on one part of the windway (*linguetta*) to adjust it. When playing the recorder in dry weather or in summer, use a feather to oil the inside of the pipe with high-class olive, sweet almond or jasmine oil, to soften the recorder and make the high notes come in tune.

In his repetitive style, Bismantova insists that all wind instruments should be played 'in a singing manner and not otherwise, and also in imitation of one who sings'. His tonguing syllables are mostly similar to the renaissance ones. The direct tongue (*de*) is used for all note-values from a breve to a quaver; the reverse tongue (*de re le re*), for quavers, semiquavers and demisemiquavers; two other types of sylla-bles (*de che* and *der ler*) are little used, except (curiously for the first one) in accompanying in cantabile style. What is new is the importance now given to the smooth tongue (*lingua legata*), or slurred pairs of notes: *de a de a de a*; this presumably reflects the influence of violin technique.[24] Bismantova gives a practical method for learning a piece of music: speak the various articulations first in rhythm; only after mastering that, practise the fingerings on the instrument. His fingering chart is marked with the sign 't' to indicate the appropriate finger to shake for trills.

Although the French approach to the new type of recorder is not documented until later in the seventeenth century, we can gain some idea of it from the tutors of England, where the taste for French music and instruments brought first the flageolet, then the recorder into vogue among amateurs. Thomas Greeting, a royal violinist who supplemented his income by teaching amateurs such as the famous diarist Samuel Pepys and his wife, wrote a tutor for the flageolet, *The Pleasant Companion*,[25] that served as a model for such books for over a century: a few rudiments of music are followed by a fingering chart and a selection of 'lessons', or popular tunes of the day. Those who had already learnt the flageolet by 'dot-way', as its tablature was known, were presented the recorder by the same method.[26]

A few tutors were aimed at children: J[ohn] B[anister II]'s *The Most Pleasant Companion* (1681) announces 'plain and easy rules and instructions for young beginners'; *The Compleat Instructor to the Flute* (1700) has similar 'directions'. Robert Carr's *The Delightful Companion* (1682, 2nd edn 1684) has 'plain and easy instructions for beginners', to be used in conjunction with a teacher. Banister is the only significant professional author represented among the tutors; the remainder are anonymous or else put together by unknowns (Carr) or music sellers (John Hudgebut's *A Vade Mecum* (1679) (pl. 30), Humphrey Salter's *The Genteel Companion* (1683)). When John Walsh entered the music publishing business in 1695, he immediately issued a recorder tutor, *The Compleat Flute-Master*, with the most extravagant claim: 'The whole art of playing on the recorder, laid open in such easy and plain instructions, that by them the meanest capacity may arrive to a perfection on that instrument'.[27]

The four earliest tutors – Hudgebut, Banister, Salter and Carr – are the most revealing because of their use of the flageolet tablature, which indicates slurs and fingerings for ornaments.[28] The ornaments dis-cussed are elementary ones derived from the French style: the trill,

Plate 30 The title-page engraving probably intended for a later edition of John Hudgebut's tutor for the 'Rechorder' (*A Vade Mecum*), first published in 1679. Like Ganassi's frontispiece (pl. 29) it also shows three recorder players with a singer – who also keeps time with his left hand. And again there is one recorder not being played. There is no descant recorder, but treble, tenor (or two trebles? or two tenors?) and a bass with bocal (not 'direct blow'), in rather slender versions of the new French 'baroque' recorder design introduced to London in (or before?) 1673. Hudgebut claims his tutor as being 'the first Essay of this kind', and it probably was the first English instruction book for the recorder to be published. But Pepys must have used some instructions, or at least a fingering chart, when as a flageolet player he first took up the recorder with its unfamiliar fingerings in April 1668, for he refers to 'perfecting my getting the scale of music without book' (*Diary*, 9 April 1668). This might have been compiled for him by Thomas Greeting or by Samuel Drumbleby the instrument-maker. WB 23

beginning on the main note or upper auxiliary (at first called the 'beat', later the 'shake' or 'close shake'); the mordent, beginning on the main note or with a rising appoggiatura ('shake', then 'beat' or 'open shake'); the slur; the slur and mordent; and the 'double shake', a warbling trill across the registers on g''. Carr also has a chart for trill fingerings, some of which are ingeniously conceived. Since enharmonic sharps and flats are generally distinguished in the fingering charts, the authors of these tutors were apparently sensitive to good intonation. We should there-fore take seriously the fingerings for ornaments that show not simply semitones and whole tones but 'a rich diversity of intervals ... ranging from microtones to expanded whole tones'.[29]

The ornament instructions in *The Compleat Flute-Master* also mention the 'sigh' (equivalent to the French *accent*) and the 'double relish' (trill with turn), and give directions for adding graces on ascending, descending and repeated notes when they are not marked.[30]

The 'sweetning', which on the face of it is listed simply as an alternative name for 'open shake or beat', may in fact be a fingered vibrato (equivalent to the French *flattement*).[31] Curiously, these instructions were pirated and incorporated into most English tutors until as late as 1780, when they must surely have puzzled the performers of classical songs and dances.

The first French method for the baroque recorder was written by Etienne Loulié, a musician and music director in the celebrated ensemble attached to the household of Marie de Lorraine (better known as Mademoiselle de Guise), then music teacher to the Duke of Chartres (later regent of France).[32] In the 1680s Loulié wrote the first draft of a recorder tutor[33] and several other tutors and treatises, perhaps for Mademoiselle de Guise's academy for children of the nobility, later presumably putting all these manuals to good use in his instruction of Chartres. The tablature and some of the wordings in Loulié's recorder tutor seem to derive from the earliest English tutors. As his tutor was intended for adolescents, it is fairly elementary – failing, for example, to discuss ornaments, which depend on taste and can only be formed under a good teacher. Yet we learn that he taught the tonguing syllables *tu* and *ru*.[34]

La veritable maniere d'apprendre a jouer en perfection du haut-bois, de la flute et du flageolet (Paris 1700) by Jean-Pierre Freillon-Poncein, the Prévost of the Grande Ecurie at the Versailles court, was the first published French tutor for the baroque recorder.[35] It was intended primarily for the oboe, however, and adds little to our knowledge of recorder technique. The fingering chart, shown by means of schematic figures of a recorder, introduces fully chromatic fingering for the first time, apparently with equal half-steps. Trill fingerings are described for the first octave only. Of considerable interest are the extensive instructions for articulation (again using the tonguing syllables *tu* and *ru*) and ornaments.[36]

As the order of instruments named on the title page suggests, Jacques Hotteterre le Romain's *Principes de la flûte traversière, ou flûte d'Allemagne, de la flûte à bec, ou flûte douce, et du haut-bois, divisez par traitez* (1707)[37] was conceived primarily as a tutor for the transverse flute, which had recently become 'one of the most fashion-able instruments' in France. Although, as Hotteterre says, the recorder had 'its merits and partisans, just like the flute', he gives the recorder a secondary role by placing its section after that of the flute and referring recorder players to the flute section for information on articulation and ornaments. Hotteterre held the position of *Flûte de la chambre du roy*, and we have approving contemporary reports of his performance on the flute and the musette. Although the engraving in his tutor of two hands playing a recorder has become strongly identified with the

baroque recorder in modern writings, his familiarity with the instrument has been questioned.[38]

In his fingering charts, Hotteterre seems to have been the first author systematically to divorce from a picture of a recorder those now familiar symbols of black circles for closed finger-holes, white circles for open finger-holes and half-blackened circles for half-closed or 'pinched' finger-holes. Although his method of showing trill fingerings is equivalent to Carr's, Hotteterre's adoption of these symbols makes them much easier to comprehend. He devotes a chapter to explaining the fingerings for *battements* (mordents) and *flattements* (a fingered vibrato). The other ornaments – *port-de-voix* (ascending appoggiatura), *coulement* (descending appoggiatura), *accent* and *double cadence* (trill with turn) – are described in a manner that leaves their rhythm and accentuation open to interpretation.

Hotteterre's instructions on articulation, once again using the syllables *tu* and *ru*, constitute the classic explanation of the late baroque French approach. The brilliant researches of Patricia Ranum have recently shown that these syllables need to be understood in the context of declaimed and sung French texts of the period.[39] *Tu* was a 'rigorous' sound, used for all long notes as well as any shorter notes performed 'equally'. *Ru* was a 'gentler' sound, always part of what Ranum calls 'a basic building block', *tu-ru-tu*, or else the pattern *tu-ru-tu-tu* for 'concluding statements'. Two, three or more notes could also be slurred together; Hotteterre freely notates slurs – including long ones – in his improvisatory *traits* and preludes.[40]

The recorder method published around 1710–15 by the prolific German woodwind composer Johann Christian Schickhardt is disappointing, apparently being intended largely to sell the forty-two recorder duets that form the major part of it.[41] Schickhardt borrows Hotteterre's fingering and trill fingering charts with minor alterations. The main interest of the tutor is a couple of musical examples that show the iambic pair of articulation syllables *ti-rí* in dotted figures, a modification of the French vowel sound (as well as of the complex French practice of using syllables based on a knowledge of declaimed

Plate 31 (opposite) Frontispiece engraved by John Smith (1652–1742) to the (plagiarised) *Directions for Playing on the Flute* from Prelleur's *The Modern Musick-Master* (1731). This fine gentleman, complete with sword, plays his recorder by a mountain lake to enjoy the echo – rather like singing in the bath. Having learnt his Air by heart (it was quite usual for baroque musicians to play from memory) he has left the open book of music on the ground, together with his hat which could have muffled his enjoyment of the recorder's resonance. Pepys was also a lover of 'mighty fine' echoes, for example in the wine cellar of Audley End House while returning to London from Cambridge (*Diary*, 27 Feb. 1659/60). WB 114

or spoken texts) for Dutch and German speakers. Similar modifications
in the French articulation practice were made by the German flautist
Johann Joachim Quantz in his celebrated flute method, *Versuch einer
Anweisung die Flöte traversiere zu spielen* (Berlin 1752).[42] Since
Quantz was himself a recorder player in his early days and wrote a
trio-sonata involving the recorder, his treatise is worthy of intense
study by recorder players.[43]

The most unusual eighteenth-century instructional document about
the recorder is by the celebrated maker Thomas Stanesby, Junior,
'humbly dedicated to all those gentlemen who like the instrument': *A
New System of the Flute a'bec, or Common English-Flute* (London
c1732).[44] Stanesby proposed to make the tenor, rather than the treble,
the standard size of recorder, and included a comprehensive fingering
chart containing several notes above the customary baroque upper
limited of *d'''* (the equivalent of the treble's *g'''*). Several other
eighteenth-century sets of instructions published in Germany, the
Netherlands, Norway and Spain are notable mainly for their inclusion
of fingering charts containing such high notes.[45] The many eighteenth-
century English tutors, with their long outdated instructions on
ornaments, are really of interest only for the selection of up-to-date
music they contain and their frontispieces (pl. 31).[46]

Modern instructions

The typical modern recorder tutor consists of musical examples,
generally drawn from folk or early music, that enable the reader
progressively to learn all the fingerings and perhaps a little about
articulation and ornaments. In addition, modern tutors have attempted
to teach their readers more and more about early performance
practices. Since about 1960, the rapid rise in the number and standard
of players, both amateur and professional, and the use of the recorder
in avant-garde music have prompted some novel and significant
contributions on more advanced aspects of recorder technique.

Anthony Rowland-Jones's *Recorder Technique* (Oxford 1959), still
directed at the amateur, showed the way forward with an intelligent
and detailed look at such neglected topics as breathing, intonation, the
use of alternative fingerings, high notes, dynamics, practising and
performing, and an insightful survey of the recorder's repertoire.[47]
(Kenneth Wollitz's popular *The Recorder Book* (New York 1982) covers
much of the same territory.) Hans-Martin Linde's *Handbuch des
Blockflötenspiels* (1962), based on his course for students at the Schola
Cantorum Basiliensis, demonstrated the breadth of both recorder
technique and history that the budding professional player was now
expected to absorb.[48]

Michael Vetter's pioneering book on avant-garde technique, *Il flauto dolce ed acerbo* (Celle 1969), was largely a compilation of hundreds of fingerings for both single notes and multiphonics, although it contains brief instructions on embouchure, articulation, breathing, vibrato and dynamics.[49] More recent comprehensive treatments of this subject are Hermann Rechberger's book *Die Blockflöte in der zeitgenössischen Musik*[50] and a series of articles by Robin Troman.[51]

After a decade of promoting the bell-key recorder, Daniel Waitzman published a stimulating book on recorder technique, *The Art of Playing the Recorder* (New York 1978), that received a mixed reception for its concentration on the use of such an instrument. Walter van Hauwe, the present-day performer who has pushed recorder technique the furthest, has distilled the essence of his phenomenal command of the instrument into a non-traditional tutor entitled *The Modern Recorder Player* (3 vols., London 1984–92). Significant studies of individual aspects of recorder technique include Edward L. Kottick's *Tone and Intonation on the Recorder* (New York 1974), Johannes Fischer's *Die dynamische Blockflöte* (Celle 1990), and articles by Abraham Greenberg on the phonetics of articulation,[52] Linde Höffer-von Winterfeld on fingering combinations and tone-colour,[53] and Eugene Reichenthal and Scott Reiss on shading and leaking.[54]

Notes

1. I would like to thank Marianne Mezger and Anthony Rowland-Jones for looking over drafts of this chapter and making many helpful suggestions.
   The most important studies of pre-modern recorder instruction books are in Hildemarie Peter, *The Recorder: its Traditions and its Tasks* (Berlin-Lichterfelde and New York 1958); Edgar Hunt, *The Recorder and its Music* (London 1962; 2nd edn 1977); Thomas E. Warner, 'Indications of performance practice in woodwind instruction books of the 17th and 18th centuries' (Diss., New York U. 1964); Mary Vinquist, 'Recorder tutors of the seventeenth and eighteenth centuries: technique and performance practice' (Diss., U. of North Carolina 1974); Andrew Hornick, 'Early eighteenth-century treatises on the recorder', *The American Recorder* 19/2 (1978), pp. 62–4; and E. Hunt, 'Early recorder methods', *Recorder & Music* 6/6 (June 1979), pp. 166–70. The tutors published between 1654 and 1818 were first listed in T. E. Warner, *An Annotated Bibliography of Woodwind Instruction Books, 1600–1830* (Detroit 1967); those published between 1654 and 1780 are relisted with some additions and corrections in Vinquist, 'Recorder tutors', Appendix A (pp. 145–242). The early articulation syllables are well summarised and discussed in Richard Erig and Veronika Gutmann's introduction to their edition of *Italienische Diminutionen: die zwischen 1553 und 1638 mehrmals bearbeiteten Sätze = Italian Diminutions: The Pieces with more than one Diminution from 1553 to 1638* (Zurich 1979); and Scott Reiss, 'Articulation: the key to expressive playing', *The American Recorder* 27/4 (1986), pp. 144–9. The early fingering charts are collected in David Lasocki, '17th and 18th century fingering charts for the recorder', *The American Recorder* 11/4 (1970), pp. 128–37; and Jean Claude Veilhan, *La flûte à bec baroque selon la pratique des XVIIe et XVIIIe siècles: Technique, modes de jeu, tablatures*

132   *David Lasocki*

originales = The Baroque Recorder in 17th- and 18th-Century Performance and Practice: Technique, Performing Style, Original Fingering Charts (Paris 1980).

For modern tutors, Jean W. Thomas, 'A practical guide to recorder method books and related material: an annotated bibliography', *The American Recorder* 20/3 (1979), pp. 111–17, describes no fewer than sixty-nine available in the United States at the time of publication. Lists of German-language tutors are included in Linde Höffer-von Winterfeld and Harald Kunz, *Handbuch der Blockflötenliteratur* (Berlin 1959); and Hans-Martin Linde, *Handbuch des Blockflötenspiels* (Mainz 1962; 2nd edn 1984; English translation as *The Recorder Player's Handbook*, London 1974; 2nd edn 1991).

2. Thus we can never recreate a historical performance of early recorder music, only be inspired by some historical aspects of its performance.

3. Facsimile edns, Cassel 1931 and 1970, New York 1966. English trans. by Beth Bullard as *Musica getutscht: A Treatise on Musical Instruments (1511) by Sebastian Virdung* (Cambridge 1993). An earlier English trans. is in William E. Hettrick, 'Sebastian Virdung's method for recorders of 1511: a translation with commentary', *The American Recorder* 20/3 (1979), pp. 99–105. See also Laurence Wright, 'Sebastian Virdung: Musica getutscht und auszgezogen (Basel 1511)', *The Recorder and Music Magazine* 1/10 (1965), pp. 301–3. A loose, partial French translation was published in Antwerp in 1529 under the title *Livre plaisant et tres-utile*, and that in turn was translated into Flemish and also published in Antwerp in 1568 as *Dit is een seer schoon boecxken* (joint facsimile, Amsterdam 1973).

4. Virdung's English translator, William E. Hettrick, plausibly suggests 'It is possible that Virdung's relative silence on [breath and articulation] and other aspects of recorder technique is due simply to a lack of knowledge on his part'. 'Sebastian Virdung's method for recorders', p. 105, note 3.

5. 'Diplomatic edition' (Leipzig 1896). Facsimile of 1529 edn (Hildesheim 1969). English trans. and facsimiles of woodwind sections from 1529 and 1545 edns in William E. Hettrick, 'Martin Agricola's poetic discussion of the recorder and other woodwind instruments', *The American Recorder* 21/3 (1980), pp. 103–13; 23/4 (1982), pp. 139–46; and 24/2 (1983), pp. 51–60; reprinted in *The Recorder and Music Magazine* 8/4 (1984), pp. 127–9; 8/5 (1985), pp. 139–48; 8/6 (1985), pp. 171–9; and 8/7 (1985), pp. 202–12. Hettrick has recently produced a complete translation and edition of *The 'Musica instrumentalis deudsch' of Martin Agricola – A Treatise on Musical Instruments, 1529 and 1545* (Cambridge 1994).

6. 'Martin Agricola's poetic discussion', p. 112.

7. Facsimile reprints, Milan 1934, Bologna 1969. German trans. as *La Fontegara: Schule des kunstvollen Flötenspiels und Lehrbuch des Diminuierens, Venedig, 1535*, ed. Hildemarie Peter, trans. Emilia Dahnk-Baroffio and H. Peter (Berlin-Lichterfelde 1956). English trans. as *Opera Intitulata Fontegara, Venice 1535: A Treatise on the Art of Playing the Recorder and of Free Ornamentation*, ed. H. Peter, trans. Dorothy Swainson from the German trans. (Berlin-Lichterfelde 1959). See also H. Peter, 'An introduction to Ganassi's treatise on the recorder (1535)', *The Consort* 12 (1955), pp. 18–23.

8. On his life, see Howard Mayer Brown, 'Sylvestro di Ganassi dal Fontego', in *The New Grove*.

9. Swainson trans., p. 9.

10. *Embellishing Sixteenth-Century Music* (London 1976), p. 25.

11. Trans. and ed. Clement A. Miller in Hieronymus Cardanus, *Writings on Music* (n.p. 1973). See also Miller's article, 'Jerome Cardan on the recorder', *The American Recorder* 12/4 (1971), pp. 123–5. In a second treatise, also entitled *De Musica* (1574), Cardan discusses the use of the recorder and other woodwinds in ensemble, stressing the need to keep together to match intonation, tone and mood.

12. A diesis is half a small semitone (the difference in pitch between the second note of the scale and a flat minor third).

13. See François Lesure, 'L'épitome musical de Philibert Jambe de Fer (1556)', *Annales musicologiques* 6 (1963), pp. 341–6, [i–xl]. Also published separately, Neuilly-sur-Seine 1964.

14. Facsimile, Kassel 1958. English translations: *The Syntagma musicum of Michael Praetorius. Volume Two: De Organographia, First and Second Parts*, trans. Harold Blumenfeld (New York 1962, 1980) and *Syntagma Musicum, II: De Organographia, Parts I and II*, trans. and ed. David Z. Crookes (Oxford 1986).

15. Facsimile, Paris 1965. See also Wolfgang Köhler, 'Die Blasinstrumente aus der "Harmonie Universelle" des Marin Mersenne und ihre Bedeutung für die Aufführungspraxis heute', *Tibia* 13/1 (1988), pp. 1–14; and W. Köhler, *Die Blasinstrumente aus der 'Harmonie Universelle' des Marin Mersenne: Übersetzung und Kommentar des 'Livre cinquiesme des instrumens à vent' aus dem 'Traité des instruments'* (Celle 1987).

16. Elsewhere I have suggested that the prominence of the Bassano family of recorder players, composers and instrument makers in England led to this name (David Lasocki, 'The Anglo-Venetian Bassano family as instrument makers and repairers', *The Galpin Society Journal* 38 (1985), pp. 112–31). See also p. 222.

17. 'Douce' can mean sweet or soft.

18. The same three names are given by Pierre Trichet in his *Traité d'instruments* (*c*1640). See François Lesure, 'Le Traité des instruments de musique de Pierre Trichet, Les instruments à vent', *Annales musicologiques* 3 (1955), pp. 283–387, at 348. Unfortunately Trichet has nothing else of value to say about recorders.

19. See Ruth van Baak Griffioen's *Jacob van Eyck's* Der Fluyten Lust-Hof *(1644–c1655)* (Utrecht 1991), pp. 377–81. We should not, therefore, refer to 'van Eyck's fingerings'.

20. Two other, little-known Dutch seventeenth-century fingering instructions for C recorders are in Christiaan Huygens, *Tons de ma flute* (MS 1686) (reproduced as a chart in Griffioen, *Jacob van Eyck's* Der Fluyten Lust-Hof, p. 380), and Claas Douwes, *Grondig Ondersoek van de Toonen der Musijk* (Fraeneker 1699; facsimile, Amsterdam 1970).

21. *Jacob van Eyck's* Der Fluyten Lust-Hof, p. 419.

22. Biblioteca Marciana, Venice, MSS Ital. Cl. IV. No. 486. See also Nikolaus Delius, 'Die erste Flötenschule des Barock?' *Tibia* 1/1 (1976), pp. 5–12. If this tutor really was written in 1630, we need to revise our notions of the development of the recorder in the seventeenth century; it may turn out with further research, however, that the tutor dates from the third quarter of the century.

23. Facsimile edn, Florence 1978. Transcription in Adriano Cavicchi, 'Prassi strumentale in Emilia nell'ultimo quarto del seicento: flauto italiano, cornetto, archi', *Studi musicali* 2/1 (1973), pp. 111–43. English trans. in Bruce Dickey, Petra Leonards and Edward H. Tarr, 'The discussion of wind instruments in Bartolomeo Bismantova's Compendio Musicale (1677): translation and commentary = Die Abhandlung über die Blasinstrumente in Bartolomeo Bismantovas Compendio Musicale (1677): Übersetzung und Kommentar', *Basler Jahrbuch für historische Musikpraxis* 2 (1978), pp. 143–87. See also Marcello Castellani, 'The Regola per suonare il flauto italiano by Bartolomeo Bismantova (1677)', *The Galpin Society Journal* 30 (1977), pp. 76–85.

24. Although the slurred pairs are also found in Fantini's trumpet tutor, *Modo per imparare a sonare di tromba* (Frankfurt 1638).

25. London 1672. 1st edn not traced but claimed to be as early as 1661 or 1667 and definitely published by 1668 (see Warner, *Annotated Bibliography*, pp. 1–2). The relative chronology of Greeting's tutor with respect to the anonymous *Directiones ad pulsationem* and Thomas Swain's *Directions for the Flagellett* (both London 1667) remains to be ascertained.

26. As proclaimed by the title of a tutor that has not survived: *The Recorder or Flute made easie; by exact and true directions, shewing the manner and way of playing on that fashionable Instrument by the Notes of the Flagelet; whereby the meanest capacity may, with a little spare time, attain his desire* (London 1683). Title quoted in Vinquist, 'Recorder tutors', p. 159.

27. See David Lasocki, 'The Compleat Flute-Master reincarnated', *The American Recorder* 11/3 (1970), pp. 83–5.

28. Herbert W. Myers, 'Three seventeenth-century English recorder tutors', *The*

American Recorder 7/2 (1966), pp. 3–6, discusses Hudgebut's *A Vade Mecum*, Banister's *The Most Pleasant Companion* and Salter's *The Genteel Companion*. The ornaments in those tutors and three later English ones are compiled into two handy charts published with Marianne Mezger's edition of Jacques Paisible, *Five Sonatas for Alto Recorder and Continuo* (Brighton 1993).

29. Mezger, preface to Paisible, *Five Sonatas*.
30. A similar set of instructions, 'Rules for Gracing on the Flute', is found in London, British Library, Add. MS 35043 (f. 125), a volume of miscellaneous instrumental music from the last decade of the seventeenth century. See Thurston Dart, 'Recorder "gracings" in 1700', *The Galpin Society Journal* 12 (1959), pp. 93–4. Reprinted in Vinquist, 'Recorder tutors', p. 293.
31. This is the opinion of Marianne Mezger.
32. On Loulié's life, see especially Patricia M. Ranum, 'Etienne Loulié (1654–1702): Musicien de Mademoiselle de Guise, pédagogue et théoricien', *'Recherches' sur la musique française classique* 25 (1987), pp. 27–76; 26 (1988–90), pp. 5–49; and 'Etienne Loulié: recorder player, teacher, musicologist', *American Recorder* 32/1 (1991), pp. 7–11, 34.
33. See Richard Semmens, 'Etienne Loulié's "Method for Learning How to Play the Recorder"', *Studies in Music from the University of Western Ontario* 6 (1981), pp. 7–23; and 'A translation of Etienne Loulié's Method for Learning How to Play the Recorder', *The American Recorder* 24/4 (1983), pp. 135–45. See also Patricia Ranum's additions and corrections in 25/3 (1984), pp. 119–21 as well as her two articles cited in note 32. As Ranum shows, Loulié made a revised draft of his recorder tutor in 1701 or 1702, after seeing Freillon-Poncein's.
34. Using them more in the manner of Freillon-Poncein than that of Hotteterre (see below).
35. Facsimile, Geneva 1972. English trans. by Catherine Parsons Smith as *On Playing Oboe, Recorder, & Flageolet* (Bloomington, Ind. 1992). Earlier versions of her translation were published as *The True Way to Learn to Play Perfectly the Oboe, the Recorder, and the Flageolet Along with the Principles of Music for Voice and All Kinds of Instruments* (Brooklyn 1969), and also in *The American Recorder* 23/1 (1982), pp. 3–10. See also the transcription and English trans. of the part devoted to the recorder in David Lasocki, 'Freillon-Poncein, Hotteterre, and the recorder', *The American Recorder* 10/2 (1969), pp. 40–3.
36. The best discussion of the instructions of Freillon-Poncein and Hotteterre is in Betty Bang Mather, *Interpretation of French Music from 1675 to 1775 for Woodwind and Other Performers* (New York 1973).
37. Facsimile of *c*1710 Amsterdam ed. with German trans. by H. J. Hellwig, Kassel 1942 and 1982. Facsimile of 1720 Paris edn, Geneva 1973. English trans. by David Lasocki as *Principles of the Flute, Recorder & Oboe* (London 1968); English trans. by Paul Marshall Douglas as *Rudiments of the Flute, Recorder and Oboe* (New York 1968) and as *Principles of the Flute, Recorder & Oboe (Principes de la flûte)* (New York 1983). Hotteterre adds to his instructions on ornaments in the preface to his *Pièces pour la flûte traversière et autres instruments, avec la basse continue*, Op. 2 (Paris 1708; 2nd edn. 1715).
38. For example, Edgar Hunt asserts that Hotteterre 'seems to be writing from the point of view of a flute player, not as someone who has made an intimate study of the recorder', criticises four of his trill fingerings as being unnecessarily out of tune and/or ugly, and suggests that recorder players should follow flautists in finding fingerings that are as in tune as possible. See his 'Thoughts on Hottteterre's recorder fingerings', *The American Recorder* 27/4 (1986), p. 151.
39. 'A fresh look at French wind articulations', *American Recorder* 33/4 (December 1992), pp. 9–16, 39; extended in '*Tu-Ru-Tu* and *Tu-Ru-Tu-Tu*: toward an understanding of Hotteterre's tonguing syllables', in David Lasocki (ed.), *The Recorder in the 17th century* (Utrecht 1995).
40. See his *L'art de préluder sur la flûte traversière, sur la flûte-a-bec, sur le hautbois et autres instruments de dessus* (Paris 1719; facsimile, Geneva 1978; modern edn Michel Sanvoisin, Paris 1966).

41. *Principes de la flûte* (Amsterdam c1710–1715). Facsimile, Rome 1987. See also David Lasocki, 'A newly rediscovered recorder tutor', *The American Recorder* 9/1 (1968), pp. 18–19; and 'Johann Christian Schickhardt (c1682–1762): woodwind composer, performer and teacher', *Recorder & Music* 5/8 (1976), pp. 254–7; 5/9 (1977), pp. 287–90.

42. English trans. by Edward R. Reilly as *On Playing the Flute* (London 1966; 2nd edn 1985).

43. For an application of Quantz's instructions on affections to his trio-sonata in C major for treble recorder, flute and basso continuo, see David Lasocki, 'Quantz and the passions: theory and practice', *Early Music* 6/4 (1978), pp. 556–67.

44. The pamphlet is reproduced in facsimile in Dale Higbee, 'A plea for the tenor recorder by Thomas Stanesby Jr.', *The Galpin Society Journal* 15 (1962), pp. 55–9.

45. As Dale Higbee drew attention to in 'Third-octave fingerings in eighteenth-century recorder charts', *The Galpin Society Journal* 15 (1962), pp. 97–9. The sources are: Joseph Friedrich Bernhard Caspar Majer, *Museum musicum theoretico practicum* (Nuremberg 1732, 2nd edn 1741; facsimile, Kassel 1954); see also Joel Newman, 'The recorder in Majer's *Museum musicum* 1732', *The American Recorder* 3/1 (1962), pp. 6–8; Pablo Minguet y Irol, *Reglas, y advertencias generales que enseñan el modo de tañer todos los instrumentos majores* (Madrid 1754; facsimile, Geneva 1981; and see pl. 25); see also David Lasocki, 'A Spanish recorder tutor', *The American Recorder* 9/2 (1968), pp. 49–50; and Joos Verschuere Reynvaan, *Muzijkaal Kunst-Woordenboek* (Amsterdam 1795). A source that has turned up since Higbee wrote his article is Johann Daniel Berlin, *Musicaliske Elementer* (Trondheim 1744); see also John Mosand, 'Ein wenig bekanntes Buch über Musik und Instrumentenspiel: Johann Daniel Berlin, Musicaliske Elementer, 1744', *Tibia* 8/1 (1983), pp. 276–9.

46. For discussions of them see Hunt, *The Recorder and its Music*, pp. 72–5; and Vinquist, 'Recorder tutors', *passim.*

47. An extensively revised second edition with the subtitle *Intermediate to Advanced* (Oxford 1986) skilfully incorporates recent developments in the field.

48. Mainz 1962, 2nd edn 1984; English trans. by James C. Haden, *The Recorder Player's Handbook*, London 1974; English trans. of 2nd edn (revised and enlarged) by Richard Deveson, London 1991.

49. The title celebrates the transformation of the recorder into 'a new instrument which combines and mixes the characteristics of the flauto dolce with that of a "flauto acerbo"'.

50. 1987. Available from the Finnish Music Information Center, Runeberginkatu 15 A 1, 00100 Helsinki, Finland.

51. 'Technique contemporaine de la flûte à bec', *Flûte à bec & instruments anciens* 11 (1984), p. 12; 'Souffle', *ibid.*, 13/14 (1984–5), p. 15; 'Flûte à bec contemporaine (suite)', *ibid.* 15 (1985), pp. 6–8; 'Flûte à bec contemporaine: Respiration continue', *ibid.* 16 (1985), p. 2; 'Flûte à bec contemporaine (suite): Whistle tones', *ibid.* 19 (1986), pp. 3–4. The first article promised twenty-four instalments in all.

52. 'Articulation in recorder playing: a phonetic study', *The American Recorder* 24/3 (1983), 99–101.

53. 'Griffkombinationen und Klangfarben auf der Blockflöte', *Tibia* 1/2 (1976), pp. 77–80.

54. Eugene Reichenthal, 'Partial venting', *Recorder & Music* 5/6 (1976), pp. 193–5; Scott Reiss, 'Pitch control: shading and leaking', *The American Recorder* 28/4 (1987), pp. 136–9.

Plate 32 Further evidence of recorder and flute being played together in the 1750s (see pl. 25). During his visit to Rome for study and portrait-painting in 1749–52, it seems that the young Joshua Reynolds was commissioned in 1751 to paint, for their and his own amusement, a series of 'caricatures', rather in the manner of Hogarth, of English and other gentlemen who were visiting Rome as part of their Grand Tour. Several of these pictures – which Sir Joshua later regretted painting! – are now in the National Gallery of Ireland, including the one shown here. This portrays four musically minded characters, an Englishman, Welshman, Scotsman and Irishman, each with his national emblem on his hat. It is the Irishman who plays a beautiful recorder with ivory rings, for the recorder had declined in fashion in England by 1751. The Scotsman, with a blue and white St Andrew's cross perched on his hat, plays a one-keyed flute, the Welshman a cello and the Englishman, whose head-gear sports a red St George's cross, may be singing – or just standing by.

Three of the four figures appear in place of Pythagoras and his students in Reynolds's 1751 *Parody of 'The School of Athens'*, Raphael's fresco in the Vatican. They play the same instruments, but their hats are without emblems. Our painting may be a study for this larger work. The recorder player, James Caulfield, later the first Earl of Charlemont, takes the place of Pythagoras himself, with Sir Thomas Kennedy of Culzean (flute) and Mr Richard Phelps (cello) among his pupils.

Perhaps another Irishman, George Bernard Shaw, wryly recalled these pictures when he became acquainted with the recorder.

8 The recorder revival i: the friendship of Bernard Shaw and Arnold Dolmetsch

JOHN MANSFIELD THOMSON

When Bernard Shaw heard eight visiting wind players from the Brussels Conservatoire at the 1885 International Inventions Exhibition in the Albert Hall, London, he was deeply shocked. The Band of Lansquenets, as they were called (after mercenary military fifers),

had a drum of the sort used by the *virtuosi* that accompany Punch and Judy shows; and the flutes are brown keyless flageolets, not very accurately pierced, and not absolutely identical in pitch. They are of various sizes, the largest resembling a leg of an old-fashioned bed, and the smallest – a most dreadful instrument – a leg of the small stool belonging to the same suite of furniture. They are eight in family, and when they discoursed the March of the Lansquenets ... the effect was voted 'quaint'.

Shaw proceeded to discourse of flutes generally, noting that although these instruments were called '*flauti dolci* or sweet flutes ... the "sweet flute" has an inimitable plaintive silliness that is all its own; but it is not sweet'.[1]

Recorder players can take courage from the thought that perhaps these instruments were indeed flageolets, close relations to the recorder, for Shaw uses both terms even adding 'lansquenet flute' in a subsequent reference, concluding that their most agreeable tones 'may be compared to the cooing of an old and very melancholy piping crow ...'.[2]

Having bought a season ticket on 25 May 1885, Shaw attended the Exhibition frequently, his reviews showing the intense interest of the period in musical instruments of every kind. Hotteterre's flute, oboe and bassoon had been transformed, new inventions such as the saxophone demanded attention, the piano was turning into a steel-sprung fortress, the brass was acquiring a new power. Yet amidst all this flurry a few ardent spirits were moving in the opposite direction and dedicating themselves to the restoration and revival of the sonorities of the past.

The Exhibition took place in the topmost circular area of the Albert

Hall, now used by the promenaders, but then arranged as a suite of drawing rooms, furnished in the fashions of the sixteenth, seventeenth and eighteenth centuries, with the instruments displayed in their appropriate epochs.

Thus the visitor can fancy himself in the very room in which Shakespear read his sonnets to 'the dark lady', and watched her fingers walk with gentle gait over the blessed wood of the virginals, whilst the saucy jacks leapt to kiss the tender inward of her hand. The illusion is greatly strengthened by the band of the Coldstream Guards playing a selection from the *Mikado* outside.[3]

The seeds had already been sown for Shaw's championing of Dolmetsch, which began some six years later. In rereading his writings of this period one is strongly aware of his intense response to the tonal nature and character of instruments, of their pitches and intonation. Again and again we find discussion of the qualities, or lack of them, of a newcomer such as the cornopean (the dreaded cornet), of the effect of the Boehm system on the timbre of the flute, of the way the newcomers and 'improved' versions blended with the voice and other instruments and of their general capacities for further development. Despite this intuitively musical background his motivation has raised doubt in some present-day commentators, such as Richard Taruskin: 'Though a muckraking critic like Shaw might, as we would now say, coopt him as a stick with which to beat the Establishment, the professional musicians of his day by and large wrote Dolmetsch off as a rustic crank'.[4] As the nineteenth century progressed and music became increasingly sentimental and vulgar in texture, harmony and melody, so Shaw's impatience and anger at the misuse of instruments increased:

... Trumpet parts are habitually played upon the cornopean [cornet] (I prefer to give the thing its hideous English name): an instrument that, accompanied by the harp, can, in skilful hands, draw tears from a crowd at the door of a gin-palace by 'The Pilgrim of Love', or 'Then You'll Remember Me', but the substitution of which for the trumpet in the concert room is an imposture and an outrage. ... Herr Julius Kosleck, of Berlin, shewed us on Saturday that the old trumpet parts are as feasible as ever.[5]

Shaw's wide range of feelings for instrumental timbres included a keen response to Berlioz: when he heard the endless Strauss waltzes of the resident Austrian Quadrille Band at the Exhibition he became furious in that the organising commission had not engaged an orchestra of 200 able to play such monumental works as the *Symphonie Funèbre et Triomphale* and the *Te Deum*, both of which had so far defeated ordinary London instrumental forces.

Apart from crack military bands like the Coldstream and Grenadier Guards, the Court Band of the King of Siam did its valiant best. Despite the fact that their scale contained no leading note they still attempted 'God Save the Queen', an act of valour which proved 'rather trying'.[6]

Much worse happened when they announced a composition entitled 'Krob Chakewarn or The Glory of the Universe', but which turned out to be the soldiers' chorus from Gounod's *Faust.*[7]

In the regular series of 'historic concerts' Shaw heard a double quartet of singers called The Round, Catch and Canon Club, and the Bristol Madrigal Society of 120, especially strong in boys' voices, conducted by the well-known musicologist W. S. Rockstro, whose concerts of Old English and Italian Music 'it would not be easy to overpraise'.[8] The singing in the first of three concerts of Dufay, Josquin, Ockeghem and other early Netherlandish masters by eight artists of Daniel de Lange's small A Capella choir from Amsterdam was 'excellent beyond description'.[9] A 'masterly' organist played Sweelinck, 'a musician of remark-

Plate 33 The recorder (?) in the nineteenth century. This picture (detail) is by Carl Spitzweg (1808–85) who painted eccentric small-town characters in the Biedermeier manner. It is called *Flötenkonzert im Waldesinnern* (A flute recital in the middle of the forest). The instrument is probably the Viennese czakan, a small duct flute based on a Hungarian original, but often supplied with keys (see p. 70, note 1 and p. 153), though the position of the fingers makes it look as if this is an eight-holed unkeyed version, rather than the flageolet type, making it very similar to a descant recorder. The picture admirably captures the mood of the salon music written for the czakan – variations on Tyrolean songs and so forth, composed by Krähmer, Heberle and others, and now appearing in LPM Dolce and other editions for recorder. The costumes indicate a scene from about 1835, and the picture, which is now in the Bundespräsidialamt at Bonn, was painted about 1855. At least in Austria and Germany, where recorders continued to be made, our instrument did not quite die out in the nineteenth century. WB 106

able genius, hitherto practically unknown to us'.[10] Shaw repeatedly advocated the adoption of a standard pitch. He seemed to know from inside the intricacies of tuning wind instruments, though he had never been a regular player himself.

If he had a blurred impression of any future potential of the recorder (or flageolet) he was undoubtedly not to blame. The harpsichord demonstration at the Exhibition proved just as misleading: 'All that can now be said for the harpsichord is that it checkmated slovenly and violent playing; that it forced composers to cultivate clearness of construction and intelligent part writing ...'.[11] If it was easy for the musically literate to form an adverse assessment of instruments such as the recorder, the one-keyed flute and the harpsichord, that were soon to be reinstated, how much more so it would have been for the uninitiated. Shaw felt no such antipathy to the viols. It is salutary to recall that in the mid-1960s in London similar doubts were repeatedly expressed about the advisability (and practicality) of reviving baroque wind instruments; those who persevered to the point of being ready to give professional performances were regarded in some ways as martyrs, struggling against unequal odds.

In 1891 Arnold Dolmetsch (1858–1940), a French-born instrument-maker, musician and scholar who had settled in England in 1883, began giving his own 'Historical Concerts'.[12] The paths of these two highly individualistic figures first crossed in 1893, the year in which Shaw had previously heard A. J. Hipkins, another pioneer of the revival, talking on the spinet, harpsichord and clavichord at the Incorporated Society of Musicians Annual Conference in January 1893. Shaw's views of early keyboard instruments were beginning to change. In praising Hipkins's proficiency he wrote: 'For my own part, I hope Mr Hipkins will find many imitators. There is no sort of doubt that the pianoforte must succumb sooner or later to the overwhelming objection that you can hear it next door.'[13]

There followed a lecture on the lute and viols by Arnold Dolmetsch, which yielded Shaw's now memorable lines: 'How much pleasanter it would be to live next door to Mr Arnold Dolmetsch, with his lutes, love viols, and leg viols, than to an ordinary string quartet! But if we went back to the old viols with sympathetic strings and the old harpsichords, I suppose we should have to begin making them again; and I wonder what would be the result of that.'[14] Apart from their historical interest these viol concerts 'were highly enjoyable from the musical point of view, his own playing and that of his daughter (on the viol da gamba) being excellent'. Nevertheless Shaw never shirked advancing what he felt to be deserved criticism, either of Arnold or of members of his family whenever he felt they fell below their own achievable standards. He was devastating, for instance, about Cecile's singing.

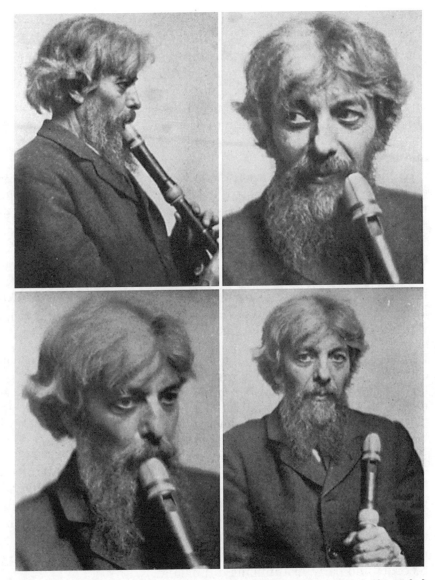

Plate 34 Arnold Dolmetsch with recorder, four portraits (from his wife Mabel Dolmetsch's book *Personal Recollections of Arnold Dolmetsch* (London 1958)). He plays the Bressan recorder shown in Plate 35A, which later cracked at the mouthpiece and was strengthened with a brass banding, a repair that can restore a recorder to its previous playing condition. In making his recorders, Dolmetsch shortened the baroque original so that it played at modern pitch (a′ = 440) rather than the generally lower baroque pitches. He reverted to a flat labium with a large deep windway which required more breath and so made the recorder loud enough to do battle with a modern piano, and he used unequally sized and spaced finger-holes (including double holes for the bottom two fingers) to improve intonation in an equal-tempered system, especially for the treble upper C♯, although this required some other fingering modifications, for example at the B♭s. Further improvements were made by Carl Dolmetsch to increase the recorder's power and versatility. This is today's common modern recorder, seen in action in Plate 28. It is discussed in Chapter 11, p. 178.

At the concert the following month Shaw enjoyed 'the unexpected sensation of having one of my criticisms read aloud to the audience', considering it an excellent precedent that might agreeably enliven the Philharmonic concerts and those of the Bach choir, 'nay, the very Opera itself'.[15] Following pertinent observations on how to enlighten and at the same time instruct an audience Shaw put forward a basic concept of educational technique: 'Mr Dolmetsch's answer to the question "What is a pavan or galliard?" should be to have it played and danced on the spot'.[16]

As the relationship between the two men progressed from admiration and respect to friendship, it may well be wondered what had happened to the recorders. While a student at the Brussels Conservatoire from 1879 to 1883, Dolmetsch heard several concerts using harpsichords, virginals, regal and viol. In her biography of Dolmetsch, Margaret Campbell describes a lecture on early wind instruments by one of the professors at which students demonstrated, each being allotted the instrument which came closest to his or her own speciality. Thus the bassoonist was given the bass recorder, the clarinettist the tenor, the flute and piccolo players the treble and descant.

Derisive laughter greeted every attempt and one student remarked that he could not understand our forebears using such dreadful instruments .... But Dolmetsch was not at all satisfied at this total rejection of the instruments, and thereby in a sense also the music, of a bygone age; he remembered thinking that we do not dismiss the painters and writers of the same period merely because their style is not identical to our own.[17]

Such a disastrous misuse of recorders because of an ignorance of the correct fingering proved to be a major obstacle to their revival. Not until 1905, when he was forty-seven, did Dolmetsch acquire his own instrument when he bought a fine early eighteenth-century boxwood and ivory Bressan treble at Sotheby's (pl. 35A).[18] In the meantime a number of enthusiastic amateurs had been promoting the cause of the recorder and early instruments in England.[19]

In 1898 Christopher Welch (1832–1915), an Oxford MA, musician and bibliophile, delivered a lecture on 'Literature Relating to the Recorder' to the Musical Association. In a section entitled 'Decay and Extinction of the Recorder' Welch commented: 'Just as the harpsichord was giving way to the pianoforte, so the recorder, yielding to the inexorable law of the survival of the fittest, was succumbing to its rival the German flute, the surpassing beauty of its tone failing to ward off its impending fate. The decay of the instrument is to be attributed to the altered state of music.'[20] In 1886 Dr Joseph Cox Bridge, then organist at Chester Cathedral, had discovered what became known as the Chester Recorders, a consort of four notable instruments made by Bressan. As Christopher Welch wrote later in his *Lectures on the Recorder*,

The case which contained them was so worm-eaten when they were discovered, that, with the exception of the green baize lining, it fell to pieces on being handled. There was no record to show how they found their way to the museum, but a very old member of the society had 'some recollection' that the box had been brought there by a Colonel Cholmondley. They were sent for repair to a local music seller, who had a new key made for the alto, and the tube for carrying the wind from the player's mouth to the top of the instrument added to the bass.[21]

Welch refers to this consort in his lecture on 'Hamlet and the Recorder': 'It is needless to say that, in any case, even the discant would be so stout as to make Hamlet pause, unless he were a Milo, before he attempted to snap it like a twig'.[22]

The first demonstration of their qualities had taken place at one of three lecture concerts in 1892 where the performers included two celebrated flute virtuosi, John Finn and John Radcliffe, as well as the Rev. J. L. Bedford, a player of the Welsh pibcorn or pibgorn, an obsolete single hornpipe with mouth horn, and Bridge himself. It was an odd occasion. Without knowledge of the fingering, the players treated the instruments like whistles, covering the thumb-holes with stamp paper – similarly they lacked understanding of their pitch.[23] In 1939 Carl Dolmetsch restored them to playing condition, revoicing them and checking their tuning so they could be played again as a consort. Before this, as Margaret Campbell states, 'One had been mute and the pitches did not agree'.[24]

Welch gave further papers to the Musical Association in the following years which eventually formed his *Six Lectures on the Recorder and Other Flutes in Relation to Literature* published in a handsomely illustrated edition by Oxford University Press in 1911, with the figure from the frontispiece of the section 'Directions for Playing on the Flute' from *The Modern Music Master* (1731) embossed in gold on the front cover (pl. 31).

In June and July 1904, an important Music Loan Exhibition, organised by the Worshipful Company of Musicians, included a highly successful lecture series (although Welch did not take part), subsequently published as *English Music (1604–1904)* (London, 1906). This volume gives an intriguing sidelight on the various strands of what might now be called the 'authentic' approach, though such labels were then undreamed of. The Exhibition contained instruments, scores, portraits, books and other objects all displayed in the magnificent Hall of the Fishmongers, the lectures taking place each afternoon in the handsome courtroom. Speakers included Henry Watson on 'The Early English Viols and their Music', A. H. D. Prendergast on 'Masques and Early Operas' and another collector and enthusiast, the Rev. F. W. Galpin (1858–1945), on 'The Water-Organ of the Ancients and the Organ of Today'.

Galpin had amassed a valuable collection of instruments which he used in the entertainments, fêtes and musical occasions he organised and which in 1916 he subsequently sold to the Boston Museum of Fine Arts, some 500–600 items in all, retaining only a few. Margaret Campbell describes a 'graphic lecture on music common in England during the reign of "Good Queen Bess"', given in 1890 by Mr C. F. Abdy Williams in which Galpin and his wife took part, using instruments from their private collection. The recorder, played by Canon Galpin, made a less than favourable impression and the combined cornett and regal a disastrous one, chiefly, it seems, from a similar lack of knowledge of the correct fingering.[25] In 1910 Galpin's important *Old English Instruments of Music* was published (revised in 1965), and in the year following his death the Galpin Society for the study of instruments commemorated his lifework with an influential annual *Galpin Society Journal*, elegantly designed by Thurston Dart and still flourishing.

John Finn, who had taken part in the unveiling of the Chester recorders, gave a lecture demonstration during the 1904 Exhibition on 'The Recorder, Flute, Fife and Piccolo' which looked at the contemporary scene from the point of view of a performer to whom Boehm's achievements in redesigning wind instruments appeared as the harbinger of the new. Finn played recorder pieces from Humphrey Salter's *Genteel Companion* of 1683, followed by others for the flageolet, double flageolet, one-keyed flute, eight-keyed flute, piccolo, alto flute and cylinder flutes. A pair of the latter dazzled the audience with one of the most florid cadenza-strewn show pieces of the period, an Andante and Rondo, which when played by the virtuosi Doppler brothers used to create a furore because of its effervescent passage-work. Finn further entertained his audience by telling them the story of Wagner's response to hearing the new silver cylinder flutes at Bayreuth as against those traditionally made of wood. When the flautist Rudolph Tillmetz and a colleague made their entries, Wagner, who was conducting, protested: 'They're not flutes', he complained angrily, 'they're cannons'.

No brief for earlier instruments, including the recorder, was put forward, for Finn's views implied that the processes of natural selection had quite justly brought their lives to an end: 'Undoubtedly there was something attractive about the old flutes', he conceded. 'We are still interested in them but they are of the past. The present and future are for us, and the art of today requires the use of musical instruments duly advanced in the stage of perfection as will serve it worthily.'

Finn had played 'Hail to the Myrtill Shades'[26] on the tenor recorder but from those very shadows forces were now gathering to refute not only his own words, but those authorities who held similar views. The eminent scholar and organist Dr Albert Schweitzer's book on Bach[27] also dismissed the recorder: 'The disappearance of the flûte-à-bec is not a very great misfortune ... . The overtones being completely lacking, the timbre was soft but inexpressive. The parts for flûte-à-bec hardly suffer at all from being played on the modern transverse flute ...'.[28] Dolmetsch's name was not mentioned once in the published version of the Music Loan Exhibition lectures – nor did he take part in a single concert. He was ignored by the entire musical establishment.

The following year he bought a Bressan treble recorder at Sotheby's: 'Enfin vers la fin j'ai acheté pour £2 un beau old English recorder 1630 boxwood and ivory. Perfect preservation. Sweet tone ..., Cela me sera très utile'. ('Finally, just before the end, I bought for £2 a beautiful old English recorder 1630. ... It will be very useful to me.'[29]) Dolmetsch took the recorder with him on his trip to America, practising each evening in his cabin after his wife had gone to bed, apparently coming to terms with the appropriate fingering through a copy of *The Compleat Flute-Master or The Whole Art of Playing on ye Rechorder*, published around 1695 by J. Walsh and J. Hare of London, which he had acquired from Mr Taphouse of Oxford.[30] Subsequently the members of the Dolmetsch family learned the recorder and Arnold used it thereafter from time to time in his concerts and demonstrations. Primarily interested in strings and keyboard, he may well have been content to let it play a subsidiary role had not a certain event taken place, well known in the folklore of the recorder world.

On 30 April 1919, while waiting on Waterloo Station with the family for a train back to Haslemere, his seven-year-old son Carl left behind the instrument, a Wildean contretemps, like the hand-bag abandoned at Victoria in *The Importance of Being Earnest*. 'Concert Londres AWG. Grd. Succes – Baba abandonne mon sac à main contenant le recorder et mes outils etc., à Waterloo en face de la Plateforme No 5. Désespoir! Belle Journée', wrote Dolmetsch in his diary that night.[31] This alarming loss precipitated him into fashioning a replacement. (The original recorder subsequently turned up in the window of a pawnshop opposite the station and was bought by an accomplished amateur clarinettist, Mr F. G. Rendall of the British Museum, for five shillings, and returned to the family.) Dolmetsch spent the next year 'experimenting, rejecting model after model because the right intonation constantly eluded him. ... On August Bank Holiday, when he finally solved the problem, he rushed into the kitchen shouting "Eureka! Eureka! I've got it!" and danced round the room repeating his newly-found note like a two-year old with a birthday whistle', writes Margaret Campbell.[32] By 1920 Arnold could offer instruments to friends including Bernard Shaw, Judith Masefield, daughter of the poet, and the cartoonist Edmund X. Kapp.[33] In 1925 at the first Haslemere Festival the treble recorder made its first appearance when Arnold's gifted son Rudolph, with Miles Tomalin, a virtuoso student, played the F major version of

Bach's Brandenburg Concerto No. 4, for harpsichord, two recorders and strings.[34] 'Innumerable people were thumping pianos throughout the length of Britain', wrote Miles Tomalin, 'but here was an instrument which perhaps a score of people in the world were playing, and the Dolmetsch family accounted for half a dozen of those. ... Although I was learning other instruments I loved the recorder best.'[35] The following year the first recorder consort of soprano, two altos, tenor and bass appeared in a Purcell Chaconne in three parts from *Dioclesian* and Couperin's *Les Fauvettes Plaintives*, in three parts. Five-part consorts for descant, two trebles, tenor and bass were performed on 30 August.[36] But the opening night of the Festival proved most notable with the Brandenburg Concerto No. 4 in G major, Dolmetsch on solo violin, his son Rudolph and Miles Tomalin playing the two recorders in G.

The subsequent history of the recorder has been charted by various writers, including Margaret Campbell, Edgar Hunt and Eve O'Kelly, who have described the way in which it was taken up in Germany, spread throughout Europe and the rest of the world, how the first plastic recorders came to be made and how the instrument acquired an almost unassailable position in music education and in the manifold activities of amateurs.

Arnold Dolmetsch's friendship with Bernard Shaw continued, although by 1895 Shaw had stopped writing about music and turned to drama: 'Now that I have taken to dramatic criticism I find that the theatre keeps me away from concerts almost as completely as the concerts used to keep me away from the theatre. I was quite unable to get to the Salle Erard on either of your evenings', he wrote apologetically on 31 January 1895.[37] On 19 July 1898 he offered Dolmetsch a loan of £50 having heard he was 'going into the hands of the surgeons'. And on 25 September 1899 he told Dolmetsch of the travails of hearing a cornet in the ship's band of the *Lusitania* while on a six-week Mediterranean cruise:

One of the attractions of this ship is a first-class band. One double bass, two violins, a piano (ad lib), and a cornet. The cornet is the star: he plays The Lost Chord on Sundays. Nothing more horrible can be imagined. ... They are playing a skirt dance (pizzicato) in my ear just now – I can no more. We return to London (if I am not hanged for murdering the band first) on the 31 October.[38]

On 26 January 1906 he asked Dolmetsch if he ever studied the pianola. 'A pianola that will play the clavichord is indispensable if the clavichord is to be a success.'[39] On 5 March 1918, he regretfully had to decline a request for a loan of £50 from Dolmetsch, at the same time chastising him for charging such low prices for his instruments. 'I have no patience with you as to the virginals', he writes. 'If you had a

factory with steam sawmills and a thousand men turning out fifty
instruments a week, or a Ford factory turning out complete harpsichords in three minutes you could no doubt afford to sell them for £25
apiece, or even 25 shillings; but such prices under existing circumstances are simply pawning your future for the sake of a few guineas in
hand. ... You can't get a really good Wheatstone concertina for less
than double or treble your £25.'[40]

In the garden of Shaw's house at the village of Ayot St Lawrence,
north of London, where he lived, there stands a hut connected to the
house by phone, where he used to work in solitude. In the mid-1960s,
amongst the books and papers, visitors who peered through the
window could see a wooden tenor recorder that appeared to be of
twentieth-century origin, without a visible number. In 1965 Carl
Dolmetsch, Arnold's son, ventured the opinion that this was one of his
father's instruments: 'He built Shaw a clavichord in the early 1920s
and it's very likely he also made him a tenor recorder', he said. 'It's
almost certainly based on a recorder, probably a Stanesby, belonging to
Sir Francis Darwin, the son of Charles.' The custodian of the house at
the time felt sure that Shaw would have used the instrument; she gave
a vigorous demonstration of the way he pedalled the exercise bicycle
inside the front door to impress on visitors that nothing was for show.
'He sang and played the clavichord right to the very end, so why not
the recorder?'

'It should be made a felony to play a musical instrument in any
other than a completely soundproof room', wrote Shaw in the 1935
Preface to the reprint of his *Corno di Bassetto* criticism, perhaps
recalling his response to the Dolmetsch clavichord. Obedient to his
own precepts, it is perfectly in character for him to have kept this
instrument where it could be a solace in times of need and no
imposition on his neighbours.[41] Arnold Dolmetsch and Bernard Shaw
recognised and respected each other as equals, albeit in different
fields. Their friendship proved crucial in the re-establishment of the
recorder and just as forcefully in their joint recognition of the glories
of those earlier periods of English musical history then buried, and
which Dolmetsch, with Shaw's help, was enthusiastically uncovering.

Notes

1. Bernard Shaw, *Shaw's Music, The Complete Musical Criticism in Three Volumes*,
   ed. Dan H. Lawrence, vol. I, 1876–1890 (London 1981), pp. 301–2. First published
   in *The Dramatic Review*, 4 July 1885. Shaw's description continues: 'The incessant
   beating of the loosely stretched drumhead; the weak whistling of the soprano
   flutes; and the mournful woodiness of the tenors and basses, moving in thirds,
   sixths, and fifths, with them all being more or less out of tune from defects of
   construction that no skill on the part of the players could neutralize made a whole

which was certainly quaint enough: almost as quaint as the waits at Christmastide. But a little of it was calculated to go a long way.' Enquiries made in Brussels as to the instruments used by the Band of Lansquenets have so far (1994) yielded no results.

2. *Ibid.*, p. 322. First published in *The Magazine of Music* (August 1885).
3. *Ibid.*, p. 358. First published in *The Dramatic Review* (19 September 1885).
4. Richard Taruskin, 'The pastness of the present', *Authenticity and Early Music, A Symposium*, ed. Nicholas Kenyon (Oxford 1988), p. 198.
5. *Shaw's Music*, p. 222. First published in *The Dramatic Review* (28 March 1885).
6. *Ibid.*, p. 293.
7. *Ibid.*, pp. 334–5.
8. *Ibid.*, p. 292.
9. *Ibid.*
10. *Ibid.*, p. 293.
11. *Ibid.*, p. 322.
12. See Margaret Campbell, *Dolmetsch, the Man and his Work* (London 1975).
13. *Shaw's Music*, vol. II, p. 781.
14. *Ibid.*, p. 782.
15. *Ibid.*, pp. 815–16.
16. *Ibid.*, p. 817.
17. Margaret Campbell, *Dolmetsch*, p. 12.
18. *Ibid.*, pp. 164–5.
19. Mention should also be made of other lecturers such as C. K. Salaman on the history of the pianoforte, which included illustrations on a Kirkman harpsichord. See Percy Scholes, *The Mirror of Music II* (London 1947), pp. 775ff; Ernst Pauer (1826–1905) and J. H. Bonawitz (1839–1917) likewise. Carl Engel (1818–82) is amongst the most celebrated of these early performer–lecturers, being connected with what became the Victoria and Albert Museum and its collection, compiling several of their catalogues. A. J. Hipkins (1826–1903) has a special importance having been in charge of the musical arrangements at the 1885 Inventions Exhibition. Principally a piano recitalist and important writer on instruments, he also assembled an outstanding collection, now the nucleus of that of the Royal College of Music. His *Musical Instruments, Historic, Rare and Unique* (Edinburgh 1888, 3rd edn 1945) is sumptuously illustrated and ranges as far as India, China, Japan and South Africa.
20. Christopher Welch, *Six Lectures on the Recorder and Other Flutes in Relation to Literature* (Oxford 1911; rpt of Lectures I–III with Introduction by Edgar Hunt, Oxford 1961), pp. 85ff.
21. *Ibid.*, p. 163.
22. *Ibid.*, p. 165.
23. Described by Edgar Hunt, as from Dr Bridge himself, in *The Recorder and its Music*, rev. edn (London 1977), pp. 128–9.
24. Campbell, *Dolmetsch*, p. 55.
25. *Ibid.*, pp. 24–5.
26. This tune is from Henry Purcell's theatre music for Nathaniel Lee's *Theodosius or the Force of Love*, his first venture into the genre, performed in autumn 1680. It quickly appeared in the 1680 edition of Greeting's *Pleasant Companion* for the flageolet. 'Hail to the Myrtill Shades' from Greeting was illustrated and transcribed from tablature on p. 86 of Sir Frederick Bridge's *Samuel Pepys, Lover of Music* (London 1903). Finn may have used Bridge's transcription. (Information from Anthony Rowland-Jones.)
27. Albert Schweitzer, *J. S. Bach* (Leipzig 1905; London 1911) pp. 432–3.
28. See *English Music (1604 to 1904)* (London 1906).
29. Campbell, *Dolmetsch*, pp. 164–5. The Sotheby catalogue lists the recorder as being 'about 1730'. Dolmetsch (or his 'agent'), actually paid £5.2s.6d.
30. Campbell, *Dolmetsch*, p. 166. She mentions that a copy of this book is held in the Dolmetsch Library at Jesses, Haslemere.
31. 'Concert at AWG (Artworkers' Guild Hall), London – great success. "Baba" [Carl

Dolmetsch] left my bag with the recorder and my tools etc. in it on Waterloo Station in front of platform No 5. Despair! Beautiful day!', Campbell, *Dolmetsch*, pp. 208, 212.

32. *Ibid.*, p. 209.
33. See Eve O'Kelly, *The Recorder Today* (Cambridge 1990), p. 6. Edmund Kapp (1890–1978), a notable cartoonist, had a particular sympathy for musical occasions and musicians, his drawings of Delius, Schoenberg and Vaughan Williams, for instance, have now acquired the status of icons.
34. Miles Tomalin, with Rudolph Dolmetsch, was the first English recorder virtuoso. See his 'Early days', *Recorder & Music* 4/8 (Dec. 1973), pp. 271–4 and also editorial mention p. 270. The author met Miles Tomalin through his son Nicholas, a distinguished London journalist, at a party. 'When he asked me what I did I told him I edited the *Recorder Magazine*. "You must meet my father", he replied, "he used to play the recorder at Haslemere". I had no idea then of the crucial role of Miles in the recorder revival'. Nicholas was tragically killed on the Syrian front of Israel in the last days of the first Arab–Israel war. He was described in *The Times* as 'one of the finest reporters of his generation'.
   Rudolf Dolmetsch, Arnold's brilliant eldest son, also excelled as a composer and conductor. He was lost at sea during World War II on 6 or 7 December 1942.
35. Quoted in the editorial of the special recorder issue of *Early Music*, 10/1 (Jan. 1982), p. 2.
36. Campbell, *Dolmetsch*, pp. 219–20.
37. Bernard Shaw, *Collected Letters 1874–1897*, ed. Dan H. Lawrence (London 1965), p. 481.
38. *Ibid.*, *1898–1910* (London 1972), pp. 55, 104.
39. *Ibid.*, p. 602.
40. *Ibid.*, *1911–1925* (London 1985), p. 533.
41. Edward Goetz [J. M. Thomson], 'Did Shaw play the recorder?' *Recorder and Music Magazine* 1/11 (Nov. 1965), pp. 326–7. The most distracting aspects of living next to Shaw at Ayot St Lawrence were apparently the crises caused when he had mislaid or lost a paper and strode through his garden cutting off the tops of the tallest flowers in a frenzy of exasperation.

150

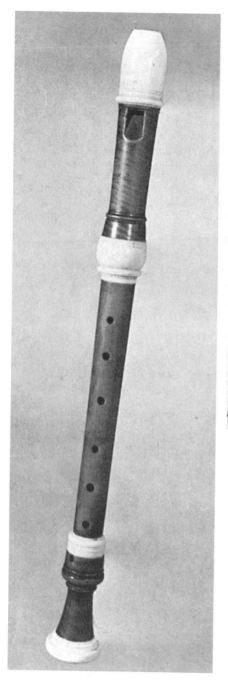

Plates 35A and 35B   The Bressan recorder

Plate 35A (Opposite left)   The lost Bressan, made in London about 1700, that started it all! (see pp. 145 and 153). Photograph by Colin G. Futcher. Compare this instrument with the one in Plate 32 and with the well-known picture of a recorder player by János Kupezky in Budapest (see cover of *The Recorder Magazine* 12/2 (June 1992)), a self-portrait from 1778. There are some beautiful still-life depictions of baroque recorders, with delicious fruit and other food (even turnips!), by Cristoforo (or '— fano') Munari (1667–1720) in the Pitti and Uffizi galleries in Florence.

It will be seen that, with baroque elegance and symmetry, the holes of the Bressan are equally sized and spaced, fine tuning being achieved by undercutting, expanding the hole inwards to the bore. Double holes for the bottom two fingers are rare in surviving baroque recorders, although they are referred to by Hotteterre in his 1707 tutor. The bore of the instrument is mainly cylindrical at the head-joint, then becomes mainly conical (tapering) though this is slight and varies in different parts of the bore giving a complex bore profile. To facilitate the difficult task of reaming and under-cutting, the instrument is in three sections with waxed thread joints, and this also eliminates the need for left and right alternative little-finger holes. The windway of a baroque recorder is broad and shallow, curved to fit the exterior contour of the mouth-piece; and the labium is consequently also arc-shaped. This voicing gives greater resistance to the player's breath-pressure, providing more dynamic flexibility within negligible intonational fluctuations. The tone, with a smaller amount of breath input than a renaissance or modern recorder, is less loud and open, but compensates through its limpid, reedy and penetrating quality, so that a focused (rather than disseminated) sound can be projected out to an audience. It is by no means less powerful than a baroque flute, and is capable of discourse with a baroque oboe or violin played sensitively. Boxwood was the baroque makers' favourite material for wind instruments. There was no one standard baroque 'low pitch' but modern copies are usually constructed at a'=415, a convenient semitone below modern pitch.

Plate 35B (Opposite right)   Dolmetsch judged well in using a fine Bressan instrument as the model for his first recorders. The dominance of this design in England is apparent from the two trophies carved on the front of the organ case at Christ's College, Cambridge. It is ideal for Handel's sonatas as the lower notes are stronger than they are in German baroque instruments with a narrower bore which favours the higher tessitura of Bach and Telemann's recorder music. The woodwork in the chapel is by John Austin, completed in 1703 except for the organ which was opened with a concert, presumably including recorders (and this music?), in the spring of 1705. The upper illustration opposite, also reproduced in colour on the front of this book, shows the left-hand carving. The trophy on the right of the console (lower illustration) is almost identical except that the open book is headed 'Sinphony Flauto Secundo'. The music has not yet been identified. One possibility is that it is by Lord William Biron, an ancestor of the poet, who received an LL.D. at Cambridge in 1705, and who composed some not dissimilar (brief and equally uninspired) *Symphonys for 2 Flutes*, a copy of which is in the Rowe Library at King's College. Another is that it was composed by Charles Quarles, Organist of Trinity College, and of Christ's College, who was responsible for the installation of the new organ. The recorders look so real that they could almost be taken down and played. Photographs by Anthony Rowland-Jones with kind permission of the Master and Fellows of Christ's College.

9 The recorder revival ii: the twentieth century and its repertoire

EVE O'KELLY

When surveying the revival and development of the recorder in the twentieth century, one of the most striking features is the existence of a large and innovatory contemporary repertoire. Other early instruments have had modern works written for them, of course, but in no other case has this repertoire come to be such a highly significant extension of the historically defined boundaries of the instrument. These new pieces, and in particular those composed in the last thirty years, have brought forth a whole new set of playing techniques, taking the possibilities of the instrument far beyond the accepted norms of its heyday in the seventeenth and eighteenth centuries. Again, there is no real parallel. Extended techniques[1] have been developed for other early instruments, but for the recorder it seems fair to say that mastery of them is now central to every serious player's apprenticeship.

There are several interrelated reasons for this development, which will become clear as we survey the progress of the revival. The difference between 'conventional' recorder music – a term adopted in default of a better one to describe those works that are completely traditional in their approach – and the modern, innovatory pieces referred to above, is great.

The recorder revival

The progress of the recorder revival during the first half of the twentieth century has been described and discussed in several publications,[2] and it is not the intention of the present writer to go over this ground again here. Suffice it to say that evidence suggests that when interest in the recorder first began to develop, it was as part of a wider interest – one might even say a fashion – for early music and instruments in general which arose independently in England, Germany and other countries in the late nineteenth century. The recorder had fallen into decline towards the end of the eighteenth century, although it has been suggested that the essential techniques of making and playing recorders survived in the traditions of the French and English flageolets and the czakan, which were widely played throughout the nineteenth century.

Be that as it may, if a tradition survived it was not an overt one, to judge by the difficulties encountered when the first recorder players of modern times tried to come to grips with the instrument. There are several accounts of the work of notable figures such as Canon Francis Galpin, Dr Joseph Cox Bridge and Christopher Welch in England, and Willibald Gurlitt and Werner Danckerts in Germany, whose research first advanced knowledge of the instrument in the late nineteenth and the early twentieth centuries.[3]

The single most important pioneering force, however, was Arnold Dolmetsch (1858–1940). Again, the life of this extraordinary man has been very well documented elsewhere.[4] His researches in libraries and auction rooms made use of his twin skills as a trained musician and instrument-builder. He unearthed old scores and was able to repair and reconstruct the instruments on which to perform them. In 1891, with members of his family, he embarked on a series of 'Historical Concerts' which brought early music before the fashionable London public.[5]

Because he is so much associated with the revival, it is easy to forget – or fail to realise – that for many years the recorder occupied a peripheral role in Dolmetsch's music-making. His first recorder was acquired at an auction in 1905 and, although he later began to use it in nearly every concert, his programmes were usually dominated by instruments of the bowed- and plucked-string families. It is interesting to speculate, indeed, whether Arnold Dolmetsch would ever have had the motivation to make a recorder at all had it not been for the irritating circumstance of the loss of his own Bressan alto fourteen years after he bought it.[6] He was sixty-two when, after some unsuccessful experiments, his first recorder was made in 1920 as a replacement. By this time his reputation was long established as a maker of viols, harpsichords, lutes and other early instruments.

Recorder-making

Arnold Dolmetsch's work undoubtedly created the climate in which a revived recorder could flourish, but it was the missionary efforts of others which really re-established it. Initial experiments had been carried out by musicologists in somewhat rarefied circumstances. The recorders that Arnold Dolmetsch began to make and sell in the 1920s and 30s were individually handmade and therefore were not cheap. They were certainly beyond the means of most ordinary players, and the Dolmetsch workshop at that time did not have any interest in entering the mass market. A popularising force was needed if recorder playing was ever to spread beyond the province of specialists.

As well as the growth of interest in early music, impetus was also provided by the development of a number of similar socio-cultural movements, all dedicated to restoring values of simplicity and innocence in an increasingly mechanised age (Youth and Hausmusik in Germany, Arts and Crafts in England and, to a certain extent, the parallel development of bamboo pipes in England and France). All of these found in the recorder a practical and attractive means of making music, particularly suitable for children and adult amateurs. The unsophisticated sound of the instrument, the naive nature of much of the musical material that was adapted for it, and the simplicity of playing it, appealed greatly. The onset of World War II further encouraged the development of recorder playing, because it was one of the few practical musical outlets in difficult times.

The demand thus created encouraged several firms to go into mass-production of low-priced recorders. In Germany Peter Harlan (1898–1966) played an important role in ensuring a supply of instruments for the German recorder movement. Edgar Hunt recalls examining recorders by Harlan, Herwig, Merzdorf, Moeck and Bärenreiter in the trade exhibition at the Kasseler Musiktage in 1934[7] and this indicates a high level of production in Germany at a time when the only other recorders being made were the handmade 'professional' Dolmetsch instruments. Hunt arranged to import Herwig recorders to England but, having investigated the German fingering then being used, specified that they must be made with baroque, or English, fingering.[8] In this way, modestly priced instruments became readily available in England to all who cared to play them.

Repertoire

The modern repertoire for the recorder is now, at the end of the twentieth century, large, diverse and challenging. It is not possible to survey it in depth in this chapter and so the works mentioned are those that the present writer considers to have been in some way influential or innovative. Many excellent compositions are omitted for reasons of space, and not all of those discussed will meet with universal approval.

The growth of recorder playing in the 1930s, 40s and even into the 50s remained firmly rooted in early music, so it was natural that what was available at this time consisted mainly of rediscovered seventeenth- and eighteenth-century pieces, together with many arrangements of folk material. The few new works that were written fell largely into the category of 'Spielmusik', that is, music intended for the education and enjoyment of amateurs, but without any serious compositional pretensions. A number of significant works may be noted from this period, however.

One of the earliest known twentieth-century pieces is a suite for three recorders entitled *Fantasy, Air and Jigg*, a light-hearted piece written by Arnold Dolmetsch in 1928 for the family to play. When he heard it many years later, Dolmetsch did not recognise it as his own. Another very early work, but one that has kept its place in the repertoire, is Paul Hindemith's *Trio* from the Plöner Musiktag (1932). Hindemith was himself a recorder player and had a great interest in early music, which he made a point of introducing in his composition classes. He gave the first performance of the *Trio* himself with two friends at a music workshop in the German town of Plön.

Also noteworthy are a group of sonatas for alto recorder and piano commissioned by Manuel Jacob, a student of Edgar Hunt, in the late 1930s. Among these were the *Sonatina* (1940) by Lennox Berkeley (1903–89), an excellent piece but more suited to the transverse flute than to the recorder; the *Partita* (1938) by Franz Reizenstein (1911–68), again a good work but one which seems to need the more forceful sound of the clarinet; and the *Sonatina* (1939) by Walter Leigh (1905–42). The latter comes closest to success in bringing out the best in the instrument, perhaps because Leigh played the recorder himself. Interestingly, the *Suite* for recorder by Alan Rawsthorne, which was one of these commissions but was subsequently withdrawn by the composer, has recently come to light.[9] It also seems more than a coincidence that Leigh, Reizenstein and several other composers who wrote for recorder, such as Arnold Cooke, Hans Ulrich Staeps, Harald Genzmer, Hans Poser and Stanley Bate, had studied with Hindemith.

The 1950s

By the mid- to late 1950s, playing standards had risen considerably and knowledge of the instrument had moved on a great deal. A second generation of recorder players had come on the scene and were keen to stretch their abilities by mastering new music. In Germany, for instance, the students of Gustav Scheck and Willibald Gurlitt, two of the very early pioneers of the recorder, included Ferdinand Conrad, Linde Höffer-von Winterfeld, Hildemarie Peter, Hans-Conrad Fehr and Hans-Martin Linde, all to become influential as players, teachers and, in Linde's case, as a composer. In England, Edgar Hunt, Walter Bergmann, Carl Dolmetsch and Freda Dinn were active in promoting the recorder. Hunt's influence, through his work with the publishers Schott and his teaching at Trinity College of Music, London, has been enormous, while Dolmetsch's annual Wigmore Hall concerts, commenced in 1939, have included a newly commissioned British work each year ever since. Composers who have written for Carl Dolmetsch include Arnold Cooke, Cyril Scott, Alun Hoddinott, Colin Hand,

Edmund Rubbra, Gordon Jacob, Robert Simpson, Alan Ridout, William Mathias, Nicholas Maw and Michael Berkeley.

Other compositions that stand out from the 1950s and early 60s are Henk Badings's *Sonata* (1957) for alto recorder and harpsichord, and Arnold Cooke's *Concerto* (1957) for alto recorder and string orchestra. Benjamin Britten's *Alpine Suite* and *Scherzo* for recorder consorts from 1955 were unfortunately followed by nothing more substantial for the instrument; Michael Tippett wrote *Four Inventions* for two recorders in 1954; and there are attractive pieces by Herbert Murrill and Francis Baines. All of these works are traditional in their approach, though they are by no means easy to perform. The recorder is treated largely as a sort of younger sister of the flute, and there are sometimes problems of range and balance arising because the individual qualities of the instrument were not always fully understood. Nevertheless, they have their place in the repertoire and composers such as Hans Ulrich Staeps, Arnold Cooke and Edmund Rubbra, who have written recorder music consistently throughout the 1950s, 60s and 70s, have had a lasting influence.

The 1960s and after

By the 1960s the recorder was firmly established and it was at this point that the traditional view of it as a simple melody instrument, incapable of any great depth of expression, began to be reconsidered and ultimately strongly challenged. It was by then taught in many schools and the amateur movement had grown greatly in strength. Recorders even began to appear in 'beat' and pop groups. The Falling Leaves, Manfred Mann and the Rolling Stones all used it in their backing groups,[10] to the disapproval of some high-minded aficionados. As perceptions began to change so the recorder's potential for development became apparent. This was a big step forward and, happening as it did during a period of intense change and ferment in society in general, it is not surprising that it produced many of the most innovative works in the entire repertoire.

The first breakthrough came with the realisation that there is more than one possible fingering for any given note on the recorder and, further, that it can play more than one note at a time.[11] Like any instrument, the fingering system developed for the recorder through custom and usage is simply that which has been found to be most effective. There are literally thousands of other possible combinations of closed and open holes (known as 'non-standard fingerings'), each producing a note and many several notes at once. This realisation opened up new possibilities in terms of tone-quality, intonation, dynamics and range. The next step, inevitably, was to explore what else the recorder could do, and experiments with different forms of articulation, vibrato and various special effects followed. These in turn required new methods of notation, which proliferated in the music of the 1960s as composers devised their own solutions to notational problems, often without any reference to previous conventions.

It is important to realise that this development was not exclusive to the recorder; many other instruments were undergoing a similar reappraisal at much the same time. Bruno Bartolozzi's book, *New Sounds for Woodwind*,[12] is generally agreed to have been particularly influential in opening up new possibilities for extended techniques on wind instruments. The detailed studies of, for example, flute, clarinet, trombone and double bass which followed in later years have raised the level of technical expertise required out of all recognition. In the case of the recorder, development of extended techniques came about not so much as a conscious investigation but as a gradual cross-fertilisation and drawing-together of new ideas.

The avant-garde

The term 'avant-garde' has been widely applied to any recorder music using extended techniques and unconventional notation. More properly, however, it should be used only to refer to the innovatory works of the 1960s and early 70s. Some of the first and most important of these were written for Frans Brüggen (*b*.1934) and Michael Vetter (*b*.1943), two of the leading players at the time. Both performers were interested in contemporary music and wanted to extend their own repertoire beyond the somewhat restricted possibilities of renaissance and baroque music. Brüggen in particular, the most influential player of the twentieth century, felt that a concert career could not be sustained with the historical repertoire alone. Consequently, he began to commission new works which made no concessions to the supposed limitations of the recorder. Over the years an enormous number of new pieces have resulted from Brüggen's influence, either directly as commissions or indirectly as a result of the inspiration of his playing.

Among the first of these was *Muziek* (1961) for alto recorder solo by the Dutch composer Rob du Bois (*b*.1934). It takes a note-row and transforms it in various ways, using note-sequences that hitherto were regarded as unplayable, extremes of range, rapid alternations of awkward fingerings in complex rhythms, big dynamic changes. Flutter-tonguing, glissando and finger vibrato are also employed. Technically, it requires a skill far above that called for in earlier works. At roughly the same time, the German composer Jürg Baur (*b*.1918) wrote *Mutazioni* (1962) for Michael Vetter. Also for solo recorder, *Mutazioni* was Baur's second piece and it uses multiphonics and other special effects within an overall open form which also contains improvisatory passages. This was the kind of music which was being written for mainstream instruments by composers like Stockhausen, Nono and Berio, but nothing like it had yet been written for recorder: the effect was far-reaching. Vetter's attitude, in particular, was highly original from the beginning, and he may be credited, in conjunction with Baur, with the early development of non-standard fingerings.

A work that has held its place and even grown in stature since it was written is *Sweet* (1964) by the leading Dutch composer Louis Andriessen (*b*.1939). Composed for Brüggen, this piece is now in every performer's repertoire and learning it has come to be regarded as a sort of rite of passage for aspiring students. *Sweet* was deliberately designed to be 'unplayable', and the title mocks the traditional image of the baroque suite and the supposedly 'sweet' sounds of the recorder. As the work develops, using highly complex, rapid chromatic writing, the performer reaches a frenzied climax which is interrupted, in a sort of black-out, by an outside sound-source of some kind, leaving the player unable to continue. This 'interruption' can take many different forms – auditory, visual, electronic, theatrical – and when it subsides, the player continues, subdued, to the end of the piece.

Perhaps the most well-known and still the most frequently performed of all contemporary works is *Gesti* (1966) for alto recorder solo by Luciano Berio (*b*.1925), written for Brüggen: 'I tried to celebrate a divorce between your fingers and your mouth...'.[13] In other words, the piece separates the functions of breathing, tonguing and fingering which the player has spent so many years learning to coordinate and, having explored the sound possibilities thus revealed, reunites them only at the end of the work. The notation is largely graphic and is very individual and precise. Berio's series of *Sequenzas* for solo instruments, each written with a particular performer in mind, is well known; *Gesti* may be said to belong in spirit to this group.

The 1970s

By the end of the 1960s recorder performers were far more theatrical, outgoing musicians, with greatly improved technical skills. The novelty of extended recorder techniques had worn off as far as they were concerned, although audiences, still unprepared for the sounds they heard, found them difficult to understand. The greater leeway allowed – indeed, encouraged – in improvisatory scores, had motivated players to involve their own personality to a far greater extent in the overall effect of the piece. Inevitably, this also began to feed back into their performance of the historical repertoire.

A major area of influence has been the music written by Japanese composers. There seems to be a particular understanding of the recorder in these works, probably because the Japanese shakuhachi has much in common with the recorder. *Fragmente* (1968) for solo tenor recorder by the Japanese composer Makoto Shinohara (*b.*1931) – again written for Brüggen – was the first avant-garde work of note for the tenor, and provides perhaps the best synthesis of extended techniques within the overall construction of a single piece. The 'fragments' of the title are fourteen short musical units which the performer may put together in any order, subject to certain conditions. Each uses a different technique, thus giving a palette of very varied sounds, some of them noisy and highly aggressive. The use of the tenor – or voice flute in D which many players nowadays prefer – also gives a full and substantial timbre.

A composition now central to the repertoire is *Black Intention* (1975) by Maki Ishii (*b.*1936), an extraordinary theatre piece in which one soloist plays successively two soprano recorders together, tenor recorder, Japanese tam-tam or gong, and also uses his or her voice. It is a dramatic and musical *tour de force*, strongly influenced by Japanese traditional music and very difficult to perform successfully. Ryohei Hirose's *Meditation* (1975) for alto recorder solo is another very important work, as is the same composer's *Lamentation* for recorder quartet, from the same year.

Other influences

Hans-Martin Linde (*b.*1930), the German player, composer and teacher, has been on the faculty of the Schola Cantorum of Basel, Switzerland, since 1957 and has made an important contribution to the growth of modern recorder music. One of the seminal avant-garde works – frequently used as a first introduction to extended techniques for young players – is *Music for a Bird*, written in 1968. This short, relatively simple piece is, as its name suggests, an evocation of birdsong. It connects, therefore, with the historical association between the recorder and birds, but here its seven short movements use glissandi, trills, tremolos, multiphonics and vocal effects to reinterpret this connection in the light of the twentieth century. Linde has written many other works for solo and consort, among them *Amarilli mia bella* (1971), inspired by the music of the seventeenth-century carillon and recorder player, Jacob van Eyck. One of his most recent pieces is *Browning, Fantasia on 'The Leaves be Green'* (1988), a reworking of the famous William Byrd fantasia.

Gerhard Braun (*b.*1932), one of the chief exponents of modern techniques, has led the German contemporary recorder movement for many years as player, teacher, composer, writer and editor. His works are difficult to play and, in most cases, allow a great deal of autonomy in interpretation. He has devised several quite unusual techniques of his own for which the recorder is dismantled, and pitched and unpitched sounds are produced in several unorthodox ways. These are best shown in works such as *Monologe I* (1968–70) where the composer's designation 'for one recorder player' has a significance of its own. Other notable works are *Nachtstücke* (1972) for recorder player and pianist, and *Schattenbilder* (1980) for solo recorder. His more recent compositions, such as the *Five Meditations for Tenor Recorder* published in 1992, are more restrained in their use of new techniques.

Modern techniques

At this point it may be useful to take a closer look at extended techniques for recorder. The first attempt to codify these was made by Michael Vetter. His book, *Il Flauto Dolce ed Acerbo*,[14] appeared only two years after Bartolozzi's *New Sounds for Woodwind* and several years before similar treatises on other instruments. This presented the results of Vetter's investigations into non-standard fingerings. In 1967 he had written:

The recorder has at its disposal hand positions which far exceed the number of 1000, an average of up to eight or ten possibilities of overblowing and underblowing, and finally a mechanism of sound-production which can be enriched in many different ways, and spontaneously, as can no other, to give a corresponding increase in possible sounds.[15]

Vetter's interest in extended techniques derived from his studies of improvised music and from his performances of works by Stockhausen and Sylvano Bussotti. Later, he was greatly influenced by Japanese traditional music, in particular that of the shakuhachi and the Noh flute and this, together with a very charismatic stage presence, served to open up another area for the recorder, that of music theatre. Vetter's own compositions are complicated improvisatory works involving electronics and graphic notation, with a strong theatrical dimension.

Non-standard fingerings produce a huge range of single and multiple sounds with many variations in timbre and intonation. Martine Kientzy, who researched multiphonics in the early 1980s, wrote in *Les Sons multiples aux flutes à bec*[16] that the publication presented 'a selection of only 1191 fingerings from the 2170 classified during preliminary research work'. Hermann Rechberger's manual, *Die Block-flöte in der zeitgenössischen Musik*,[17] is even more extensive, and gives tables of non-standard fingerings for harmonics, multiphonics, micro-tones, dynamic variations and so on.

To discuss modern techniques or the notation of them in detail is beyond the scope of this book[18] but it may be useful to give some general information on the subject. As has been mentioned above, there is no question of extended techniques having been developed in any deliberate, coherent way. Rather, they have cropped up as new

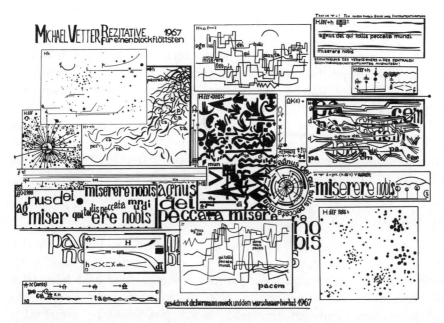

An example of graphic notation: Michael Vetter, *Rezitative* (actual size 54 × 38 cm)

ideas suggested by composers or players and, having been introduced in a new piece, have been accepted, modified or rejected.

For those who are unfamiliar with them, extended techniques are most readily understood by reference to the area of conventional usage to which they relate. All, one might say, are a distortion of the 'normal' playing technique. Thus a simple classification would divide them into four groups as follows: (1) *Non-standard fingerings*, i.e. any sound created by finger combinations outside the accepted pattern; (2) *Articulation*, i.e. any tonguing method, including flutter-tonguing (a rapid oscillation of the tongue, as in rolling an 'r'), that creates an unusual attack on the note; (3) *Vibrato*, i.e. any one of several methods of adding vibrato to the note, ranging from an exaggeration of normal diaphragm vibrato, to that created by the throat, tongue, finger, hand or even knee; (4) *Special effects*, i.e. sound or noise created on, with or by the whole or the dismantled parts of the instrument, by the mouth (other than by normal blowing), by the hands (as in percussive finger noises, etc.), or by more conventional effects such as glissandi.

All of the above may be performed in combination with one another, and to different degrees of loudness, softness, aggression or sweetness, subject only to the technical facility of the player. Here, a good musician will make something extraordinary out of his or her playing, where a good technician will merely impress with the strangeness of the sounds.

Initially, the use of extended techniques was somewhat haphazard, but during the 1970s, as the novelty wore off, they were able to be used with more discrimination and therefore to greater effect. In the 1980s this trend continued and, together with a marked movement in music in general away from the sensational and back to a strong sense of melody and line, their use has now decreased. This does not mean that avant-garde techniques have been rejected, but rather that they have been thoroughly assimilated. They have permanently broadened the horizons of the recorder player. Technique has had to develop to cope with these demands, and this in turn has raised playing standards in general, also to the benefit of the historical repertoire.

Electro-acoustic music

The recorder first ventured into the area of electro-acoustics in the 1960s and most of the experiments of this period are associated with Michael Vetter. Amplification via normal microphones and later tiny contact microphones attached to the instrument produced some interesting effects. The development of synthesisers has opened up many possibilities in recent years, perhaps the most significant being the work of the Netherlands-based American player and teacher, Michael Barker. He has adapted the square contrabass recorder made by Herbert Paetzold and, by connecting the keys to sophisticated synthesisers, can make an enormous range of extraordinary sounds on his Interactive MIDI Performance System, or 'midified blockflute', as he calls it. Barker's performances of his own compositions are compelling, but the very sophisticated equipment and the amount of technical knowledge it requires suggests that this will remain a specialist area.

The recorder consort

Much of the modern professional recorder repertoire – that is, music composed specifically for concert performance as opposed to that written with amateurs in mind – is for solo recorder or recorder with keyboard. The consort repertoire has received a major boost from the playing of the Amsterdam Loeki Stardust Quartet, which has commis-sioned many new pieces in recent years. This group (Daniel Brüggen, Bertho Driever, Paul Leenhouts and Karel van Steenhoven – see pl. 36) first became known through the 1981 Musica Antiqua Competition in Bruges, where their jazzy arrangement *When shall the sun shine?*, based on Stevie Wonder's 'You are the sunshine of my life', was first performed as one of their test-pieces. Since then they have gained an international reputation not only for early music but also for the contemporary pieces they play with immense musicality and flawless technique. Their repertoire contains such important works as Ryohei

Plate 36 The Amsterdam Loeki Stardust Quartet, photographed for this book in a cloister at Utrecht, where Jacob van Eyck played. From left to right its members are: Daniel Brüggen, Bertho Driever, Paul Leenhouts and Karel van Steenhoven. They hold a 'great consort' of recorders, being (again from left to right) great bass in *B* flat, bass in *f*, contra-bass in *F* and great bass in *c*. These carefully matched instruments were made by Ture Bergstøm of Denmark.

As mentioned on p. 164, the quartet's repertoire is extremely wide ranging, including contemporary music specially composed for them. They recently (1994) recorded some of the baroque ensemble concertos discussed in Chapter 6, with The Academy of Ancient Music and Christopher Hogwood, an immaculate performance full of baroque elegance and springy rhythms, but no unnecessary showiness (L'Oiseau-Lyre 436 905).

This photograph has been generously sponsored by Decca U.K. Decca's L'Oiseau-Lyre recordings of the Amsterdam Loeki Stardust Quartet have set new standards for recorder consort playing, and have also inspired some excellent new compositions. References to these recordings are made in this book on p. 27, p. 41 (pl. 14), p. 44 notes 3 and 4, p. 47, note 26, p. 48, note 36, p. 88, note 9 and p. 118, note 25.

Hirose's *Lamentation* (1975) and Tristan Keuris's *Passeggiate* (1990); works by Frans Geysen such as his *Installaties* (1983); Chiel Meijering's *Een Paard met Vijf Poten* ('A Horse with Five Legs', 1982, rev. 1984); *Wolken* (1984) by Karel van Steenhoven; and many jazz and 'fun' pieces from Pete Rose's *Tall P* (1991) to Paul Leenhouts's *Loeki the Lion on the trail of the Pink Panther* (1987). Their influence has been enormous and many consort groups have been formed in imitation, none of them as yet able to surpass their role model.

Conclusion

In 1965 Richard Noble wrote in *The Recorder and Music Magazine*[19] that *Muziek* by Rob du Bois 'has the disadvantage of being almost unplayable except in the hands of a performer of genius'. A correspondent (the recorder player and teacher John Turner, a lifelong advocate of modern music) was quick to jump in with a letter[20] in the next issue pointing out 'the amazing difference in standards of performance between the recorder and other wind instruments. ... No professional or good amateur flautist would have a heart attack at seeing a passage of double-tonguing looming ahead ... yet the average good recorder player would I suspect jib at them, though I fail to see why he should.' To show how things have changed since then, one can quote Walter van Hauwe writing in 1992: 'several times as many *original* compositions for the recorder have been composed in the thirty years since 1960 as in the entire history of recorder music up to that date'.[21] This view is shared by the Australian expert, Malcolm Tattersall, who maintains that more contemporary music has been written for recorder in Australia since 1980 than in the previous forty years.[22]

   The search for repertoire is a problem for any instrumentalist, but for the recorder player possibly more than most. Very few of the established masterpieces that constitute the backbone of, for instance, a pianist's or a violinist's repertoire exist. By its very nature, the recorder has more weaknesses than strengths, so that any music chosen for it must carefully maximise what it has to offer, rather than expose its potential inadequacies. There are also very few substantial works in terms of duration; the average piece is somewhere between five and ten minutes long, and this tends to create programming problems. A new work by the British composer Anthony Gilbert is of interest here. *Igorochki* (1992) for recorder and chamber orchestra is a substantial five-movement piece taking its title from the Russian for 'little games' and showing deliberate Stravinskian references. It uses the full range of recorders from sopranino down to bass with an inventiveness that combines extended techniques with folk influences from Balinese gamelan to Japanese ritual lament.

The whole question of instrument-swopping causes difficulties, yet changing from one member of the recorder family to another during the performance of a work such as *Igorochki* has become standard practice because it avoids monotony of sound. The practicalities of where to put the instruments and how to change them with the minimum of fuss need as much thought as the coherence of the concert programme itself. As Daniel Brüggen has said: 'A good programme remains good even if you play it not so well; a bad programme is good only when you play it brilliantly, and then it doesn't matter!'[23]

Recent compositions, such as *Rotations* (1988) for solo recorder by the Dutch composer Jan Rokus van Roosendael, have shown a new confidence in integrating extended techniques and improvisatory and theatrical elements into carefully planned concert works – the music is arranged on stands set in a circle around the player. *The Circle* (1985), Kees Boeke's forty-minute improvisatory piece, is a complex journey through the circle of keys: never the same twice, yet following strict rules. Some players have struggled against the restrictions of the repertoire, early and modern, and have gone right outside it to steal from other instruments. Walter van Hauwe's CD, *Ladder of Escape*, issued in 1988, shows to what extent he had by then become frustrated with the standard repertoire. The CD contains performances on recorder of Varèse's *Density 21.5* and Debussy's *Syrinx*, two classics of the flute repertoire, with some thirteenth-century Japanese and fourteenth-century Italian pieces, and Stravinsky's *Pièces I* and *II*, originally for clarinet. Van Hauwe is one of the leading players and most influential teachers of his generation, so he has started a fashion, and every young performer is now playing these pieces. What does this musical piracy say, however, about the ability of the recorder to sustain its own existence in the future?

It might be said that the definition of a living as opposed to a museum instrument is the continuous appearance of new compositions for it. It must be owned, however, that the modern recorder repertoire contains few real masterpieces; good music, certainly, but little that is comparable with those composed for mainstream instruments. Most of the works are the direct result of the stimulus of a few master performers with a specific interest in contemporary music. Does the recorder have the necessary impetus to carry it into the twenty-first century if first-rank performers like van Hauwe find they must depart so far from the core repertoire in order to sustain their interest?

Notes

1. The term 'extended technique' refers to any instrumental technique which takes the player outside the area of conventional, melodic playing.
2. Edgar Hunt, *The Recorder and its Music* (London 1962; rev. edn 1977); Harry Haskell, *The Early Music Revival* (London 1988); Eve O'Kelly, *The Recorder Today* (Cambridge 1990).
3. O'Kelly, *The Recorder Today*, pp. 4–5.
4. Margaret Campbell, *Dolmetsch: the Man and his Work* (London 1975).
5. See Chapter 8, 'The recorder revival i'.
6. Campbell, *Dolmetsch*, pp. 208–9.
7. Hunt, *The Recorder and its Music*, p. 135.
8. 'English' and 'German' fingering: see Chapter 11 on professional recorder players and their instruments.
9. John Turner, 'Rawsthorne's recorder suite', *The Recorder Magazine* 13/1 (March 1993), pp. 13–14.
10. Richard Noble, 'The new recorder sound', *The Recorder and Music Magazine* 1/9 (May 1965), pp. 275–6, and 'The recorder in pop: a progress report', *The Recorder and Music Magazine* 2/5 (May 1967), pp. 135–6.
11. This was not a new discovery, of course. Alternative fingerings, multiphonics, playing and singing simultaneously and so on, are mentioned in several of the early treatises, and there are many precedents in ethnic music. The new factor was the influence of these techniques when used within modern composition.
12. London 1967.
13. Frans Brüggen, 'Berio's *Gesti*', *The Recorder and Music Magazine* 2/3 (Nov. 1966), p. 66.
14. Celle, Moeck, 1969.
15. Michael Vetter, 'The challenge of new music', *The Recorder and Music Magazine* 2/5 (May 1967), p. 133.
16. Paris 1982.
17. Helsinki 1987.
18. Further details may be found in O'Kelly, *The Recorder Today*, pp. 82–115. Also in Ursula Schmidt, *Notation der neuen Blockflötenmusik: ein Überblick* (Celle, Moeck, 1981).
19. Richard Noble, 'The recorder in twentieth century music: a personal view', *The Recorder and Music Magazine* 1/8 (Feb. 1965), pp. 243–4.
20. John Turner, Letters to the Editor, *The Recorder and Music Magazine* 1/9 (May 1965), p. 277.
21. Walter van Hauwe, *The Modern Recorder Player*, vol. III (London 1992), p. 7.
22. Malcolm Tattersall, 'Australian music for recorder', *The Recorder* (Melbourne) (March 1984), pp. 19–22; and 'Wider horizons: more Australian recorder music', *The Recorder* (Melbourne) 6 (June 1987), pp. 5–8.
23. Eve O'Kelly, 'Daniel Brüggen', *The Recorder Magazine* 11/4 (Dec. 1991), pp. 107–11.

10 Professional recorder players i: pre-twentieth century

DAVID LASOCKI

Which professional musicians played the recorder before the twentieth century? What repertoire did they perform, where and for whom? The answers to these questions are now known in some depth for England but remain to be researched seriously for other European countries.[1] For that reason this chapter will concentrate on the professional recorder player in England, drawing only occasional parallels with other countries.

The renaissance recorder

The recorder had arrived in England by the 1390s.[2] As numerous poems depict, fifteenth-century minstrels usually played a number of instruments, including the recorder, although we know next to nothing about their use of it.[3] The traditional distinction between players of *haut* (loud) and *bas* (soft) instruments disappeared during the second half of that century.[4] The 'Arnold, player at recorders' who was rewarded by Henry VII in 1498 was probably a minstrel associated with the court.[5] In 1501 Guilliam van der Bourgh, one of the king's three 'sackbuts' (shawm and sackbut players), was paid 'for new recorders' he had purchased for the court, presumably for himself and his colleagues to play.[6]

Henry VIII introduced to England the fashionable French and Italian practice of having complete consorts of like instruments: violins, flutes and recorders. In 1540 he appointed to the court, the Venetians Alvise, John, Jasper, Anthony and Baptista Bassano, 'brothers in the art or science of music', whom his Venetian agent described as 'all excellent and esteemed above all other[s] in this city in their virtue'. The Bassanos were significant makers of instruments, including recorders; their products can be traced on the Continent as well as in England. Although the Bassano brothers (and their descendants) could play several wind and string instruments, in England they specialised in the recorder, Alvise's son Augustine joining them in 1550 to complete a six-member consort.[7]

Recruitment to the consort came partly from second- and third-generation members of the Bassano family (Augustine, Lodovico, Arthur, Edward I, Jeronimo II, Anthony II, Henry; see p. 222), partly from other foreign musicians (William Daman) or descendants of them (Alphonso and Clement Lanier), and eventually from native English musicians (Robert Baker senior and junior, John Hussey, William Noke). In the sixteenth century the recorder consort played dance music as well as entertainment and dinner music. In the early seventeenth century it was used at special ceremonies and perhaps also in masques and in the Chapel Royal.[8] It lasted until the reorganisation of the court's wind musicians around 1630 into a single group divided into three 'companies', each playing cornetts, flutes, recorders, shawms and sackbuts. The royal musicians were highly paid, received extra rewards, grants and gifts, and held the rank of 'gentleman' (two of the Bassanos with large property holdings even became esquires).

During the second half of the sixteenth century, the consort of recorders was taken up by the other types of professional musicians in England, who generally also played many other wind and stringed instruments. At least one recorder player (Daman) was employed by Sir Thomas Sackville, and Sir Thomas Kytson's six household musicians had the use of 'one case of recorders, in number seven'. The travelling troupes of musicians who wore the livery of noblemen – notably the troupe of the Earl of Leicester, a favourite of Queen Elizabeth – also seem to have employed recorders.

Few documents about waits (city and town musicians) mention which instruments they played, besides the ubiquitous shawm. But recorders are known to have been used by the waits of London (1568), Exeter (1575), Norwich ('five recorders, being a whole noise' 1584; 1589, 1618, 1622), Chester (1591) and Gloucester (1594).[9] All or most of the members of these groups of three to six musicians played the instrument – presumably for indoor functions, although at Gloucester the waits used recorders outdoors during the nightly city watch.[10]

The consort of recorders was used extensively by the groups of six musicians attached to the several London theatres, especially from about 1610 to 1642. Recorders had strong associations for the dramatists, being used to depict the supernatural, death and appearances of gods; to express love; and to announce entrances of royalty or nobility. The theatre musicians were trained by apprenticeship for periods of at least seven years, thereafter becoming freemen of the City of London in their early twenties.[11]

In the late sixteenth and early seventeenth centuries, the recorder occasionally substituted for the flute in the mixed consort[12] consisting of treble viol (sometimes treble violin), bass viol, lute, bandora, cittern and flute.[13] This distinctive grouping of unlike instruments probably originated with travelling troupes of liveried players, and later, as well as being used in noble households, became popular among waits, theatre musicians and amateurs.

The baroque recorder

According to received opinion, the baroque recorder – like the flute, oboe and bassoon – was developed from its renaissance counterpart by a group of French makers around the middle of the seventeenth century.[14] French woodwind players then took the remodelled instruments all over Europe.[15] By all indications, baroque recorders arrived in England from France in 1673, when the opera composer Robert Cambert brought with him some French musicians, including Maxant De Bresmes, Pierre Guiton, (Jean?) Boutet and James Paisible, who all played oboe, recorder and strings.[16] The recorder soon became known by its French names, *flute douce* or plain *flute*. When Cambert's theatrical projects failed, one of these players probably left the country (Boutet), two others worked briefly at the court and then also left (De Bresmes, Guiton), and the fourth stayed on and became the most important recorder player of the day (Paisible). A fifth French recorder player, François Mariens, served at court, 1685–9.

The baroque recorder quickly found its way into the London theatres. In Etherege's play *The Man of Mode* (1676), a character says: 'What, you are of the number of the ladies whose ears are grown so delicate since our operas, you can be charmed with nothing but flute doux [*sic*] and French hautboys?' Within a decade, three different groups were playing the recorder in the theatre: the actors, the theatre band and the 'fiddlers' who appear on stage (in Shadwell's *The Squire of Alsatia* (1688) they are said to be 'always fluting or scraping').[17]

The public concert as we know it – a performance for which a fixed admission charge is made – was invented by a court violinist, John Banister I, in 1672 and quickly assumed great importance. Banister also played the flageolet and used the recorder in some of his concerts. The concert series at York Buildings and other halls in the 1690s were promoted by such musicians as the recorder-playing court violinists Robert King and Banister's son, John II.

By the 1690s the recorder had also become such a feature of the London stage that Nicholas Brady's play *The Rape* (1692) uses the expression 'flute and voice' to represent the normal music heard there. The United Company regularly employed two oboists, who sometimes played pairs of simple recorder parts, as in all Purcell's dramatic operas and other large-scale works from 1690 to 1694. When the United Company split into two companies at Drury Lane and Lincoln's

Inn Fields, the bands of both regularly used oboes and up to four recorders. Their interval 'entertainments' had similar performers and repertoire to the public concerts, featuring the recorder players Paisible and Banister II in music by Corelli, Corbett, Croft, Fedeli, Finger, Keller, Daniel Purcell, Weldon, Williams and others, most of it soon published for amateur consumption. Paisible's own virtuoso recorder sonatas remained in manuscript.

At court, between about 1692 and 1708, Princess (later Queen) Anne's prince consort, George of Denmark, had an 'oboe band' made up of newly arrived foreign musicians, among them Peter La Tour and Johann Ernst Galliard, with a few natives such as James Graves. Paisible was the house composer for the royal couple. The band's repertoire included the sonatas by Finger and Keller for two recorders, two oboes and basso continuo.

In the 1710s, the interval entertainments of both Drury Lane and the new Lincoln's Inn Fields Theatre featured recorder concertos, performed by John Baston at the former and Paisible at the latter. In the advertisements many such concertos are said to be for small sizes of recorder, no doubt the surviving concertos for fifth and sixth flutes (descant recorders in C and D) by Baston himself, the amateur oboist and recorder player Robert Woodcock,[18] and two composers associated with the theatres, William Babell and Francis Dieupart.

James Brydges, Earl of Carnarvon and later Duke of Chandos, briefly had George Frideric Handel and Johann Christoph Pepusch as his house composers (1715–21). His band of eight to fourteen instrumentalists, the Cannons Concert, included the Dutch woodwind player Jean Christian Kytch, the French recorder player Louis Mercy, and 'Signor' Biancardi, apparently the first Italian oboist to arrive in England.[19] Their repertoire included a number of works with recorder parts: two of Handel's Chandos Anthems, his *Te Deum*, and his masque *Acis and Galatea*, and cantatas and anthems by Pepusch.

Between its founding in 1705 and the decline of the recorder in the 1730s, the band of the opera house in the Haymarket engaged the efforts of the best London composers and musicians. At least ten of these who primarily played other instruments – Paisible (bass violin), Banister II (violin), La Tour, John Loeillet, Galliard, Kytch, Francesco Barsanti and Giuseppe Sammartini (oboe), and John Festing and Carl Friedrich Weidemann (flute, also oboe?) – would have all used the recorder there as the occasion demanded, notably in the obbligatos in operas and oratorios by Handel. Sammartini, who arrived in London around 1729, was considered one of the greatest oboists in Europe; he represents the second migration of the French woodwind players, since his father was an oboist who had emigrated from France to Milan around 1690. Like Paisible's, Sammartini's recorder sonatas, as well as his famous descant recorder concerto, remained in manuscript.

The most heavily advertised participants in the public concerts of the first three decades of the eighteenth century included the recorder players we have already encountered in the theatres – especially Banister II, Paisible, La Tour, Kytch, Mercy and Sammartini – as well as the Huguenot Daniel De Moivre (who also played in taverns and coffee houses)[20] and the occasional foreigner such as Johann Christian Schickhardt who was merely visiting.[21] They played sonatas and concertos by Corelli and other Italians as well as local composers (Pepusch, Dieupart, Galliard, Corbett and Visconti). In the 1720s, Kytch specialised in arrangements for bassoon, oboe or recorder of opera arias by Handel and Bononcini.

Most of the players in London seem to have taught the recorder. In 1695 an abortive attempt was made to set up two Royal Academies to provide instruction in several arts and sciences, including music.[22] The three men named as recorder teachers were Banister II (also a violin teacher), Paisible and De Moivre. Roger North wrote that Banister was an excellent singing teacher. Graves advertised himself in 1696 as a teacher of the violin, recorder and oboe. A visiting German, Uffenbach, reported in 1710 that Paisible frightened off a prospective pupil by asking £3 3s 0d for eighteen lessons.[23] According to Sir John Hawkins, Barsanti taught the recorder and Loeillet the harpsichord.

The recorder player of this era who seems to have made the best living is Loeillet.[24] As Hawkins tells us, Loeillet gave up the post of first oboist of the opera house (which he had held from 1708 to 1711) and began giving private concerts in his own house, becoming successful at attracting gentleman participants, who rewarded him handsomely. His recorder sonatas were presumably written for these concerts. He left bequests totalling £1,700; his instruments, paintings and other possessions were impressive enough to be auctioned off; and Hawkins reckons he had accumulated a fortune of some £16,000. Of course, it was not by public performance that he had grown rich – least of all on the recorder – but by a judicious combination of private performing and promoting, capitalising on the good impression created by his convivial, self-effacing character.

Conclusion

Apart from the Bassanos at court and the lowly De Moivre working in taverns and coffee houses, all professional recorder players of the Renaissance and Baroque earned their living primarily playing other instruments, sometimes supplemented by composing, teaching and promoting concerts. Most of the music they played was written by local composers (including themselves) specifically for their working situations. Although the recorder's role in English musical life was minor, it was not insignificant. The instrument was valued for dinner and dance music at court and for its depiction of certain 'affections' in theatre and vocal music; and, in the hands of such virtuosos as Paisible, it participated widely in chamber music and concertos at public and private concerts.

Notes

1. Unless otherwise referenced, the material in this chapter is taken from David Lasocki, 'Professional recorder players in England, 1540–1740' (Diss., U. of Iowa 1983) as well as the articles derived from it: 'Professional recorder playing in England, 1500–1740', *Early Music* 10/1 (1982), pp. 23–9; 10/2 (1982), pp. 183–91; 'The recorder in the Elizabethan, Jacobean and Caroline theater', *The American Recorder* 25/1 (1984), pp. 3–10; 'The recorder consort at the English court 1540–1673', *The American Recorder* 25/3 (1984), pp. 91–100; 25/4 (1984), pp. 131–5; 'The Anglo-Venetian Bassano family as instrument makers and repairers', *The Galpin Society Journal* 38 (1985), pp. 112–32; and 'The French hautboy in England, 1673–1730', *Early Music* 16/3 (1988), pp. 339–57.
2. Brian Trowell, 'King Henry IV, recorder player', *Galpin Society Journal* 10 (1957), pp. 83–4.
3. The most useful discussion of these poems remains that in Dietz Degen, *Zur Geschichte der Blockflöte in den germanischen Ländern* (Cassel 1937; rpt. 1972), pp. 133–9.
4. For evidence, see Keith Polk, 'The Schubingers of Augsburg: innovation in renaissance instrumental music', in *Quaestiones in musica: Festschrift für Franz Krautwurst zum 65. Geburtstag*, ed. Friedhelm Brusniak and Horst Leuchtmann (Tutzing 1989), pp. 495–503.
5. Eileen Sharpe Pearsall, 'Tudor court musicians, 1485–1547: their number, status and function' (Diss., New York U. 1986), vol. I, pp. 54, 58; II, p. 21.
6. Pearsall, 'Tudor court musicians', vol. II, p. 38.
7. This seems to have been common among sixteenth-century Italian musicians. The sixth Bassano brother, Jacopo, returned to Venice. In 1559 he and his son-in-law Santo Griti drew up a contract with three musicians working for the Doge of Venice, the makers agreeing to make cornetts, crumhorns, curtals, flutes, recorders and shawms – presumably the instruments the musicians played (see Giulio Ongaro, '16th-century Venetian wind instrument makers and their clients', *Early Music* 13/3 (1985), pp. 391–7). The leader of a company of Italian musicians, Giovanni Pietro Rizeffo, in seeking employment from the Duke of Parma in 1546, claimed that all six musicians in his company could play the trumpet, sackbut, shawm, cornett, cornemuse, recorder, flute and violin, were all excellent at improvising from a vocal part, and could sing excellently besides (see N. Pellicelli, 'Musicisti in Parma nei secoli XV–XVI: la capella alla corte farnese', *Note d'archivio per la storia musicale* 9/1 (1932), pp. 42–3).
8. About twenty pieces by Augustine and Jeronimo II Bassano and William Daman, surviving in consort versions and/or lute or keyboard arrangements, seem to represent part of the repertoire over a period of fifty years. See Peter Holman (ed.), *The Royal Wind Music, Vol. I: Pavans and Galliards in 5 Parts by Augustine Bassano* and *The Royal Wind Music, Vol. II: Four Fantasias in 5 Parts by Jerome Bassano*, and William Daman, *Fantasia di sei soprani*, ed. P. Holman (all London 1981). Some of the early seventeenth-century repertoire, including ten dances probably by Augustine and Jeronimo II Bassano, seems to be contained in the Fitzwilliam Wind Manuscript (Cambridge, Fitzwilliam Museum, Mus. MS 734).
9. See Walter L. Woodfill, *Musicians in English Society from Elizabeth to Charles I* (Princeton 1953; rpt. New York 1969), pp. 34–5; *Devon*, ed. John M. Wasson, Records of Early English Drama (Toronto 1986); *Norwich 1540–1642*, ed. David Galloway, Records of Early English Drama (Toronto 1984); *Chester*, ed. Lawrence

M. Clopper, Records of Early English Drama (Toronto 1979); *Cumberland, Westmorland, Gloucestershire*, ed. Audrey Douglas and Peter Greenfield, Records of Early English Drama (Toronto 1986), p. 313: 'James [blank's] musicians, having played on the recorder as the waits for this quarter of the year past at four of the clock in the mornings in the chief streets of this city …'.

10. This may seem surprising, but there is at least one foreign parallel. In 1775 Charles Burney reported that the large sixteenth-century recorders in Antwerp 'in times when commerce flourished in this city … used to be played on every day, by a band of musicians who attended the merchants, trading to the Hans towns, in procession to the exchange'. See *An Eighteenth-Century Musical Tour in Central Europe and the Netherlands*, trans. Percy A. Scholes (London 1959), vol. II, p. 15.

11. See David Lasocki, 'Musicians and apprentices in City of London companies other than the Musicians Company during the 17th century' (forthcoming).

12. Modern scholars have until recently called this grouping the 'broken consort', although this term was never used for it historically. There is some evidence that it was understood by the plain word 'consort'. My preferred term 'mixed consort' is that of Warwick Edwards (see his 'The sources of Elizabethan consort music' (Diss., Cambridge U. 1974), vol. I, pp. 44–8). Scholars have recently also called it the 'English consort' and the 'consort-of-six'.

13. For editions of this repertoire, see Warwick Edwards (ed.), *Music for Mixed Consort*, Musica Britannica 45 (London 1979).

14. But for evidence of more gradual development of the oboe, see Bruce Haynes, 'Lully and the rise of the oboe as seen in works of art', *Early Music* 16/3 (1988), pp. 324–38; and Rebecca Harris-Warrick, 'A few thoughts on Lully's *Hautbois*', *Early Music* 18/1 (1990), pp. 97–106. Some recently discovered evidence from Italy, moreover, suggests that Italian recorder-makers may have at least made parallel experiments. See Nikolaus Delius, 'Die erste Flötenschule des Barock?' *Tibia* 1/1 (1976), pp. 5–12; Bartolomeo Bismantova, *Compendio musicale* (Ferrara 1677; facsimile, Florence 1978); Adriano Cavicchi, 'Prassi strumentale in Emilia nell'ultimo quarto del seicento: flauto italiano, cornetto, archi', *Studi musicali* 2/1 (1973), pp. 111–43; Marcello Castellani, 'The *Regola per suonare il flauto italiano* by Bartolomeo Bismantova (1677)', *The Galpin Society Journal* 30 (1977), pp. 76–85. Furthermore, unpublished research by several scholars is beginning to suggest that Richard Haka in Amsterdam may also have had some hand in the transition from renaissance to baroque types of woodwinds.

15. It is possible that the French oboe players who went to Spain in 1679 in the suite of the new queen, Marie-Louise d'Orléans, also played the recorder. In 1690, Miguel and Joseph Hauteloche, two brothers from Cambrai, then part of Flanders, began to appear in court records. They played violin and recorder (described as a new instrument that was harmonious when accompanied by others). See Beryl Kenyon de Pascual, 'The recorder revival in late 17th-century Spain', in *The Recorder in the 17th Century*, ed. David Lasocki (Utrecht 1995).

No fewer than fifteen French oboists were active in Germany between about 1681 and 1732; and as late as 1714, J. B. Richter, the principal oboist of the celebrated Dresden orchestra, was sent to Paris to complete his training. (Bruce Haynes, 'Johann Sebastian Bach's pitch standards: the woodwind perspective', *Journal of the American Musical Instrument Society* 11 (1985), pp. 62–4; on oboists in Germany see also Werner Braun, 'The "hautboist": an outline of evolving careers and functions', in *The Social Status of the Professional Musician from the Middle Ages to the 19th Century*, ed. Walter Salmen, trans. Herbert Kaufman and Barbara Reisner (New York 1983), pp. 123–68.)

French oboists were also absorbed into Italian musical life. For example, Giuseppe Sammartini's father was a Frenchman, referred to in one Italian source as 'Alessio S. Martino francese'; he had settled in Milan by the early 1690s. (Claudio Sartori, 'Giovanni Battista Sammartini e la sua corte', *Musica d'Oggi* 3/3 (1960), pp. 107–8.)

16. Paisible probably received his training at the Versailles court from one of the twelve 'joueurs de violons, hautbois, sacquebouttes et cornets' of the Grande

Ecurie, the members of which played the oboe, tenor oboe, bassoon, violin, tenor violin, bass violin, cornett and sackbut. Each player was nominally responsible for two instruments of different types – generally the upper, middle or lower ranges of the double reeds or violins – although they may well have been able to play most or all of the sizes, as well as the recorder. (See Marcelle Benoît, *Musiques de Cour, Chapelle, Chambre, Ecurie. 1661–1733* (Paris 1971).) Paisible specialised on oboe and bass violin.

I am inclined to believe that the famous reference in Samuel Pepys's diary to his hearing recorders at a revival of *The Virgin Martyr* in 1668 is still to renaissance-style recorders being brought back to the theatres for one of the first times since the Restoration (the theatres having been closed during the Civil War and Commonwealth, 1642–60). If baroque recorders had come over to England before 1673, would we not have had the change of name etc. earlier? For an elaboration of this point, see David Lasocki, 'Professional recorder players in England', pp. 316–18.

17. See Curtis A. Price, *Music in the Restoration Theatre* (Ann Arbor 1979).
18. See David Lasocki and Helen Neate, 'The life and works of Robert Woodcock, 1690–1728', *The American Recorder* 29/3 (1988), pp. 92–104.
19. See Graydon Beeks, 'Handel and music for the Earl of Carnarvon', in *Bach, Handel, Scarlatti: Tercentenary Essays*, ed. Peter Williams (Cambridge 1985), pp. 1–20.
20. See David Lasocki, 'The life of Daniel De Moivre (fl. 1687–1731)', *The Consort* 45 (1989), pp. 15–17.
21. Schickhardt's career is a good illustration of how a less than first-rate baroque woodwind musician and composer earned his living, constantly moving from one minor musical centre to another, despite publishing no fewer than twenty-eight sets of sonatas and concertos for the flute, oboe and recorder, as well as methods for the oboe and recorder. He was born around 1682 in Braunschweig and received his musical training under the protection of the heir to the dukedom of Braunschweig-Wolfenbüttel. By his early twenties he was working in the Netherlands, at first for Friedrich of Hesse-Cassel, later for Princess Henriëtte-Amalia of Nassau-Diez and her son, Johann Willem Friso, the Prince of Orange, accompanying both Friedrich and Friso on their military campaigns. After soliciting employment from several noblemen, Schickhardt worked in Hamburg around 1712, acting as an agent for the publisher Estienne Roger of Amsterdam. By 1717 Schickhardt was in the service of Johann Friedrich, Count of Castel-Rudenhausen, then moved on to Scandinavia. In 1732 he gave some concerts in London, primarily playing the fashionable small sizes of recorder, but does not seem to have stayed. In 1745 he was enrolled as a student at the University of Leiden and retained connections with that university until his death in 1762. (See David Lasocki, 'Johann Christian Schickhardt (c1682–1762): a contribution to his biography and a catalogue of his works', *Tijdschrift van de Vereniging voor Nederlandse Muziekgeschiedenis* 27/1 (1977), pp. 28–55; and 'Schickhardt in London', *Recorder & Music* 6/7 (1979), pp. 203–5.)
22. See Michael Tilmouth, 'The Royal Academies of 1695', *Music & Letters* 38/4 (1957), pp. 327–34.
23. To put this in perspective, Paisible was earning 15s per night at the opera house in 1708–9; and at Drury Lane in 1716 'five shillings per diem and one guinea every time he performs anything upon the stage'.
24. See David Lasocki, 'A new look at the life of John Loeillet (1680–1730)', *Recorder & Music* 8/2 (1984), pp. 42–6; also in *Concerning the Flute*, ed. Rien de Reede (Amsterdam 1984), pp. 65–73.

11 Professional recorder players (and their instruments) ii: the twentieth century

EVE O'KELLY

The relationship between a musician and his or her instrument is always special. It has often been observed that two performers on the same instrument will make a different sound. This is not just a question of differing technical abilities or physical attributes; it has more to do with that indefinable quality called musicality, which is individual to every musician. A happy relationship between the player and his or her instrument makes possible the expression of the most deep and complex feelings and it is often difficult to say what makes it work.

Recorder players, like any other performers, are always in search of the ideal instrument and share the same preoccupations with design, tuning and physical condition of their recorders. There is an added complication, however. A violinist may own and use, say, three different violins, but no one will expect him to play viola and cello as well. A professional recorder player, on the other hand, needs to be able to play the entire family and, because of the specialised nature of the historical repertoire, also needs instruments appropriate in design and pitch to each period. In addition, because recorders are particularly susceptible to overuse, changes of climate and so on, performers on tour always bring spares for practice and to save the day when the inevitable occurs and a crack or fault develops just before a concert. Most, therefore, will have anything from six or eight to more than twenty recorders in constant professional use, and this requires a considerable financial investment.

Unlike stringed instruments which improve with age and playing, even over a period of several hundred years, those of the wind family tend to have a limited lifespan, and this is another practical considera-tion. The effects of constantly blowing moist air into a wooden tube begin to build up and may eventually cause considerable deterioration. Many performers reckon recorders are played out after as short a period as five years, and it is perhaps for this reason that few historical recorders have survived in good condition. So here is another difference between the recorder player and the violinist referred to above. Whereas a violinist aspires to own an old violin by a famous maker, the recorder player must find a modern maker with the skill to make a recorder that embodies all the qualities of an instrument that died out 200 years ago, leaving no continuity of tradition.

Twentieth-century recorder-making

As is well known, the first notable recorder-maker of modern times was Arnold Dolmetsch.[1] Nowadays, the profession has expanded but it still divides into two areas: large firms making wooden and plastic instruments by mass-production, and specialist master craftsmen and women producing handmade ones in small numbers in their own workshops.

Mass-production of recorders first began in the 1930s in Germany, when the rapid growth of school and amateur music-making produced a demand for them in quantities and at prices that individual makers could not satisfy. Among firms which began to make recorders at this time are those of Bärenreiter, Herwig, Heinrich, Adler, Mollenhauer, Nagel and Moeck, many of them still in production today. The first mass-produced recorders to be played in England were imported by Edgar Hunt in the 1930s. He approached the German firm of Herwig, at that time making the so-called 'German fingered' recorders[2] for the home market, with a request to adapt their design and make 'English' or baroque fingered instruments for export to England. This meant that the disadvantageous German fingering was never adopted in England. Later the firms of Dolmetsch and Schott started making mass-produced plastic and wooden recorders in England and these and the German ones were exported all over the world as the revival gathered momentum. Technology and materials have improved greatly nowadays, and most beginners and amateurs use good plastic, rather than wooden, recorders. Here the Japanese firms of Aulos and Yamaha have accomplished something of a takeover of the market.

Authenticity

Having gone through a stage in the 1970s and early 80s when every recorder was a 'Denner copy', a 'Stanesby copy', a 'Bressan copy' and so on, a change has taken place in recent years. The latest thinking suggests that historical makers worked to a 'sound ideal' rather than to an exact template. This conclusion is based on the fact that no two Bressans, for instance, are exactly identical in dimensions, although they will certainly *sound* like Bressans. Present-day makers, it has been suggested, should therefore adopt a way of thinking based on a knowledge of the methods of the past, rather than slavishly copying dimensions taken from a museum instrument which might be hope-lessly distorted by age. The risk of unknowingly copying a maker's bad habits, for instance, is one that must be recognised. Furthermore, it seems clear that Arnold Dolmetsch worked with such a 'sound ideal' in mind and it was probably this, together with his uncanny instinct, that enabled him so successfully to revive the techniques of recorder-making.

With relatively few surviving instruments left, some aspects of design remain open to question and interpretation. Until the 1970s or there-abouts most makers based their designs on extensive study and measuring of museum models. Nowadays, such institutions recognise that many old instruments were damaged by this process, however unintentionally, and access is greatly restricted. Published sheets of measurements and drawings must suffice. An interesting, if quirky, possibility pointed out in this connection by recorder-maker Tim Cranmore is nevertheless worth considering: were the surviving originals in museums preserved because they were very good and so were treasured, or because they did not work and so were forgotten in the attic?

Now that a new tradition of recorder-making has been established, however, present-day makers feel more free to forge a personal reputation for the quality of their instruments which, while based on sound research and experience, will nevertheless be very identifiably theirs.

The craft of recorder-making

A solo career demands specially made recorders and, for these, performers go to one of the relatively few master craftsmen and women with a small hand-crafted output. These recorders are very often made to order for a particular player, who will have discussed his or her exact requirements before the instrument is even begun, and may sometimes bring it back for many minute adjustments after it is finished. A close relationship thus develops between the maker and the player and, in working together, a comment from one may lead to the solution of a persistent musical or technical problem for the other.

It is not nowadays considered acceptable to perform early music on instruments inappropriate to the period. There are many good reasons for this, not least the fact that the ranges and timbres of renaissance and baroque recorders are quite different from one another and, clearly, the music of each period was written within the boundaries of what was possible at the time. Basically, recorders may be divided into renaissance, baroque and modern types, each with differing dimen-sions and external appearance, timbres and ranges, and built at various appropriate historical pitches. Without going into too much detail, we can say that renaissance recorders are generally louder and stronger in tone, particularly in the lower register, and are typically built at high pitch (a' = 466 being one of several historical standards). Baroque recorders are sweeter and more reedy in tone, with a range of at least two octaves and a note and are generally at low pitch (a' = 415, for instance).[3] The definition of a 'modern' recorder is harder to arrive at, and many would dispute that there is such an instrument, but it is useful to be able to apply this term to recorders with wide windways and bores, double finger-holes or keywork, and a powerful, carrying sound. An example of these would be the recorders made in the early part of the twentieth century by Carl Dolmetsch, but the modern recorder is still evolving, as will be seen below.

In pursuit of some elucidation of the relationship between recorder players and their instruments, the present writer talked to three very different performers and one maker who, between them, represent something of a cross-section of the profession.

The soloist

Robert Ehrlich, the young British performer and teacher, is a strong advocate of recorder-makers Bob Marvin and Fred Morgan. Ehrlich does not espouse the view that recorders – or indeed players – are delicate and need special coaxing. He believes that a recorder should be able to stand up to three to four hours practice every day, and that it is up to makers to ensure that their instruments are made of high-quality wood which can do this. The best recorders, he feels, have a flexible and interesting sound that can produce a uniform colour across the range without becoming monotonous. Another important quality he referred to is that of resonance, which creates a feeling of 'presence' in the concert hall.

Most recorder-makers voice their instruments for a quick attack, that is, so that they speak instantly when they are blown. Ehrlich finds this unsatisfactory, because, he says, 'there is only one way you can start the note, like a pre-programmed synthesiser'. For this reason among others, he likes recorders made by Fred Morgan, because 'they feel open, yet have a stable pitch and flexible articulation'. He also emphasises the importance of resistance to the airstream when blowing a recorder. A Moeck Steenbergen model with a very narrow windway would be very different, for instance, to an Arnold Dolmetsch recorder with a wide, straight, 'letter-box' windway. The Steenbergen he would find limiting, whereas the Dolmetsch, although more difficult to play, he finds much more exciting.

Robert Ehrlich is unusual in admitting to liking both wide-windway recorders and their early twentieth-century repertoire which, he feels, is 'a lot better than much of the music being written today'. The possibility of developing a true 'modern' recorder greatly attracts him, and he mentions an alto now being designed by Morgan which will incorporate many interesting features. Among these are a wide usable range – quiet at the top and loud at the bottom – with closed-standing keys for the bottom two holes. It will be at modern pitch of $a' = 440$, of course, and will have a loud and powerful sound. It will also be able to play top F sharp perfectly, and Ehrlich who, with Walter van Hauwe, has been involved in testing and working on the prototype, believes it will be a major step forward in instrument technology.

Asked what instruments he brings on a concert tour, Ehrlich lists his Morgan voice flute and Morgan alto at $a' = 440$ which has a *corps de rechange*[4] at $a' = 415$. He also takes an Arnold Dolmetsch alto at $a' = 440$; a Yamaha plastic alto for practice and teaching; a Morgan 'Ganassi' G alto with *corps de rechange* at $a' = 466$, $a' = 440$ and $a' = 415$, and a 'Ganassi' soprano in C with *corps de rechange* at $a' = 415$ and $a' = 440$. He does not own a sopranino or a tenor, although he is hoping to buy a Bob Marvin renaissance tenor in the near future, and if he needs a bass he has to borrow one. He uses the Dolmetsch for early twentieth-century repertoire such as the Berkeley *Sonatina* and also for avant-garde pieces such as Andriessen's *Sweet*. For contemporary ones that do not need a big range, as well as for typical baroque sonatas, he uses the Morgan alto because the *corps de rechange* makes it playable at $a' = 415$ as well as $a' = 440$. The flexibility that this gives in terms of repertoire makes the high price for the instrument seem, to him, very reasonable.

The ensemble player

The importance of choosing the right instrument for the repertoire was stressed by Daniel Brüggen of the Amsterdam Loeki Stardust Quartet (pl. 36), as well as by Ehrlich. In the course of a concert this Quartet may play thirty or thirty-five recorders and these are selected carefully not just to take account of the repertoire, but also keeping in mind the climate, the halls they will play in, and the practicalities of who needs which instrument in each piece. There is constant assessment of how the instruments are responding and consideration of possible improvements. Between them, the members of the group now own a very large collection of excellent matched recorders, but the first consideration remains the sound. Any combination of instruments that works well for a particular piece is considered legitimate, even a mixture of wood with plastic, historical with modern. The musical snobbery that can afflict this area does not affect the Amsterdam Loeki Stardust Quartet.

Daniel Brüggen made the point that the group rules out much music from its repertoire because of the instruments:

Normally with us it goes together: you play a piece and when the sound you have on the instruments is great, then the piece is great. And vice versa, if it doesn't sound good you look for several other combinations of instruments and when it still doesn't come out as you think it should, then you forget about the piece. And there are a lot of pieces we play because of the instruments we have and don't play because we can't find a sound to match.

He also made the point that recorders with too strong a character of their own can be a drawback in that they lack versatility and the ability to project the musical intentions of the player.

The recorder-maker

Tim Cranmore has been making instruments since about 1980, and is one of very few recorder-makers working in Britain. He makes mid-price baroque recorders, most of which are purchased by serious students and teachers, and over three-quarters of his instruments are sold at the major music-trade exhibitions in Europe to which he travels regularly. They sell by reputation, rather than by active marketing, because they are widely recommended by teachers to their students and by friends to one another.

His recorders are mostly made of English boxwood, which is said to be the best in the world. Cranmore likes working in it because it is easy to turn and carve and, with the light colour, one can see what one is doing. He also makes recorders in rosewood, partridge wood (a rare species) and sometimes acid-stained boxwood – an effect achieved with the dangerous-sounding combination of nitric acid and ammonia. This has no effect on the instrument's performance but gives an attractive dark finish. He has occasionally used plastic, but finds it chips and bends and he regards it as a novelty.

Cranmore makes recorders in batches, which allows time between the various stages of the process for the wood to rest. Most of it is bought from a dealer who specialises in supplying instrument-makers with blocks of wood already cut into the appropriate basic sizes and shapes. Before it can be used, it needs to be seasoned – either naturally for five to six years, or in the microwave for about forty-five minutes! The first stage of making a recorder is to bore the inside of the tube, then leaving it to rest for a couple of weeks before reaming it and letting it rest again. When the bore is complete or almost so on the inside, the tube is turned on a lathe to produce the characteristic shape and decorative rings of the outside. Then the voicing is carried out, to make the sound-producing area in and around the beak, the finger-holes are drilled and the block is made. The latter is usually of cedar, an inexpensive and effective wood. When the block has been fitted, it is removed again and the whole instrument (except the block) is immersed in a bath of linseed oil for two weeks, to impregnate the wood, protecting it against cracking. Afterwards, the upper surface of the windway needs to be cleaned of oil with acetone or dry-cleaning fluid, to avoid any future problems with moisture clogging it.

Cranmore uses a cutting machine to make the basic shape of the windway. This clever gadget, developed by the New Zealand maker Alec Loretto, is now widespread and involves a curved knife guided by hand using a template of each maker's own design. Cranmore's template is designed according to the dimensions of one of his own most successful handmade altos. The shape of this he regards as one of his only two trade secrets, the other being a knife which allows him to undercut finger-holes and make minute modifications inside recorders. The secret of recorder-making lies in the subtle final adjustments to the instrument and one of the biggest skills needed, according to Cranmore, is the ability to do this entirely by hand. 'You have to be able to take a knife and a piece of wood and cut a curve that any engineer would swear had been made by a machine', he says, and cites cutting the chamfers at the exit of the windway as an example.

Asked whether he ever gets tired of making recorders, Cranmore says:

I occasionally get sick of making *parts* of recorders, because there are boring parts and interesting parts. Drilling holes is boring – ten fingerholes per instrument gets tedious. But it's nice when they start to work, and it's very rewarding when they start to play. The most interesting bit of making a recorder is fighting with its deficiencies and trying to make a small improvement and see if it works. The problem with recorders is that as you blow them they get better, so you quite often find that a problem you were trying to rectify has gone away when they have been blown for a month. It's very easy to over-adjust, so you have to be quite subtle.

Cranmore says that he can see himself making recorders for the rest of his life. One does not make a great deal of money fast, but there is a comfortable living in it once one is established. Looking at it as a business, the overheads for recorder-making are quite low. The cost of the wood is only about 3 to 4 per cent of the finished item, for instance, and second-hand machinery is perfectly adequate, so the capital investment is small. Cranmore considers that you could certainly set up a complete woodwind-making workshop for a couple of thousand pounds sterling, and it would last you for the rest of your life. Basically it is the skill and experience, not the equipment, that is valuable, although there needs to be a satisfactory relationship between the number of instruments you can make and those you can sell – in his case about sixty to seventy per year, which is as many as he wants to produce. Here experience plays a major part. Most of the procedures are not particularly difficult, but one needs to be able to carry them out quickly enough to achieve the right ratio between productivity and sales. When Cranmore first started, he reckons it took him two to three hours just to make a block; now he can do it in fifteen minutes. Overall, he can now make a recorder in much less time than it used to take – about eight to ten hours in total from the block of wood to the finished article.

The authenticity debate is something he has little time for. 'Authenticity is usually used as an excuse by people whose instruments don't work', he says. 'In a commercial situation, you've got to produce instruments that do. Professional players will put up with an instrument that doesn't perform very well for a certain quality they might like, but students – and that's where the majority of the market lies – would rather have an instrument that works.'

The twentieth-century specialist

The American recorder player and composer Pete Rose specialises in twentieth-century music. As well as writing his own pieces, many of them founded in the jazz tradition which forms his own background, he performs the major works of the twentieth-century avant-garde. He also plays the most battered recorders I have ever seen.

Rose admits himself that his instruments are 'virtually unplayable' and says this is because he does not have any money to replace them. Nevertheless, he makes these old, battle-scarred recorders speak with great eloquence and subtlety. 'What my recorders do have', he says, 'is the one aspect in the development of the recorder which has been the most important of all time: the hole down the middle. Before this, players used to blow their brains out and not get any sound!'

Pete Rose owns a soprano Dolmetsch 'from Year One'; two Moeck altos, one with and one without a cracked windway, both modern pitch and about twenty years old; a von Huene tenor; an old Moeck Meister bass; and a Küng sopranino. He feels strongly that the player creates the sound, and he claims always to know when someone is playing his or her own instrument, rather than someone else's.

Suspecting that he is really very comfortable with his elderly instruments, I asked him whether he would get better ones if he had the means? He replied – though without much conviction – that if he had the money he would buy new instruments, but that he does become attached to objects and has a kind of personal relationship with his recorders. He is used to their shortcomings, even though they are a point of frustration for him. He also feels that 'many players buy new instruments all the time and make the same old sound on all of them'. Pete Rose seems to know the sound he wants and can therefore call it forth, where other players place more dependence on the instrument itself. Many players are looking for one that makes the sound they want, he thinks, instead of realising that it comes from themselves.

So it would appear that there are several divergent views on the art and craft of recorder-making. Is the quality of the instrument all-important, or does the ability of the player to communicate transcend everything? Does authenticity matter, or is anything that works legitimate? Are there possibilities for developing a modern recorder, or are all new modifications merely the instrument-making equivalent of reinventing the wheel?

Notes

1. See Chapters 8 and 9.
2. 'German' fingering was an attempt to simplify the forked fingerings necessary on baroque recorders. The result produces recorders that play in tune in the lower octave of the 'home' key (e.g. C on a descant recorder) but that become very out of tune once the player strays into the upper octave or into more distant keys. There are additional drawbacks in terms of the tone-quality, and the overall result is an inferior instrument which offers little real assistance to the beginner.
3. See Eve O'Kelly, *The Recorder Today* (Cambridge 1990), pp. 28–31 for fuller details.
4. A specially made interchangeable middle joint that 'converts' the recorder to play at different pitches.

12 The recorder in education

EVE O'KELLY

At a conference on 'Early Music in Europe' held in London in 1991[1] Christopher Hogwood, in his opening remarks, stated that early music has ceased to be a 'frontier study' and that it can now safely be regarded as something that 'doesn't have to be justified'. In the light of this, and bearing in mind the fact that early music is the recorder's home ground, as it were, it seems fruitful now to survey the present state of the recorder in education and to review its overall development since the early decades of the twentieth century. This overview must necessarily be brief and generalised, and aims rather to raise questions for further consideration, than to attempt to answer them. Among these questions are: to what extent has recorder teaching changed, improved or deteriorated since the beginning of the revival? After some seventy years of redevelopment, is it possible to say whether the use of the recorder as a means of teaching basic music skills has been a good or a bad thing? Does the recorder still have a place within the early-music community, or has it moved away in a direction of its own?

The recorder has been closely associated with education since the early days of the twentieth-century revival. Indeed, without the huge boost that the educational use gave to its redevelopment, it seems very likely that it would have remained a relatively obscure member of the early wind family. We have seen in Chapter 9 how it was adopted by the Youth movement in Germany in the 1920s and 30s and rapidly grew in popularity. It later spread worldwide with the educational and amateur branches dominating the professional sector.

Welcome as this popularity is, there is one serious problem: the poor image of the recorder. It is difficult to think of another instrument where expectations of the technical and musical proficiency of the child are in general so low. The recorder tends to be dismissed as a toy or condemned as noisy, shrill and unmusical. Any musical instrument in the hands of a beginner is something of a trial, but in the case of the violin or the clarinet, say, everyone knows what it *should* sound like, and there are famous players to act as role models. For recorder players these are harder to come by, however, and teachers are very often non-specialists. It is, perhaps, a question of expectations. The recorder has become labelled as 'easy', suitable for introducing children to music, and therefore somehow not 'a real instrument'. Add to this the fact that children's soprano recorders are made of plastic and can be bought for a very low price, and you begin to have an image problem which even a good teacher may be unable to reverse.

Here are two illustrations of this point, written forty years apart. In 1953, a contributor to *The Recorder News*, a publication of the British Society of Recorder Players, wrote:

Although the teaching of the recorder in schools is to be commended, there is, I think, a debit side to the account. On numerous occasions it has been remarked to me on hearing that I play the recorder, 'Oh! do you? So does my Johnnie (or Annie, as the case may be). He's learning it at school. Such a pity it's always out of tune but it's very quaint, isn't it?'

I know school recorder teachers who, after a three-day course, begin to teach the instrument at school. The result is that the parents of the children being taught look upon the recorder as one of the less pleasant kinds of toy. These teachers run the danger of being worse players than some of their pupils in only a matter of a week or two. I think that teachers should be expected to be masters of the fingering, at least, before trying to teach anyone else.[2]

In 1993 Peter Bowman, writing about the impatience and incomprehension of some parents when a teacher tries to repair basic technical flaws in a pupil, illustrates the extent to which negative attitudes, rather than being dispelled, have become reinforced in the intervening forty years. He writes:

How is it possible that six people took money to teach a child how to play the recorder and not one of them could, or would, discuss the most basic aspect of instrumental discipline: how to hold the instrument correctly? ... Determining our approach to teaching the recorder in a musical environment where people are open-minded but nevertheless sceptical about the value of the instrument ... remains difficult. ... The parent who blithely explains to me that little Johnny, who has just started with me, is only learning the recorder until he can take up the saxophone, or whatever, is the biggest problem. ... Until parents are convinced that the recorder is a worthwhile instrument to study they will remain less than happy with the 'thorough and serious' approach to teaching the instrument which is undertaken by a few recorder teachers in this country.[3]

This raises two further questions: if the general public does not take the recorder seriously, is it because we have not managed to convince them, or because it does not deserve to be taken seriously? And my second question: if recorder teaching has not managed to become thoroughly professionalised in forty years, will it ever become so?

The recorder at primary level

As a school instrument, recorders are most widely used at primary level, that is, between the ages of six and eleven approximately. Edgar Hunt, in his book *The Recorder and its Music*, says:

The use of the recorder in education is basically right, as it provides instrumental training in melody after rhythm has been taught through percussion instruments. For far too long singing had been the only form of music cultivated in school and it was high time a due balance between the instrumental and vocal was restored.[4]

Most recorder specialists would be in agreement and are happy to see recorders used on these terms. Two elements of the statement should perhaps be emphasised. These are that the recorder 'provides instrumental training in melody *after rhythm has been taught*' (my italics) and that the use of them restored a 'due balance' between instrumental and vocal music. The problems arise when instruction is in the hands of non-specialists who do not understand that the recorder is not a tool for teaching music, but one of developing musical skills already acquired. Referring to the first summer courses for teachers which commenced in 1948, Hunt said 'the music comes first and the recorder is treated as a means of making music rather than as an "educational" weapon'.[5]

Since the recorder first began to be used in schools, teaching methods in all countries have changed considerably, reflecting an overall trend away from class music instruction and towards a one-to-one, child-centred approach. This is not how the recorder was first used in education, however. In Britain, for instance, until the 1950s and 60s most children were taught recorder as a class of anything from thirty to fifty or more pupils, with no concessions to ability or level of interest. One of the most immediate problems in the customary formal classroom layout of the time was a physical one. Classrooms had fixed wooden desks and the children of necessity played seated at them, with no elbow-room and no music stands. Articles giving advice on recorder teaching from this time – clearly aimed at non-specialists – are full of ideas for making cardboard desk-stands to prop the music up, exhortations not to let the children rest the end of their recorder on the tabletop and so on. Instruments were of very mixed quality, made from bakelite, plastic or wood, leading to enormous problems of tuning. The soprano or descant recorder is, of course, the most suitable for children's small hands (a modern distortion, incidentally, of the historical precedent, when the alto was the most popular), but massed soprano recorders, even when brand new and top quality, are notoriously difficult to tune. In this way many people gained an unfortunate impression of the recorder.

Nevertheless, a good teacher produces good results whatever the

Plate 37   Jan Molenaer (*c*1610–1668) *Girl with recorder*. This picture seems to match one of a boy with recorder – equally happy – by his master Frans Hals. Molenaer, his wife Judith Leyster (who stopped painting when she married him) and many other Dutch painters, as well as artists of other nationalities (e.g. pl. 38), frequently painted children with recorders. Two 'primary-school' children, and one 'secondary-school', are shown in this chapter; a university student appears in Plate 5 and there are other youthful associations in Plates 16, 20B and 28. This young lady plays a treble recorder, of the common Dutch seventeenth-century choke-bore design. Francis Bacon in *Sylva Sylvarum* §221 (1627) says, 'The Figure of Recorders, and Flutes, and Pipes are straight; but the Recorder has a less Bore and a greater; Above and below'. Reproduction by kind permission of the Witt Collection, Courtauld Institute, University of London. WB 116

circumstances, and many happy and enthusiastic school recorder bands were established in Britain and Germany in the years immediately before and after the Second World War. Interest spread gradually to other parts of Europe and to the USA, Australia and New Zealand. The recorder magazines of the period provide a fascinating insight into the enthusiasm with which recorder playing was taken up as a school activity. In England the Summer School for Recorder Players began in 1939 as part of the Downe House Summer Schools. In 1948 the Recorder in Education Summer Course, still running successfully today, was founded, and contemporary accounts speak of the enthusiasm with which participants from Britain and abroad joined to play together, taking new ideas home to put into practice in many other countries. In Germany there was a proliferation of such courses: the Arbeitskreis für Hausmusik organised nineteen courses of a week each during the summer months of 1950, for instance. Tutors included Ferdinand Conrad, among others, and the purposes were stated as

demonstrating the various ways of performing old music, and at providing an opportunity of getting to know and understand modern music by playing or listening. ... The objects of these schools, so far as the recorder is concerned, were expressed to be the improvement of technique and the raising of recorder playing above the level of mere dilettantism....[6]

In Germany, the very widespread use of the recorder in the Youth movements had given it a strong and early start. Recorder-making and the publishing of music for it was begun in the 1930s and re-established after the war. The Moeck subscription series, *Zeitschrift für Spielmusik*, founded in 1932, for instance, has been producing old and new music for pedagogical purposes ever since.

Elsewhere in Europe, the recorder became established more slowly. In France, to judge from an article written by the French player and teacher Jean Henry, there was little school or amateur recorder playing, and no professional performance either, even as late as 1961.[7] The situation in the Netherlands was closer to that of Germany, however, with fairly widespread use of the recorder in schools and among amateurs, an active early-music movement, and several enthusiastic performers and teachers such as Kees Otten and Joannes Collette.

The recorder at second level

When a student reaches second level (twelve to eighteen years) that great peril of the recorder teacher always threatens: students (or their parents) decide it is time to take up 'a real instrument'. This is more likely to happen, of course, where opportunities to play in consort groups and with other instruments are not available, and if provisions

Plate 38 Nathaniel Hone (1718–84) *The Artist's Son* (like pl. 32, reproduced by kind permission of the National Gallery of Ireland, Dublin). A favourite of the writer of this chapter! The boy with his big brown eyes and furry jacket plays a descant recorder, but not the jointed baroque model flaunted by grown-up aristocratic Irishmen, as in Plate 32. New designs were by no means immediately and universally adopted. Near-cylindrical early renaissance-type recorders were still being depicted in seventeenth-century paintings, and in Baglione's *Euterpe* of 1620 (frontispiece to *Playing Recorder Sonatas*), and choke-bore instruments seem to have persisted in Holland even after the innovatory designs of Richard Haka, and of the Hotteterres and their contemporaries (see pl. 35) had become popular in England. When the Dutch artist Edwaert Collier worked in London around 1693 he painted the new baroque recorders instead of, as before, the Dutch *hand-fluit* model; he may have seen the new French recorders on an earlier visit to London in 1676 (see p. 169).

for teaching hours and facilities are inadequate it can be difficult to provide these. No one wants to prevent talented teenagers from playing orchestral instruments, but there is no reason why a bright student should not, with encouragement, also play an orchestral instrument.

In both Germany and France the system of state music schools and third-level music institutions now established creates a much more methodical and professional approach to recorder teaching. The pupil attends a special music school outside normal school hours, receiving tuition in theory of music, perhaps also joining a choir and a consort group, in addition to recorder lessons. A teacher cannot obtain a post in one of these schools without proper qualifications gained after specialist studies. In Britain, it was acknowledged at the Early Music in Europe Conference referred to above that early music has hardly impinged at all on second-level education. In the 1970s and 80s instrumental teaching flourished in British schools with the provision of an excellent system of peripatetic, or visiting, instrumental specialists which made music lessons available to all children free of charge. Financial cutbacks in the late 1980s devastated this service, however, and the days are now returning when only those who can afford to pay have music lessons. In the USA there is no unified approach and the recorder is not taught in state schools unless an interested teacher is prepared to establish a recorder programme.

The recorder at third level

At third level it becomes clear that, so far as the recorder is concerned, the countries where systematic music teaching is provided throughout all levels of formal education are those with healthy numbers of third-level recorder students and consequently, of course, professional players and properly trained teachers. The difference between music education systems in various countries shows up directly not only in the numbers of first-study recorder players but in their level of attainment when they enter the conservatory and in their job prospects as recorder players when they graduate. Even allowing for socio-cultural influences, there are considerably more full-time third-level recorder students in continental Europe than there are in Britain, the USA, Australia or New Zealand.

As an example, in Germany in the 1991/92 academic year, one regional Musikhochschule (conservatory) in a city of 300,000 inhabitants had more first-study recorder students than there were in all of the conservatories in Britain put together. In the academic as opposed to the performance sector, a recent study of university and polytechnic (as they then were) music departments[8] in Britain offering specialist

Plate 39   Gerard van Honthorst (1590–1656) *Boy Playing Recorder* (private collection, Bremen). This serious young man practises his descant recorder, although he has yet to learn a good upper-hand position (the knuckles are too bent and the thumb too flat) – it is immaterial that he is a 'left-hand-down' player. Many seventeenth-century pictures have symbolic meanings, such as representations of Hearing, of *Vanitas* (see p. 45, note 8) and of the transitory joys of music. In the Rijksmuseum at Amsterdam there is a pastoral picture by Honthorst of a shepherd playing the recorder to four decidedly erotic nymphs, combining two of the instrument's symbolic associations – three, if nymphs are supernatural beings.

early-music courses showed that, where instrumental studies formed part of a basically academic course, most departments had between forty and sixty students taking early music, but the average number of recorder players among them was only three per department. Several major universities and polytechnics which were willing to accept and provide tuition for recorder students actually had no applicants.

In Germany, the system of well-funded Musikhochschulen with excellent facilities provides a very thorough and methodical training. And the opportunities for study provided for school-age musicians are so good that by the time a student gets to the Hochschule, he or she will already as a general rule be a highly accomplished player. All major conservatories in Europe now have at least one professionally qualified recorder teacher on the staff, probably more. In the bigger institutions this is usually someone with an active performing career, thus conferring an equal status on the recorder faculty to that accorded any other instrument. Major conservatories in the Netherlands, Germany and Switzerland now require the same high standards of performance and theoretical knowledge from a recorder player that they do of any other instrumentalist. Competition for places is fierce, and standards have risen dramatically over the last thirty years. It is noteworthy, for instance, that students nowadays perform pieces for their entrance auditions which hitherto would have been set for the final examination.

In the USA, where the recorder scene is strongly amateur-based, the opportunities for third-level study are very limited and activity is centred on the strong early-music department at the University of Indiana, an active music community in the Bay area of the West Coast and the schools of music of a number of East-Coast colleges.

The Netherlands is, of course, the Mecca for aspiring recorder players, and the performing and teaching tradition established by Frans Brüggen and subsequently developed by Walter van Hauwe and Kees Boeke has been vital here. Several generations of recorder enthusiasts were won over to the instrument by Brüggen's playing, and he was the first teacher of modern times to refuse to make any concessions to its supposed limitations. If it was a serious instrument, he believed, it needed serious study to play it well, and that included serious study of technique. Walter van Hauwe's major series of technical manuals, *The Modern Recorder Player*,[9] is a distillation of all the thinking on teaching methods that he began to try to codify when he and Kees Boeke were students in Brüggen's class, and developed when he began to teach students of his own. This method has been highly influential, proposing and developing a new and carefully judged progression from the most elementary (but frequently ignored) aspects of technique through to the very highest complexities.

Competitions

There are now a number of well-established competitions for aspiring professional players. Recorders do not always compete with other instruments in high-level events, and one of the few which does allow recorders to enter is the ARD Internationaler Musikwettbewerb in Munich.[10] This has a recorder category every ten years, the first held in 1978, and has a high-profile jury of professional players and very good prize-money. Of the major early-music competitions, that of the Musica Antiqua Competition in Bruges[11] is the best known. Although the prize-money is moderate, the prestige is considerable and the competition functions as a shop-window for new talent. It has both a solo and a consort class and it was here that the now world-famous Amsterdam Loeki Stardust Quartet launched its career. Like any international music competition, it offers the competitor a chance to be noticed by top-level teachers serving on the jury as well as by promoters and agents. A win will probably lead to a recording contract, concert bookings or a teaching job. The biennial Calw[12] competition is for recorders alone and is considered very prestigious within that community. With a first prize of DM 5000 plus a CD recording, this is worth winning. A new international competition has recently been established at Karlsruhe,[13] in conjunction with the now biennial Recorder Symposium.

The adult amateur

A major area for the recorder in education is that of amateur music-making. The appeal of the recorder for the adult late-starter or amateur hobby player is a combination of its relative simplicity together with its portability, and the availability of good-quality but inexpensive plastic instruments. This means that a keen beginner can acquire the basic equipment for a very modest outlay and can enjoy making music without the necessity of major modifications to his or her living space, or complex negotiations with neighbours over practice hours. Furthermore, recorders require no particular physical strength. The amateur recorder world is particularly active in Britain, the Netherlands, Australia and the USA, although players are to be found scattered in every corner of the globe. In the USA, provisions for amateurs are very good, with many regional Chapters of the American Recorder Society co-ordinating meetings and workshops which are generally led by professionals.

The recorder orchestra

The recorder orchestra is a concept that has achieved some success in Britain in recent years. Not to be confused with straightforward 'massed playing', where the balance of instruments playing each part is not a factor, and the music is from the ordinary consort repertoire, the recorder orchestra seeks to emulate all the features of a symphony or chamber orchestra, and it is a particularly good outlet for competent players who prefer group to solo playing. The standard grouping is forty to fifty people arranged in carefully balanced instrumental sections, each with an independent line of its own, a sectional leader and a permanent assignment of players to desks. The overall effect is not unlike that of an organ and can be particularly attractive when there are sufficient great and contrabasses. The recorder orchestra is most effective when playing specially composed music which brings out its best features. Recorder orchestras are as yet largely unknown outside Britain.

Recorder societies

There are many active recorder societies in addition to the American Recorder Society already mentioned. Among these are The Society of Recorder Players in the British Isles, the Società Italiana del Flauto Dolce, the Huismuziek organisation in the Netherlands, which caters for all amateur musicians including recorder players, the Association Française pour la Flute à Bec, and in Australia the Victorian Recorder Guild of Melbourne among others. Some of these societies publish magazines which, over the years, have provided an accumulated body of scholarship, as well as social documentation.

For professional players and teachers, the newly formed European Recorder Teachers' Association is a professional body basing itself on the successful models of the European Piano Teachers' Association and the European String Teachers' Association. With national branches already formed in Germany, Britain,[14] Austria, the Netherlands and Switzerland, it will seek to draw together teachers, performers, students, instrument-makers, composers and others with an interest in raising the recorder's status in mainstream musical life. This foundation suggests the beginning of a recognition that the works and aims of the amateur and the professional are essentially different.

Conclusion

The recorder is indeed easier to learn than many other instruments, but no one who has played it would minimise the skill needed to co-ordinate fingering, tonguing and breathing in such a way as to produce a pleasant and musical sound. It does, of course, have an important part to play in music education, but this should be as an instrument in its own right on which to put into practice skills acquired first through those most natural forms of human musical expression, singing and simple percussion. With a strong growth recently in professional playing and teaching, are we now at the peak of the redevelopment of the recorder, or is there further to go? The recorder seems to be going out of fashion as an introduction to music in schools, superseded by the now ubiquitous synthesiser. The amateur movement, many would say, has lost momentum and has not progressed with the times. The age-profile of amateur players is getting higher and higher, and young professionals are not being drawn into participation in the recorder societies. In the early years of the century everyone was, of necessity, a pioneer. Today, the 'frontier spirit' has gone, but has it been replaced by any other sustaining force?

Notes

1. Eve O'Kelly, 'Early music in Europe', *The Recorder Magazine* 12/2 (June 1992), p. 37.
2. G. Dodgson, 'On not taking the recorder too seriously', *The Recorder News*, New Series no. 8 (April 1953).
3. Peter Bowman, 'The teacher's lot', *The Recorder Magazine* 13/1 (March 1993), pp. 19–20.
4. London 1962; rev. edn 1977, p. 143.
5. *The Recorder and its Music*, p. 143.
6. 'News from abroad', *The Recorder News*, New Series no. 2 (Oct. 1950).
7. Jean Henry, 'The recorder in France', *The Recorder News*, New Series no. 35 (Nov. 1961–Jan. 1962), pp. 4–5.
8. Patricia O'Sullivan, 'The recorder in the universities: update', *The Recorder Magazine* 12 (Sept. 1992), pp. 67–8.
9. 3 vols. (London 1984, 1987 and 1992).
10. Organised by Bayerischer Rundfunk, W-8000 München 2, Germany.
11. Organised by Festival van Vlaanderen-Brugge, Collaert Mansionstraat 30, B-8000 Bruges, Belgium.
12. Calw Recorder Competition, Musikschule Calw, Lederstr. 38, Pf. 1361, 7260 Calw, Germany.
13. International Recorder Competition, Staatliche Hochschule für Musik, Karlsruhe, Germany.
14. European Recorder Teachers' Association in the U.K.: Peter Bowman, 4 Heathleigh Cottages, Maidstone Road, Horsmonden, Kent TN12 8JL.

13 Facsimiles and editing

CLIFFORD BARTLETT

Musical notation is an imprecise means of conveying information. It assumes that rhythm and pitch change by discrete, clearly measurable steps. Articulation and the grouping of notes are, especially in earlier music, indicated very imprecisely, if at all. The full subtlety of dynamic change cannot be shown on paper, even in modern pieces with dynamic signs on every note. In fact, the less the notation shows, the easier it is to read and to distinguish the essentials as determined by the composer from matters which may vary from performance to performance and which are more the concern of the performer. Over the last 200 years composers have tried to notate aspects of performance in greater and greater detail. But during the renaissance and baroque periods composers could assume that players would understand the style in which they were working and could flesh out the bare bones they notated.[1] Hence the need for ornamentation; hence too the existence of editions which try to help the less-knowledgeable modern performer.

Recorder players have an advantage over other performers of early music since their repertoire, by going underground for a century or two, missed the period when interpretative editions were most extravagant. So they are spared having to disentangle the excess of (mostly unstylish) additions which make many older editions of keyboard and violin music so confusing to read. Even were such accretions a true guide to stylish playing there is a great danger in relying on them, since they ultimately lead to a loss of historically informed creativity. (If that is not something which gives you pleasure, you are probably studying the wrong instrument.) You cannot approach the ideas of a composer unless you can react to them directly rather than through an intermediary, however well meaning.

It might appear that the ideal is always to play from a facsimile of the composer's manuscript. This is rarely possible or desirable. For a start, very few survive. In the case of Handel, we are lucky. He carefully kept them together during his lifetime and bequeathed them to his assistant

J. C. Smith, from whom they passed to the Royal Library and then to the British Museum.[2] Bach was less fortunate: the manuscripts were divided among his family, and much was lost. The lion's share went to the eldest son, W. F. Bach, who sold them off item by item when he was hard up; that so much of Bach's output still survives is due chiefly to his widow Anna Magdalene and to Carl Philipp Emanuel. Bach autographs are plentiful when compared with earlier composers, and holographs of the less famous generally only survive if they were employed by a court with well-organised archives that have escaped damage by war or revolution.

Even when autographs exist, there are problems. First, can they easily be read? An example of Handel's handwriting is reproduced on page 58. There is no difficulty in reading it at a desk; but would you really be happy to play it *Furioso*? The correction at the beginning of the second system needs disentangling, and the way the bar lines at the end of the first bar of the first two systems follow on from each other makes it easy for the eye to be led to the wrong staff. Furthermore, the accompanist has to be able, not only to read figured bass, but to be happy with quick changes to the tenor clef.

There is also the possibility that the autograph is not the most accurate version of the music. Composers can make mistakes, especially when working at speed. They may also subsequently make corrections. When Handel was writing an opera, once he had produced a complete score, he had his assistant make a working copy and subsequent changes were made, not to the autograph, but to the copyist's score. A facsimile of the autograph, therefore, gives only a partial picture of Handel's composing activity. His working pattern with instrumental music is less clear, but at some stage the Furioso in the autograph just mentioned changed to the Presto of the later sources.

An alternative is to use a facsimile of a contemporary edition. This then raises the question of its authority. Occasionally the composer took responsibility for the publication (Telemann frequently was his own publisher), so one can assume that it basically represented his intentions, allowing for an occasional misprint. But the relation between composer and publisher was often uneasy, if not downright hostile. Handel eventually came to terms with John Walsh, but not before Walsh had issued a fair number of unauthorised editions (including the recorder sonatas). When there are musically plausible discrepancies between autograph and edition, which should we follow? Few players have time to compare sources; that is one reason why we need editors.

Over the last century or so, the techniques at the disposal of editors have become more and more sophisticated.[3] Scholars study the documents themselves as physical objects, identify the individuals who worked on them to seek personal characteristics that might affect their way of writing or printing, compare all sources, and deduce a pattern of relationship between them. They can then offer an edition which represents an ideal version, arguably better than a simple reproduction of any single source (though the method has limitations when the work to which it is applied never had a fixed form).

These techniques are immensely valuable in editing music by composers like Josquin des Prez, where there is often a bewildering number of sources, none with any intrinsic authority. But the time spent by the editors on accumulating and analysing the available information is so enormous that only one volume of his new *Collected Works* has so far appeared.[4] There has been a reaction against this elaboration of methodology, and some have argued that it is better to use a single source which we know someone once played rather than attempt to construct a composite which may never have existed. A compromise is to take one version as copy text, preserving its individuality but correcting obvious errors, and, of course, listing variants.

The discrepancies between sources, however, should not be exaggerated. In most recorder sonatas, mistakes are few and self-evident. Luckily, the most common one (writing a note so that it is not clear whether it is on a line or in a space) generally makes musical nonsense and can be corrected without controversy, and music is often built on the repetition of small units so that careless slips can readily be spotted (see p. 72, note 29), though one must beware of over-tidily correcting what is legitimate variety.

It is important that, if you are studying a piece of music, you know the reliability of what lies before you. It was in reaction against the bad old editions which tried to give early music the notational detail of nineteenth- and twentieth-century music that the German term *Urtext* came into use. As far as it goes it is helpful, meaning an edition with no interpretative additions, though it begs the question of the accuracy of the edition itself. In practice it has tended to be used for reprints from out-of-copyright collected-work editions (e.g. of Bach and Handel) which have been outmoded by more careful work on the sources. It represents a negative concept, good in itself but without any implications of the positive qualities of an edition.

Apart from establishing a correct text, editors often feel the need to include additional assistance to performers. Sometimes they just tidy up the inconsistencies, just as Cambridge University Press's copy-editor will tidy up what I am writing now. But they need to make all except the most trivial changes apparent to the player. Dynamics added when the original shows a clear but not fully realised pattern should be typographically distinguishable from original ones. The extrapolation of original phrasing marks is acceptable, provided editorial slurs are shown (either by being dotted or by having a small line across them), though it is tedious if a few original slurs are repeated lavishly through a whole movement; players should be able to take a hint. The wise player will take far more seriously a couple of original slurs written by the composer in the opening bars of a movement than any systematic phrasing added by an editor. Suggestions for rhythmic changes used to be added quite frequently, but editors are now more wary; the way performances of double-dotting in French overtures have changed over the last few years is a cautionary tale.[5] Adjusting conflicting rhythmic patterns is often advisable in performance, but best suggested in general terms, either in the introduction or a footnote, not marked explicitly every time it occurs.

How much else an editor should add depends on the nature of the music and the purpose of the edition. There is certainly a case for editions for beginners that spell out some aspects of performance practice. Breathing/phrasing marks, for instance, can be useful, and there is good precedent for providing suggestions for embellishment. It is the more sophisticated sorts of free embellishment that are demonstrated in works like Telemann's *Sonate metodiche*,[6] not detailed suggestions for playing cadential ornaments; it is better to follow baroque usage and include a prefatory table of these rather than try to indicate them in the score.[7] The balance has to be drawn between offering help and cluttering the page with so much information that it is counter-productive. For most editions, other than those explicitly didactic, such matters are best left to the player. If the editor feels that he needs to offer advice, the place for that is in his introduction or, if that threatens to grow out of proportion, in a separate book.[8] This is partly because the player needs to find his own solutions for himself, partly because there is not always a single right way of doing things. Turning back to the Handel example already mentioned (p. 58), the phrasing of the recorder's semiquavers needs to relate to the continuo scales in bar 1, either by copying them or by a significant contradiction; but how they are phrased will depend, not only on the understanding of the performer, but on whether they are played by cello, gamba and/or harpsichord. An editor cannot anticipate this. All he can do is set down the evidence of the sources. On economic grounds, anyway, such caution will give his product a longer shelf-life; our ideas of how to play early music are changing more quickly than advances in editorial techniques.

More and more baroque recorder music is being published, both in apparently good editions and in facsimile. How should the player choose what to buy? The crucial point concerns, not the recorder player, but the accompanist. Whether you play solos or trios, to play from facsimiles you will need a keyboard player who can read figured bass. Players of the time seem to have found this no problem. Apart from examples for educational purposes, no sonatas or trios survive with keyboard realisations. (Sonatas with genuine keyboard parts, like Bach's six violin sonatas, are a different genre.) If they could play from the bass, so can we. It is, however, possible to use a cello, bass viol or bassoon instead of keyboard; sometimes a bass recorder will work (as in pl. 40), at least for domestic playing. But the range is often too great, and some sonatas are better two-part counterpoint than others, so you will need to experiment.

If you have a choice of realisations, what should you look for? Primarily, some sign that the editor is aware that the main function of a continuo player is to play the bass. The degree of movement in the right hand should be roughly in line with the movement of the bass. Fussy right-hand parts that interfere with that should be avoided. However tied to the notes on the page, a harpsichordist will need to vary the frequency and thickness of the chords to match the recorder-player's interpretation, and an elaborate contrapuntal part for the right hand will make this more difficult. The treble should not go too high; the rule of keeping within the staff – imagining soprano rather than treble clef, so the note above the top line is *e″*, not *g″* – should rarely be broken. Treat a part that looks 'composed' with suspicion. It may well work for the person who wrote it, but will probably sound stilted and irrelevant from the hands of someone else.[9]

There were standard formats in the eighteenth century in which music was published. 'Solos' (as sonatas for one instrument and continuo were usually termed in English) appeared in score on two staves, looking virtually indistinguishable from harpsichord music. Copies seem to have been sold singly, not in pairs, and iconographical evidence concurs that all three players shared one copy placed on the harpsichord's music stand.[10] Trios, however, appeared in part-books. In the seventeenth century, there were often separate parts for the cello/gamba and the keyboard (both Purcell's sets, for example, despite their differing titles), but later a single bass part was normal.[11] This distinction is not preserved in modern editions, which for both genres usually comprise score and parts.[12] So the solo player does not have the advantage of seeing the bass line.[13]

Accidentals may be a problem. The modern convention of an accidental lasting throughout a bar was not established until the nineteenth century, but it cannot always be assumed in earlier notation that every note that should have an accidental will have one. The modern performer needs to know the status of each accidental, and it is difficult to formulate an editorial policy that can do this without being too obtrusive. For sixteenth- and some seventeenth-century music it is sensible to retain every accidental, but that is rarely done in editions of eighteenth-century music, and editors sometimes modernise without noting possible ambiguities.[14] Those who play from facsimile

Plate 40 Bass recorder (though this could possibly be a sordun), in a breathtakingly dangerous playing position, as part of a basso continuo (see also pl. 26). It joins the bass viol in supporting flute and oboe in a trio-sonata ensemble; obviously there would be no room for a harpsichord, even if it were felt to be needed. This is a detail from a fresco (c1730) *The Heavenly Feast of the Just*, by Siard Nosecký (1693–1753), in the summer refectory of the monastery at Strahov, Prague (pl. 164 of *The History of Czech Music in Pictures*, Editio Supraphon, Prague 1977). As late as c1775 a Nuremberg engraving shows a bass recorder and bass viol, with harpsichord, as the basso continuo for a Collegium Musicum performance of a cantata with three singers, three violins, two trumpets and three woodwinds – possibly including recorder(s) as one is seen hanging on the wall, with two violins, in the background.

must make allowances for different conventions, not only in the length for which an accidental is valid, but for the use of flats to cancel sharps and vice versa. Editors should resist the temptation to modernise archaic key signatures (such as F minor with three flats); any change exacerbates the difficulty in indicating each inflection and may also involve renotating the bass figuring.

So far, most of what I have said refers primarily to solos or trio-sonatas of the eighteenth century. The seventeenth-century repertoire specifically for recorders is comparatively small (though there is plenty of music that can be played on them), so we now turn to the sixteenth century, and to music chiefly for ensembles.[15] Here the difference between original and modern notation is far greater; playing from facsimiles is not to be undertaken lightly but offers a greater satisfaction. There are some ways in which the player can prepare himself for that step. Most editions of renaissance music aimed at recorder players have their note-values halved or quartered, and a page of white notes can be a shock to the unprepared. So it is worth getting used to this by seeking out editions that preserve original values. These are mostly of vocal music, and it is anyway a very good idea to play music with words – they offer invaluable guidance to how the music should be phrased.[16]

The next stage is to get used to clefs other than the treble and bass. This is something that recorder players seem extraordinarily reluctant to undertake. Sackbut players have no difficulty reading octave-treble, alto, tenor or bass. Surely recorder players are not less intelligent than brass players? Without breaking through this limitation, it is impossible to get anywhere near thinking about music in the way players did 400 years ago. When we learn to read music, we learn that the middle line of the staff is *b'* when there is a treble clef, *d* when there is a bass clef. The renaissance attitude was different: the clef is to tell you, not what the note is, but where the semitones lie, and the notes were named by the solmisation system that indicated this. If the modern player approaches clefs in that manner, rather than trying to learn the notes separately for each C clef in the modern way, he will then be able to master another skill – transposition. For us, it is a problem as we have to rethink each note. But there is no difficulty if one is playing according to a pattern of tones and semitones. Scholars are gradually beginning to work out what pitch renaissance music was played at, and it is clear that players regularly adjusted the notated pitch to accord with the compass of their instruments.[17] Modern editions can make the necessary adjustment, but the editor can only make one choice, which may be the wrong one for the instruments available to you.[18]

Most modern editions of renaissance music for recorders are of short pieces set out in score. Players need to be proficient at reading from parts. One way of starting is to use editions of consort music prepared for viol players, who prefer parts in original note-values. Players of the middle parts will need to have mastered the alto clef, though otherwise clefs are not yet a problem.[19] There is then the difficulty of learning aspects of mensural notation which differ from modern rhythmical signs. The best step here is to get hold of one of the 'Renaissance Standards' series edited by Richard Taruskin and published by Arnold Grayson (now sadly out of print). Each of the nine volumes takes one of the ubiquitous tunes which were used by a variety of composers around 1500 and presents them in modern score, while the parts use the original notation but in clear modern printing. Each volume also contains an invaluable four-page guide to the notation. This looks more fearsome than it is, since if you confine yourself at first to music from later in the sixteenth century few of the complexities will arise in any single piece. But it is useful to keep on your music stand for quick reference when playing from any renaissance facsimiles.

By this time, players will have surmounted some of the main hurdles of playing from sixteenth-century editions (leave manuscripts till later). The next stage is to try some simple examples, perhaps of music that is already familiar (Susato, Moderne or Phalèse dances, for instance).[20] It is best to start with pieces in short sections so that anyone who gets lost does not have long to wait to know where the other players have reached. Then try more complicated music; the advantage of the Moderne collection is that it contains contrapuntal pieces as well as dances.[21]

Not everyone will wish to embark on the difficult but rewarding road towards playing from renaissance notation. The advantage is a greater understanding of how the minds of composers and musicians worked, a greater flexibility in applying music to the instruments, and access to a vast, unpublished repertoire. It is also much easier to see the shape of a melodic line when it is set out as closely compacted as it normally is in original part-books.[22]

Those preferring to stay with modern editions, however, have a wealth of material to choose from.[23] The criteria are slightly different from those for the baroque period. A sign to look for is whether there are preliminary staves, showing the original time and key signatures and the first note of the original – though beware of editions that follow the form but not the purpose and fail to give the crucial information about the notation of triple time later in the piece. If you do not know the original notation, you can only guess the correct proportional change, and relationship indications added by editors cannot always be trusted.[24] It also helps if the range of each part is given. I would avoid editions that have fussy, irregular barring, except for certain lighter forms where there is a strong metrical pulse from the text. *Mensurstrich* – placing the barlines, between rather than through the staves – gives some degree of freedom to the individual lines, but many find it an unsatisfying compromise between score and parts. Scores that survive from the renaissance period are barred.

An important part of the renaissance instrumentalist's repertoire was vocal music, and the modern player should not restrict his choice to music explicitly for instruments. While there are fine instrumental pieces from the later fifteenth and sixteenth centuries, there are far greater riches among the thousands of Masses, motets, madrigals, chansons and Lieder (see Chap. 2). As mentioned elsewhere, the great advantage of music with an underlaid text is that the words guide the playing. I cannot understand why vocal music is arranged for recorders and published with the words omitted; such editions should be avoided on principle. Beware of vocal editions that have been transposed. Renaissance music was not written for the modern SATB choir, and editors often transpose to make the music more suitable for such forces. Transposition by a tone may produce an edition useful for recorder players, but many editors of English church music have an infuriating habit of transposing up a minor third, producing multi-flat keys.

It is worth being aware of the original clef conventions, since they may show at a glance whether a piece will fit the consort at hand. Virtually all sixteenth-century music was written with two patterns of clefs, conveniently called high and low. These represent, not two different pitch levels, but two ways of writing music that would sound at the same pitch. In practical terms, though, the low clefs require a consort with *F* as the lowest note, while the high clefs rarely require a bass below *c*. Low-clef pieces can generally be played with the normal octave transposition, but consorts with a great bass in C can play high-clef pieces at eight-foot pitch.[25]

Early clef combinations with modern ranges

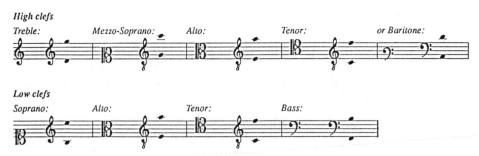

Moving back to the medieval period, we encounter even greater problems for those wishing to use the original notation. Editions aimed at recorder players are few, so those interested in finding repertoire should turn to the many publications directed primarily towards musicologists. There is no need to concentrate solely on the small number of pieces that are specifically instrumental, as all kinds of vocal music can be played on instruments. Arguments that they were not acceptable in church do not imply that they could not play religious music elsewhere, and there is no need to assume that all music with sacred words was intended specifically for liturgical use.[26]

Little is known about how medieval music was performed, so much is left to the player's imagination. There are only a few dances extant,[27] but there are plenty of songs in Provençal, Galician, French, German, Italian and Latin that can be used as a basis for improvisation. Here facsimiles are useful and help in getting beyond the rigid triple-time notation into which they have so often been transcribed. Whether any of them were played by instruments which we would define as recorders may be doubted (see p. 30), but monophonic songs provide music that is satisfying for the solitary player, needing no accompaniment and being basically simple (so playable by beginners) but permitting elaboration to a degree limited only by the player's skill and fancy.

Many recorder players may think that the suggestions made in this chapter are too demanding. But those who have read the rest of this book are clearly taking the recorder and its music seriously. It is, of course, important to take great care of your instruments and work hard on your technique. But the complete recorder player needs to exercise his mind as well as his fingers and breathing. Some aim to play as nearly as possible in the manner of the time when the music was written; others strive rather to interpret the music in a way that will communicate its meaning to a modern audience in a more contemporary way. But all need to understand what the composer was trying to say. However much we study performance practice from modern books, nothing brings us so close to early composers and performers as reading the music in the way they wrote and read it.

Notes

1. Bach and other composers sometimes wrote out embellishments, but still left most other matters of performance practice unnotated.
2. Seven volumes of sketches and shorter works, including some recorder sonatas, found their way to the collection of Viscount Fitzwilliam and are now in the Fitzwilliam Museum in Cambridge.
3. Textual criticism developed primarily in the study of the Bible and of Greek and Roman literature, and first played a significant part in musical editions with the preparation for the *Neue Bach-Ausgabe* after the Second World War.
4. *The Collected Works of Josquin des Prez* (New Josquin Edition), vol. 27: *Secular Works for Three Voices*, ed. Jaap van Benthem and Howard Mayer Brown (Utrecht,

Vereniging voor Nederlandse Muziekgeschiedenis, 1987), also separate critical commentary, 1991. This is a volume with much music of interest for recorder players, though it is badly set out with no regard to sensible page-turns.

5. Until recently, editors were expected to give explicit guidance on how the long notes should be extended and the short notes made shorter. There has been some musicological sniping at the concept, and the problem has been minimised by two factors – the existence of a wide body of players who settle such details by ear rather than by eye, and the much faster tempo at which overtures are now played.

6. Georg Philipp Telemann, *Sonate metodiche* ... (Hamburg 1728), and *Continuation des Sonates Méthodiques* ... (Hamburg 1732); edition transposed for recorders by Bernard Thomas (Brighton, Dolce Edition 1990). The elaborate written-out embellishment of many of Bach's slow movements also leave cadential ornaments to the player.

7. There are many examples; the most frequently reproduced is that which Bach prefaced to the *Clavier-Büchlein vor Wilhelm Friedemann Bach* (complete facsimile, New Haven, Yale University Press, 1959), which is similar to examples in several French keyboard publications. In general, notational signs for keyboard are more specific than signs for other instruments.

8. A good example is Anthony Rowland-Jones, *Playing Recorder Sonatas: Interpretation and Technique* (Oxford 1992).

9. Bach's practice, as described by, for example, Johann Friedrich Daube in 1756, is rather different (see *Dokumente zum Nachwirken Johann Sebastian Bachs 1750–1800 (Supplement zu Johann Sebastian Bach Neue Ausgabe Sämtliche Werke, 3)* (Cassel, Bärenreiter, 1972), p. 111; translated in Hans T. David and Arthur Mendel, *The Bach Reader* (London, Dent, 1966), p. 216). But Bach's practice was *sui generis*, and seems to have been at least in part a way of teaching counterpoint rather than just as accompaniment.

10. The article on Michel Corrette in *The New Grove* quotes a revealing anecdote from his *Méthode pour apprendre à jouer de la contre-basse* (1773). 'I suppose it is unnecessary to warn those who wear glasses to have some for distance vision. I remember having been at a concert in a little town in England where I saw a trio of spectacles at the harpsichord. Each of the players was competing for the closest position to the music desk. After the heads had knocked against one another, the singer, who was a castrato newly arrived from Italy and who was having difficulty seeing in spite of three pairs of glasses on his nose, had the idea of sitting astride the harpsichordist's hump-back. This advantage didn't last long, because the archlute player at one side of the grotesque group had – unfortunately for him – a wooden leg; and as he was playing standing up and in spite of the telescope he wore on his beet-nose saw no better than the others, he contrived through his contortions of beating time now on the castrato's back, now on the harpsichordist's hump, and of signalling the page-turn in Hebrew-fashion for the da capo, to let his wooden leg slip causing them all to fall like Phaeton.' This is obviously a story that has improved in the telling; but it clearly shows that three-to-a-part was normal (and demanded good eyesight) and reminds us that the archlute survived well into the eighteenth century (Corrette's visit to England may have been around 1740). For an example of 'inaccessible music' see plate 41.

11. H. Purcell, *Sonnata's of III Parts* (London 1683) (with parts for *Basso* and *Basso Continuo*) and *Ten Sonata's in Four Parts* (London 1697) (with parts for *Bassus* and *Through Bass for the Harpsichord, or Organ*); facsimiles of both sets published by Performers' Facsimiles, New York. It surprises me that performers never buy two copies of the scores of the facsimiles of violin sonatas that I publish. We avoid the problem in trio-sonatas by always including a second bass part in the set.

12. One exception is Bärenreiter's edition of Handel's sonatas, where a normal score is accompanied by a 'part' comprising both recorder and continuo parts in score; had the figures been included, it would be a useful representation of the eighteenth-century manner of publication.

13. Taking the Handel sonatas as examples, two movements where recorder players are more likely to get the right tempo if they look at the bass parts are the second of the

Plate 41 Chamber (or garden) concert with recorder/oboe, violin, viola, cello and harpsichord, played by 'a group of prominent Italian musicians': Scarlatti, Tartini, Giuseppe Sammartini, Locatelli and Lanzetti. Sammartini plays an instrument that is a cross between an oboe and a recorder, perhaps to show that he played both instruments. 'The location of this engraving, made in Paris at the time of the "*Guerre des bouffons*" (*c*1752–4), is unknown today' (caption from p. 361 of Janet K. Page's 'The hautboy in London's musical life, 1730–1770', *Early Music* 16/3 (August 1988), pp. 358–71; and see also *Early Music* 4/1 (Jan. 1976), p. 17). The import of the verse under this whimsical print is that the music would have been very pretty if the cat had not wanted to sing its part ('Casarelli's cat sings an Italian parody'). The writer implies that Italian opera singers spoil the 'sweet harmony' of the instrumentalists. Of course, the players who are named here would never have formed an ensemble together. The playing position of the cello is found in other (more serious) illustrations of musical performances. Note that this player and the violinist have to manage to share music placed on a table under the harpsichord! The cat, however, has its own music.

    Sonata in A minor and the last of the Sonata in G minor. Some argue that the subtleties of interaction between players are best achieved with good ears and memory; others welcome having the other part in view.
14. The policy Richard Charteris and I established for the King's Music editions of Giovanni Gabrieli, and which I recommend for renaissance and early baroque music, is to preserve all original accidentals except for consecutive notes. Repeating accidentals or adding editorial ones on consecutive notes would look too pedantic; any possible ambiguity is covered by adding a cautionary accidental, an editorial one or noting it in the critical commentary. For eighteenth-century music, this system may confuse the non-specialist, but the editor needs to be aware of the policy of his source and to mark clearly as editorial accidentals those which to the modern eye may seem to be implied but in fact are not.
15. Enthusiasts and specialists will also be using different instruments, the wide-bore renaissance recorders, perhaps with a treble in G rather than F.

16. Those of us old enough to have been brought up on hymn-books that used the minim as their basic note-value have an advantage here. *The Collected Works of Josquin des Prez*, vol. 27 (see note 4) is a fine example of the use of unreduced note-values but with modern clefs. Cheaper are the Kalmus reprints of *Tudor Church Music*. These are a bit small, and could benefit from an enlarging photocopier (there is no copyright infringement: almost by definition, if E. F. Kalmus reprints something, it must be out of copyright); the irregular barring can be a problem at first, though can be considered as a preparation for playing from music with no barlines. The series *Das Chorwerk* (Möseler, but some earlier volumes reprinted more cheaply by Kalmus) is also useful for its use of original note-values and *Mensurstrich*, though the purity of the original notation is sometimes sullied by transposition.

17. The important factor here is the pitch of what is played in relationship to what is notated. Absolute pitch is only relevant when playing with other instruments.

18. Very useful here are the old Collected Works of Palestrina and Lassus that preserve original clefs: C. P. da Palestrina, *Werke*, ed. F. X. Haberl etc. (Leipzig, Breitkopf und Härtel, 1862–1903), subsequent reprint by Gregg Press (but the Kalmus reprint is of the newer edition in modern clefs); O. de Lassus, *Sämtliche Werke*, ed. F. X. Haberl and A. Sandberger (Leipzig, Breitkopf und Härtel, 1894–1926). There are also many other older scholarly editions in such series as *Denkmäler der deutscher Tonkunst* (e.g. the works of Hans Leo Hassler) and *Denkmäler der Tonkunst in Österreich* (Heinrich Isaac or, for the more adventurous, the Trent Codices).

19. Such editions are published by the Viola da Gamba Society of Great Britain, Golden Phoenix/Corda Music, Fretwork, Northwood, PRB. Viol consort music may require a wider range than renaissance recorders can manage.

20. T. Susato, *Het Derde Musyck Boexken* (Antwerp 1551); J. Moderne, *Musique de Joye* (Lyons c1550); P. Phalèse, *Chorearum molliorum* (Antwerp 1583) – all issued in facsimile by Alamire, Peer, Belgium.

21. A modern score of these, a useful crib in case of difficulty, is *Musica nova*, ed. H. Colin Slim, Monuments of Renaissance Music 1 (University of Chicago Press, 1964); repr. Midway Reprint 1975.

22. Of the facsimiles available, most tempting is the twenty-nine-volume series *Renaissance Music in Facsimile* published by Garland in the 1980s; many of the volumes have been available at a cheap rate and are in circulation among facsimile-playing enthusiasts. Particularly suitable for the beginner are vol. 26 (*Trium vocum cantiones centum*, Nuremberg, Petreius, 1541) and vols. 27–9 (*Novum et insigne opus musicum*, Nuremberg, Berg & Neuber, 1558–9), containing sacred music from Josquin up to the mid-sixteenth century in clear prints.

23. The best way to build up a collection of renaissance editions is from the publications of London Pro Musica (15 Rock St, Brighton, BN2 1NF), whose extensive range of editions is astonishing for the combination of musicological acuity, practical experience and cheapness. Recorder players should also be aware of the catalogues of Schott, Moeck and Heinrichschofen.

24. Players who have no inclination to study renaissance notation should still be aware that, until well into the seventeenth century, a change of time signature usually implied a mathematical relationship between the new time and the old. This relationship is usually bar = bar (or, in renaissance terms, the tactus remains the same). During Monteverdi's lifetime we can see a change from this system (which applies in the 1610 *Vespers*) to *L'incoronazione di Poppea*, which has the aria for Amore in Act II scene 13 notated first in duple crotchets and later in triple semibreves; the customary use of longer notes for triple time is preserved, but there is clearly now a note = note rather than bar = bar relationship.

25. The definitive work on why and how these two clef-patterns operated has yet to be written and it is too complicated to address here, especially since the suggestion in the text actually uses the convention in a practical way rather than one which is known to be authentic. An alternative use of the convention is to take the clefs as a guide to whether players should proceed in the normal way, or finger as if for a C instrument on an F one, or vice versa.

26. The development of the motet with secular text from Notre-Dame organa is a clear example of music written for use in church being performed elewhere (see p. 31).
27. The complete dance repertoire is contained in Timothy J. McGee, *Medieval Instrumental Dances* (Bloomington, Indiana U. Press, 1989); a substantial anthology is in *Mediaeval Dance Collection*, ed. Greg Lewin (Wheaton Aston, Stafford, 1993).

14 Guide to further reading

A select bibliography of recent books and some articles in English of special interest to recorder players

ANTHONY ROWLAND-JONES
(with the help of David Lasocki)

Recorder bibliographies

The most useful comprehensive listing in English for recorder players is *The Recorder: A Guide for Players and Researchers* by Richard Griscom and David Lasocki (New York, Garland, 1994). Some of its material has appeared from time to time in bibliographic essays by David Lasocki published in *American Recorder* (hereafter '*AR*'). The first was in the November 1987 issue (24/4, pp. 145–56), followed by updates in March 1990 (31/1, pp. 11–13, 35–42), March 1992 (33/1, pp. 15–19, 38–44), March 1994 (35/2, pp. 5–11, 30–5) and March 1995 (36/2, pp. 9–13, 34–5). David Lasocki said his object was to include 'anything that advances our knowledge of the instrument, its depiction in works of art, its makers, making, players, playing technique, performance practice and repertory, in the past or present. ... I have surveyed books and periodicals in English, Dutch, French, Italian, German and Spanish. ... I wanted to write such a review for several reasons: first as an information service – to draw your attention to, and to summarize, material that you may not have the time or opportunity to read; second, to show how much worthwhile material is being written about the instrument these days all over the world; third, to indicate trends in research; and finally to stimulate further work.' Lasocki's critical summaries of each book, article and thesis are informative and concise.

Other bibliographies appear in books on the recorder. Edgar Hunt's *The Recorder and its Music* (enlarged edn, London, Eulenburg (Faber), 1977, pp. 168–77) is useful but includes no references later than 1975. Hans-Martin Linde's German-orientated list, *The Recorder Player's Handbook* (2nd edn trans. Richard Deveson, London 1991, pp. 136–41), goes up to 1978. The bibliography in Anthony Rowland-Jones's *Playing Recorder Sonatas* (Oxford 1992, pp. 203–7) is more up to date, but does not include references outside those in the text of the book. His earlier *Recorder Technique* (2nd edn Oxford 1986, pp. 153–64), however, contains a select critical bibliography under headings; the section on ornamentation includes music sources. These books are referred to hereafter as 'Hunt', 'Linde', '*PRS*' and '*RT*'.

There is much useful bibliography in the chapter-end notes of the present *Companion*, the most important books and articles being cited more than once. These references are not systematically repeated here, as this is an independent compilation.

The purpose of the present Guide is to list and briefly to comment upon books and articles, mainly in English, published since about 1985 that in the opinion of the compiler may be of particular interest to recorder players. It draws considerably from David Lasocki's reviews in *AR* (hereafter referred to as 'DL 87', 'DL 90', 'DL 92' and 'DL 94') and adds other important articles from *AR* itself. Music editions are not covered. The Guide is rather more concerned with recorder playing, music and interpretation than with individual composers or with recorder-making, players or makers, past or present. With a few exceptions, reference books and general histories of music and of musical instruments are not included, even though they may contain much of interest to recorder players.

Periodicals

The three main recorder periodicals are the quarterly *American Recorder* (from 1994 five times a year), being the journal of the American Recorder Society; *The Recorder* (now subtitled *Australia's Journal of Recorder and Early Music*, '*RV*' in later references) published by the Victorian Recorder Guild, Melbourne, usually annually but sometimes twice a year; and the quarterly *The Recorder Magazine* ('*RM*') now published by Peacock Press but containing a section prepared by the UK Society of Recorder Players. They each range from 'academic-style' short articles – these are occasionally quite long in the case of *AR* or spread across several issues – to reviews of music, books, recordings and concerts, interviews with recorder personalities, and reports of recorder activities and courses. They are unfortunately regarded as too specialist in their subject matter and diverse in the style of their contents to be available in most British academic and public libraries. Even more difficult of access are the newsletter-type journals published by various recorder society branches or chapters, although, as *AR* 34/1 (March 1993) showed in 'A chapter newsletter sampler' (pp. 14–16 and 18), they also contain material of great interest generally to recorder players. Both the American and the British recorder societies publish information booklets on subjects such as recorder care, consort skills, playing for dance, and recorder discography (see DL 94, p. 35), as well as teachers' guides. The UK Society of Recorder Players produces *The Recorder Players' Guide to Composers*, compiled by Bill Longley (1994).

The U.K. branch of the European Recorder Teachers' Association and the American Association of Recorder Teachers each has its own newsletter, but they publish jointly *The Recorder in Education Journal*. The inaugural issue, edited by David Lasocki, appeared in 1994; it contained eleven articles in its 88 pages.

More prestigious and consistently academic journals on early music, which are more often subscribed to by libraries, include, among others, *The Journal of the American Musical Instrument Society*, *The Consort* (Dolmetsch Foundation), *Early Music* (Oxford – '*EM*' in later references), *The Galpin Society Journal*, *Historical Performance: The Journal of Early Music America* (from

1995 to be called *Early Music America*), *Leading Notes* (National Early Music Association (NEMA) UK) and *Performance Practice Review*. Articles relating specifically to the recorder and its music occur only spasmodically in these journals, although there was a recorder issue of *EM* (10/1) in January 1982. A few are referred to in this bibliography, together with selected articles published in the three specialist recorder periodicals since about 1985.

Recorder care and maintenance (the starting point for good playing)

Design and acoustics

Adrian Brown, *The Recorder: a Basic Workshop Manual* (Brighton, Dolce, 1989). This book explains 'daily care and maintenance', remedies for windway clogging, etc., as well as minor surgery for tuning, which should only be attempted by players with confidence and skilled hands. It complements an equally useful earlier book, Edward L. Kottick's *Tone and Intonation on the Recorder* (New York, McGinnis & Marx, 1974). *RV* 17 (Sept. 93, pp. 15–22) has an article called 'The good oil', by Terry Simmons, on recorder oiling; he favours (unboiled) linseed oil while Brown and Rowland-Jones (*RT*, pp. 22–5) favour almond oil, which Quantz recommended for flutes in 1752. See also Linde, pp. 16–19, and p. 124 of this book.

In the June 1992 issue of *RV* (no. 15) John Martin writes on 'Flattening your recorder' (p. 8), and in this (pp. 19–23) and the following issue (no. 16, Dec. 1992, pp. 18–22) Georg Geiger gives his advice as 'The complete recorder para-medic'. 'Recorder voicing and tuning' is also discussed by Laura Beha Joof in *AR* 26/4 (Nov. 1985, pp. 155–9).

John Martin, a physicist, wrote on recorder acoustics for beginners in *RV* 2 (March 1985, pp. 26–9) and *RV* 7 (June 1987, pp. 22–7). His book on the subject was published in 1994 by Moeck (Celle), entitled *The Acoustics of the Recorder*, containing detailed measurements of instruments and mathematical models; it was enthusiastically reviewed by Raymond Dessy in *AR* 35/5 (Nov. 1994, pp. 23–4). Raymond and Lee Dessy summarised the principles of recorder design in *AR* 33/2 (June 1992, pp. 7–14). 'Tuning and acoustics' are also dealt with by Daphne Medley in *RM* 12/4 (Dec. 1992, pp. 99–101), and see also Linde, pp. 1–5. Alec Loretto wrote 'Tuning recorders' in *RM's* 1990 issues (10/1, March, pp. 2–4; 10/2, June, pp. 30–1; and 10/3, Sept., pp. 64–6). Fred Morgan's 'A player's guide to the recorder' is in the June and December 1987 issues of *RV* (no. 6, pp. 1–4, and no. 7, pp. 10–16) – he had also written 'Old recorders – our design heritage' in issue 2 (March 1985, pp. 8–11). Loretto's articles 'Recorder modifications: in search of the expressive recorder' appeared in three consecutive issues of *EM* in 1973 (1/2, April, pp. 107 and 109; 1/3, July, pp. 147–9 and 151; and 1/4, Oct., pp. 229 and 231), and Morgan wrote 'Making recorders based on historical models' in *EM* 10/1 (Jan. 1982, pp. 14–21). The recorder-maker David Ohanessian in *AR* 32/2 (June 1991, pp. 8–10 and 36–7) says 'I couldn't make an exact copy if I tried!'

Woods used in making wind instruments were discussed by Michael G. Zadro in *EM* 3/2–3 (1975: April, pp. 134–6, and July, pp. 249–51), and there is a chart analysing woods used for recorder-making on p. 6 of Hildemarie Peter's *The Recorder: its Traditions and its Tasks* (Berlin 1953, trans. Stanley Godman 1958), a book which has survived the test of time. Alec Loretto discusses the use of New Zealand woods for recorder-making in *Early Music New Zealand* (June 1987, pp. 22–7). See also Philip Levin in *AR* 27/2 (May 1986, pp. 60–3), 'Which wood should I choose?', and Linde, pp. 5–7.

For further bibliography on recorder-making and design, and on past and present recorder-makers, see DL 87, pp. 145–50, DL 90, pp. 36–8, DL 92, pp. 18–19 and 38–41 and DL 94, pp. 11 and 30–4. In particular Lasocki quotes (DL 87, p. 145) a French article defining five types of pre-baroque recorder, including the 'Ganassi' type, as well (p. 149) as Bob Marvin's article in *Continuo* 9/4 (Jan. 1986, pp. 2–7), where the author 'muses on his experiments with different types of renaissance recorders and their suitability for the music of different parts of that period'. DL also refers to articles on recorder pitch, and see also Mark Davenport's article in *AR* 34/1 (March 1993, pp. 7–10), which itself has an excellent bibliography.

Performance practice and interpretation (Renaissance, Baroque, ornamentation, and technique)

Renaissance

Paul Clark, *Adventures in Consort Playing* (Bristol, Allegro, 1993). A fifty-one-page A4 book which, though the author describes it as 'unscholarly' (it isn't), is one of the few which deal specifically with the recorder's 'assumed' renaissance repertoire, including the *Browning* fantasias and Italian canzonas. Like Freda Dinn's *Early Music for Recorders* (London, Schott, 1974) it gives direct assistance to players in tackling pieces from their own repertoire.

Timothy J. McGee, *Medieval and Renaissance Music: a Performer's Guide* (Toronto U. Press 1985). Another book designed to be of practical use to early-music players, especially members of a 'Collegium' playing early music within a specialist degree course. It is a 'must' for any serious consort group, especially mixed ensembles, even though its organisation and some rather categoric statements have been criticised by reviewers. Revwd Anthony Pryer, *EM* 15/1 (Feb. 1987), pp. 79–82.

Elizabeth Phillips and John-Paul Christopher Jackson, *Performing Medieval and Renaissance Music: an Introductory Guide* (New York, Schirmer, 1986 p.b.). Also designed for the early-music Collegium, this book places greater emphasis than McGee on editing problems. Its particular attraction is the substantial section consisting of music examples with performance notes. Useful, even though the recorder is not considered as a participant in this mainly vocal music.

Jeffery T. Kite-Powell (ed.), *A Practical Guide to Historical Performance: the Renaissance* (Early Music America 1989). This compendium by eighteen authors is for directors of early-music ensembles specialising in renaissance music. It deals thoroughly with the role of instruments, though the section on the recorder is brief. Revwd Honey Meconi, *EM* 18/1 (Feb. 1990), pp. 137–8.

Timothy J. McGee, *Medieval Instrumental Dances* (Bloomington, Indiana U. Press, 1989). All forty-seven pre-1430 medieval instrumental dances extant, prefaced by forty-five pages of helpful text and notes. This and the following are part of the Indiana U. Press 'Music Scholarship and Performance' series.

George Houle, *'Doulce memoire': a Study in Performance Practice* (Bloomington, Indiana U. Press, 1990). Twenty-four versions, for various instruments and voices, of Pierre Sandrin's chanson published by Jacques Moderne in Lyons in 1537 or 1538 (cf. pl. 8).

Christopher Page, *Voices and Instruments of the Middle Ages* (London, Dent, and Berkeley, U. of California Press, 1987); Howard Mayer Brown, *Sixteenth-Century Instrumentation* (American Institute of Musicology 1973). These two books by major scholars are given above by their promising main titles; but that of the first continues *Instrumental Practice and Songs in France 1100–1300*, before the recorder came on the scene – the instruments referred to are harp and fiddle (or vielle). The title of the second book continues *The Music of the Florentine Intermedii*, but Chapter VI is entitled 'The principles of sixteenth-century instrumentation'. The frequency of use of different wind instruments in the late sixteenth-century *intermedii* was, first, trombones, then cornetts and transverse flutes, while others such as crumhorns seem to have been reserved for special occasions or effects. Recorders, then in three sizes – G, C and F bass – are referred to on pp. 67–8.

Edmund A. Bowles's bilingual *Musical Performance in the Late Middle Ages* (Geneva, Minkoff, 1983, referred to throughout this *Companion* from its French title as 'Bowles, *Pratique*'). This is a book of musical iconography, with an excellent introduction. Like some other writers, Bowles uses the term 'recorder' for instruments which could have been duct flutes with six (or fewer) holes, or possibly even shawms. As graphic representations cannot easily show both the recorder's thumb-hole and its finger-holes, the distinguishing feature usually has to be the paired little-finger holes, clearly seen, for example, in the Dürer woodcut shown in Plate 42 and in one of the recorders in Ganassi's frontispiece (pl. 29).

Among articles in this subject-area, reference should be made to 'To play or to sing?' by Wendy E. Hancock in *The Consort* 42 (1986, pp. 15–28), to Martin Kaye's 'Cornett in context' in *Continuo* (Jan. 1987) – 'He identifies an effective, and apparently authentic, combination of soft instruments for four-part music as cornett, alto recorder, tenor recorder and bass viol' (DL 90, p. 11) – and to Keith Polk's 'Voices and instruments: soloists and ensembles in the 15th century' in *EM* 18/2 (May 1990, pp. 179–97). None of these articles gives any impression that recorders were widely used in the Renaissance compared, for example, with viols and lutes.

Plate 42 *The Men's Bath House*, woodcut (*c*1496) by Albrecht Dürer (1471–1528).
This is yet another example of the recorder being played beside water (see pls. 4, 10
and 31). Compare the shape of this recorder with those in Plate 29 – see (5) in that
caption. The two holes for the left or right little finger are beautifully clear; in this case,
for a 'right-hand-down' player, the left hole would have been blocked with wax. The
unusually shaped fiddle is held against 'the small ribs' as advocated for the violin by
Nicola Matteis 200 years later. With only a fiddle and a recorder, the former may have
played a drone to the recorder's melody. For drinking beer as an accompaniment to
recorder playing see also Plates 22 and 23B! WB 77

The New Grove Handbooks in Music: Performance Practice (2 vols.): *Music before 1600* (Middle Ages and Renaissance) and *Music after 1600* (Baroque, Classical and Nineteenth Century), ed. Howard Mayer Brown and Stanley Sadie (London, Macmillan, 1989). Each volume has substantial sections on instruments and their use. Introductions and instrumental sections in volume I for both periods are by Howard Mayer Brown. There are eighteen index references to the recorder. The woodwind and brass section under 'The baroque era' is by Alan Lumsden, with one page on the recorder. Valuable though both volumes are, it is very evident that despite a plethora of references there is a great deal yet in this field to 'try and enquire' (as Bacon would have put it). Volume II contains an excellent chapter by David Fuller entitled 'The performer as composer'. For reviews see Howard Schott's in *AR* 32/1 (March 1991, pp. 31–2), and Stanley Boorman's in *EM* 18/4 (Nov. 1990, pp. 641–5) – he ends 'Buy these books'.

Baroque

Urike Engelke, *Music and Language: Interpretation of Early Baroque Music According to Traditional Rules* (bilingual German and English, Zurich, Pan, and Frankfurt, Zimmerman, 1990). Drawing considerably, but in less than a hundred pages, on early writers, and giving many music examples, this book provides a succinct presentation, sometimes in tabular form, of early baroque performance practice, including embellishment and articulation. Very useful, though the English translation is less than perfect. It resembles and complements Jean-Claude Veilhan's *The Rules of Musical Interpretation in the Baroque Era* (Paris, Leduc, 1977) which concentrates on the later baroque period, especially French, as does his *The Baroque Recorder in 17th- and 18th-Century Performance and Practice: Technique, Performing Style, Original Fingering Charts* (bilingual French and English, Paris, Leduc, 1980). Together, these manuals would form a very sound basis for understanding performance practice across the whole baroque era.

Mary Cyr, *Performing Baroque Music* (Portland, Amadeus, and Aldershot, Scolar, 1992). The baroque equivalent of the renaissance performance-practice volumes for university students mentioned above, resembling the McGee book in its practical approach and the Phillips–Jackson one in providing substantial music examples, being pieces discussed in the text. As is only to be expected in a book covering baroque music as a whole, the recorder references are few (there is one on the splendid dust-jacket!), but one of the pieces is a Corelli Op. 5 sonata that is (or was) a set work for recorder Grade 8 examinations. Excellent bibliographies. Reviewed favourably by Dale Higbee, *AR* 34/3 (Sept. 1993), pp. 19–20, and adversely by Keith Elcombe in *EM* 22/3 (August 1994), pp. 499–500.

Peter le Huray, *Authenticity in Performance: Eighteenth-Century Case Studies* (Cambridge 1990). Six of the ten case studies are of works by J. S. Bach, Corelli, Couperin and Handel, but only one, another Corelli Op. 5

sonata, is (in arrangement) a recorder piece. But the book deals with questions of *affekt*, tempo, wide-ranging dynamics (pp. 38–41) and ornamentation that apply to all baroque music; and it is full of valuable insights.

Anthony Rowland-Jones, *Playing Recorder Sonatas: Interpretation and Technique* (Oxford 1992). Considers four baroque recorder sonatas in depth, and seven others in less detail. The only book on baroque performance practice so far written especially for recorder players (DL 94, p. 35). He has also written a short book on *Playing Recorder Duets* (Bristol, Allegro, 1995) covering the whole unaccompanied duet repertoire.

Julie Anne Sadie, *Companion to Baroque Music* (London, Dent, 1990). A very browsable work of reference on baroque musicians, by country and region, followed (pp. 349–446) by sections entitled 'Baroque forces and forms' (the chapter on instruments is by Jeremy Montagu) and 'Performing practice issues' (by Howard Schott, David Fuller and Stanley Sadie).

Betty Bang Mather, *Dance Rhythms of the French Baroque* (Bloomington, Indiana U. Press, 1987). As dance underlies so much baroque music written for recorder, this is an important 'Handbook for Performance' for the serious student, ranging more widely than its title implies. As valuable as her earlier handbooks *Interpretation of French Music from 1675 to 1775 for Woodwind and Other Performers* (New York, McGinnis & Marx, and London, Peters, 1973) and, by the same publishers and with David Lasocki as co-author, *Free Ornamentation in Woodwind Music 1700–1775* (1976) and *The Art of Preluding 1700–1830* (1984).

George Houle, *Meter in Music 1600–1800: Performance, Perception and Notation* (Bloomington, Indiana U. Press, 1987). A scholarly work on a subject much misunderstood by players of baroque music.

Frederick Neumann, *Essays in Performance Practice* (Ann Arbor and London, UMI Research Press, 1982) and, by the same author and publisher, *New Essays on Performance Practice* (1989; p.b. 1992). Controversial and challenging. The first volume has much on rhythmic inequality – see also David Fuller, 'Notes inégales' in *The New Grove*, le Huray (above; pp. 46–53 and 72–7), and Houle (above). Part two of the second volume is also devoted to problems of rhythm, and there is an interesting essay (pp. 209–20) entitled 'Matheson on performance practice' – see also George J. Buelow and Hans-Joachim Marx (eds.), *New Matheson Studies* (Cambridge 1983). Neumann's *Ornamentation in Baroque and Post-Baroque Music*, which includes an excellent section on vibrato (pp. 511–22), was published as a paperback in 1983 (Princeton U. Press), and Robert Donington's authoritative *The Interpretation of Early Music* also appeared in a slab-like revised paperback edition in 1989 (London, Faber). Neumann ties together much of his work of the last two decades in *Performance Practices of the 17th and 18th Centuries* (New York 1993).

Different approaches to the interpretation of baroque recorder sonatas are evident in articles by David Coomber (Telemann D minor) in *RV* 3 (Nov. 1985, pp. 23–7), Hans Maria Kneihs (Marcello D minor) in the same issue (pp. 15–19), and (in German) Michael Schneider (Barsanti C) in *Musica* 40/3 (May–June 1986, pp. 239–44) – see DL 87, pp. 150–1. Other articles on performance practice in the Australian journal include Kneihs, 'How do you know how to play a piece? – The relation of musical structure to historic performance practice and interpretation', *RV* 7 (Dec. 1987, pp. 7–9), and Shirley Baker, 'Playing for renaissance dance', *RV* 16 (Dec. 1992, pp. 1–4). In the British journal, Ross Winters writes on 'Historic source material', *RM* 12/3–4 (1992: Sept., pp. 77–81; and Dec., pp. 111–16) and both Alan Davis and Denis Bloodworth discuss baroque-fingered recorders in *RM* 12/2 (June 1992, pp. 47–50) and 8/5 (March 1985, pp. 151–3). *AR* articles include three by Anthony Rowland-Jones on recorder slurring (34/2, June 1993, pp. 9–15; 34/4, Nov. 1993, pp. 6–11; and 35/1, Jan. 1994 – on slurs in 'Sheep may safely graze' and Martinů's duet Divertimento – pp. 7–12). Patricia Ranum takes 'A fresh look at French wind articulations' in *AR* 33/4 (Dec. 1992, pp. 9–16 and 39) which relates to an article by Rowland-Jones in the previous issue on the interpretation of a sonata by Lavigne (33/3, Sept. 1992, pp. 9–13). Important articles appeared in May 1988 (29/2) by Theron McClure entitled 'Making the music speak: silences of articulation' (pp. 53–5), and by Scott Reiss in November 1987 (28/4, pp. 136–9) entitled 'Pitch control: shading and leaking' and in November 1986 (27/4, pp. 144–9) entitled 'Articulation: the key to expressive playing', an article which had repercussions in letters and other responses on both sides of the Atlantic.

Ornamentation

There is an excellent practical beginner's guide to renaissance ornamentation on pp. 180–4 of McGee's *Performer's Guide* (see above), and if possible this should be followed by working on Lewis Reece Baratz's two articles in *AR* on fifteenth-century improvisation, including the 'Spagna' tune (29/4, Nov. 1988, pp. 141–6; and 31/2, June 1990, pp. 7–11). These prepare the way for a study of Howard Mayer Brown's brilliant encapsulation of *Embellishing Sixteenth-Century Music* (Oxford 1976), and to playing the London Pro Musica series (Bernard Thomas) 'Ricercare e passaggi – improvisation and ornamentation 1580–1630' or the examples in the ultimate compendium (with an excellent introduction) of *Italian Diminutions* (Zurich 1979) by Richard Erig and Veronika Gutmann. See also Greg Dikmans's 'Florid Italian instrumental music *c*1600: an introduction' in *RV* 4 (May 1986, pp. 5–13), Peter Seibert's 'Ornamentation for consort players' in *AR* 25/4 (Nov. 1984, pp. 136–8), Andrew Waldo's article in *AR* 27/2 (May 1986, pp. 48–59), which includes a list of 181 ornamented pieces in sources from 1535 to 1638, and Rowland-Jones *RT* (pp. 112–14) and *PRS* (pp. 94–112 – Fontana, Sonata Terza).

An illuminating approach to baroque ornamentation, particularly with regard to Handel's recorder sonatas, may be made through the pages of *AR* and *RM*. A suggested order of reading is David Lasocki's 'Late baroque ornamentation: philosophy and guidelines' in *AR* 29/1 (Feb. 1988, pp. 7–10), and see also *PRS*, pp. 97–100; Betty Bang Mather's 'Making up your own baroque interpretation' in *AR* 22/3 (August 1981, pp. 55–9), and her 'Developing baroque ornamentation skills' in *AR* 29/1 (Feb. 1988, pp. 4–6); Edgar Hunt's 'An introduction to baroque ornamentation' in *RM* 9/9–10 (1989: March, pp. 246–8; and June, pp. 281–2); Lasocki's 'A new look at Handel's recorder sonatas' in *RM* 6/1 (March 1978, pp. 2–9) and Lasocki and Eva Legêne, 'Learning to ornament Handel's sonatas through the composer's ears' in *AR* 30/1, 3–4 (1989: Feb., pp. 9–14; August, pp. 102–6; and Nov., pp. 137–41). A bibliography on ornamentation may be found in *RT*, pp. 157–61. Roy Brewer's useful and friendly booklet *The Little Essential Graces: An Approach to Baroque Ornamentation for Recorder Players* (Bristol, Allegro, 1993) should now be added to that list together with two articles on ornaments in English baroque tutors: Malcolm Davies elucidates their confusing 'Marks and rules for gracing' in *RM* 13/2–3 (1993: Sept., pp. 39–41; and Dec., pp. 69–71) and he consequently advocates greater use of 'sweetening' or finger-vibrato (Hotteterre's 'flattements'), and Marianne Mezger writes in *Leading Notes* 4/1 (Spring 1994, pp. 13–16) on 'Performance practice for recorder players'. She concentrates on Follia divisions derived from tablature in Salter's 1683 tutor, with challenging results for she shows that the frequent ornaments – at least one in each bar of the melody – are integral to the interpretation of the music (see also p. 134, note 28).

Technique

Jochen Gärtner, *The Vibrato* (in relation to the flute) (Regensburg, Bosse, 1981). Included here not only for its historical background but, with its physiological emphasis, to remind recorder players of an insufficiently considered aspect of their technique, breathing.

Walter van Hauwe, *The Modern Recorder Player*, vol. I (1984), vol. II (1987) and vol. III (1992) (London, Schott). Van Hauwe's method certainly gives full attention to breathing techniques, and is easily the most thorough-going of all recorder tutors, both for individuals and for groups.

Anthony Rowland-Jones, *Recorder Technique: Intermediate to Advanced* (Oxford 1986), a second and much revised edn of *Recorder Technique* (Oxford 1959). A book for the advancing amateur to read, recorder in hand, different from but complementing the van Hauwe volumes which are more of a training system for aspiring professionals, with carefully staged exercises.

Johannes Fischer, *Die Dynamische Blockflöte* (Celle, Moeck, 1990). An important book not yet translated into English, but a full summary is provided by Pete Rose in his *AR* review (32/2, June 1991, pp. 22–3).

Kees Boeke, *The Complete Articulator* (London, Schott, 1986). Not a historical discussion of articulation or its interpretative functions, but a training programme of demanding studies applying principles outlined in van Hauwe's method.

(Earlier important books on technique and interpretation are described in Appendix 2 of *RT*)

Treatises and manuals (see also Chap. 7)

Sebastian Virdung (1511), *Musica getutscht: A Treatise on Musical Instruments (1511) by Sebastian Virdung*, ed. and trans. Beth Bullard (Cambridge 1993).

Martin Agricola (1529 and 1545), *Musica instrumentalis deudsch*, trans. (part) William E. Hettrick as 'Martin Agricola's poetic discussion of the recorder and other woodwind instruments', *AR* 21/3 (August 1980, pp. 103–13), 23/4 (Nov. 1982, pp. 139–46) and 24/2 (May 1983, pp. 51–60); reprinted in *RM* 8/4–7 (Dec. 1984, pp. 127–9; March 1985, pp. 139–48; June 1985, pp. 171–9; and Sept. 1985, pp. 202–12). Complete trans. and ed., William E. Hettrick, *The 'Musica instrumentalis deudsch' of Martin Agricola* (Cambridge 1994).

Sylvestro di Ganassi (1535), *Opera Intitulata Fontegara*, ed. Hildemarie Peter, trans. from German by Dorothy Swainson (Berlin-Lichterfelde, Lienau, 1959). In 1991 the Società Italiana del Flauto Dolci published *Fontegara* (Rome, Hortus Musicus), but a modern critical edition in English with a new translation direct from Italian is much needed, applying the same thoroughness in elucidating the text as David Boyden's analysis of Ganassi's bowings in his viol tutor *Regola Rubertina* (1542–3) on pp. 76–82 of *The History of Violin Playing from its Origins to 1761* (p.b. Oxford 1990) – this comprehensive work contains much of potential interest to recorder players.

Michael Praetorius (1618–19), *Syntagma Musicum II De Organographia Parts I and II*, trans. and ed. David Z. Crookes (Oxford 1986).

Marin Mersenne (1636), the books on instruments from his *Harmonie universelle*, trans. R. E. Chapman (The Hague 1957 and 1964).

Paulus Matthysz (1649), 'A translation of the Introduction to *Der Fluyten Lust-hof* of 1649' by Nicholas Humphries, *RV* 8 (July 1988), pp. 1–7.

Etienne Loulié (*c*1685–90): Patricia M. Ranum, 'Etienne Loulié: recorder player, teacher, musicologist', *AR* 32/1 (March 1991), pp. 7–11 and 34; and Richard Semmens, 'A translation of Etienne Loulié's method for learning how to play the recorder', *AR* 24/4 (Nov. 1983), pp. 135–45. For more background see DL 90, p. 12, and Ranum 'A sweet servitude: a musician's life at the court of Mlle. de Guise', *EM* 15/3 (August 1987), pp. 346–60.

Jean-Pierre Freillon-Poncein (1700), *La Veritable Manière d'apprendre à jouer en perfection du Haut-bois, de la Flute et du Flageolet*, trans. with introduction by Catherine Parsons Smith as *On Playing Oboe, Recorder, & Flageolet* (Bloomington, Indiana U. Press, 1992).

Jacques Hotteterre le Romain (1707), *'Principes ...' Principles of the Flute, Recorder & Oboe*, trans. and ed. David Lasocki (London, Barrie & Jenkins, 1968). Also trans. Paul Marshall Douglas (New York, Dover, 1968 and 1983). See also Greg Dikmans's 'Hotteterre's *Principes*' in *RV* 8 and 9 (July 1988, pp. 11–17; and Feb. 1989, pp. 9–16).

Johann Joachim Quantz (1752), *'Versuch ...' On Playing the Flute*, ed. and trans. Edward R. Reilly (p.b. 2nd edn London, Faber, 1985). For the applicability of this outstanding book to playing the recorder see *PRS*, pp. 4ff. Considerable insights into playing eighteenth-century music can also be gained from Tromlitz (1791), trans. and ed. Ardal Powell, *The Virtuoso Flute-Player* (Cambridge 1991), revwd Eric Haas, *AR* 33/1 (March 1992), pp. 26–9.

Some historical studies

Some general histories of music, often with each chapter written by a different specialist, may contain material of direct interest to recorder players, for example Chapter VII by Frank Dobbins, 'Lyons: commercial and cultural metropolis', in *The Renaissance* volume of the 'Man and Music' series, ed. Iain Fenlon (London, Macmillan, 1989). This volume even shows recorders on its cover. The following books are suggested as having bearing on the recorder's repertoire, though the best repertoire histories are those in Hunt's and Linde's books.

Reinhard Strohm, *The Rise of European Music 1380–1500* (Cambridge 1993); Tim Carter, *Music in Late Renaissance & Early Baroque Italy* (London, Batsford, 1982), especially Chap. 10: 'Instrumental music'. Generally these books describe the aesthetic, political and social background, and discuss the quality of the music, rather than becoming involved with questions of performance practice. They both have excellent bibliographies.

Tess Knighton and David Fallows (eds.), *Companion to Medieval and Renaissance Music* (London, Dent, 1992). Short essays, wide ranging and sometimes controversial, by forty-five contributors, both scholars and performers. Recorder symbolism in Italian renaissance art (including Titian) is touched upon by Iain Fenlon (p. 194). Revwd Jeremy Summerly, *Leading Notes* 4/1 (Spring 1994), pp. 18–21.

Peter Allsop, *The Italian 'Trio' Sonata from its Origins until Corelli* (Oxford 1992). Pp. 32 and 88 refer to Riccio (see also *PRS*, pp. 130–2). Brief, but more wide ranging, is Christopher Hogwood's BBC Music Guide to *The Trio Sonata* (1979), and multi-part as well as solo sonatas are covered in William S. Newman's major survey, especially in *The Sonata in the Baroque Era* (New York, Norton, 1959 and later edns).

Keith Polk, *German Instrumental Music of the Late Middle Ages 1350–1520* (Cambridge 1992), a book with many references to recorders; DL 94, p. 5, calls this 'An essential book for all players of early wind instruments'. See also Louise Cuyler, *The Emperor Maximilian I and Music* (Oxford 1973), which has many music examples. Recent books on J. S. Bach that might interest recorder players include John Butt, *Bach Interpretation* (Cambridge 1990), dealing with questions of articulation and slurring, and Malcolm Boyd, *The Brandenburg Concertos* (Cambridge 1993); this takes the debate on Bach's 'fiauti d'echo' in the fourth Brandenburg Concerto one stage further – see DL 90, pp. 15–16, and his article in *The Galpin Society Journal* 45 (March 1992, pp. 59–66), as well as Michael Marissen's comprehensive article in *Journal of the American Musical Instrument Society* 17 (1991, pp. 5–52) (DL 94, p. 7). Pippa Drummond, *The German Concerto* (Oxford 1980), included those with recorders by Bach and Telemann. There is a useful account of Telemann, Schütz and Purcell, in the *New Grove Dictionary* extracts on *North European Baroque Masters* (London, Macmillan, 1985).

Willem Elder's book on (renaissance) *Composers of the Low Countries*, trans. Graham Dixon (Oxford 1991), has a rather sketchy chapter entitled 'Instrumental music', mainly keyboard. However, moving a century on, Jacob van Eyck is well served by Ruth van Baak Griffioen's book *Jacob van Eyck's Der Fluyten Lusthof 1644–c.1655* (Utrecht 1991); revwd Jeremy Barlow, *EM* 30/3 (August 1992), pp. 485–6.

Isabelle Cazeaux's *French Music in the Fifteenth and Sixteenth Centuries* (New York, Praeger, 1975) is admirably continued by James R. Anthony's *French Baroque Music* (New York, Norton, 1981) – see esp. pp. 335–8. Occasionally a book on an individual composer is more than a discourse on one musician's work; examples are Wilfrid Mellers on François Couperin (rev. edn London, Faber, 1987), Cuthbert Girdlestone on Rameau (New York, Dover, 1969) and Michael Talbot on Albinoni (Oxford 1990). The latter has several interesting recorder references, as does H. Wiley Hitchcock's *Marc-Antoine Charpentier* (Oxford 1990) – Charpentier occasionally scored for recorder and flute together (e.g. pp. 62 and 77).

David Wulstan's *Tudor Music* (London, Dent, 1985), revwd William Metcalf in *AR* 28/4 (Nov. 1987, pp. 170–2), has an excellent chapter entitled 'Private musick'. English recorder music from the sixteenth to eighteenth centuries is the subject of many articles by David Lasocki (see Chaps. 7 and 10); additionally for 'Handel's chamber music' see Terence Best in *EM* 13/4 (Nov. 1985, pp. 476–99). Lasocki's articles 'The recorder consort at the English court 1540–1673' are in *AR* 25/3–4 (1984: August, pp. 91–100; and Nov., pp. 131–5); with Roger Prior, Lasocki has written a book on *The Bassanos: Venetian Musicians and Instrument Makers in England, 1531–1665* (Aldershot, Scolar Press, 1995). A violin parallel is *Four and Twenty Fiddlers: The Violin at the English Court 1540–1690* by Peter Holman (Oxford 1993).

The Recorder in the 17th Century, Proceedings of the International Recorder

Symposium Utrecht 1993, ed. David Lasocki (Utrecht, STIMU, 1995). Wide-ranging research in an untilled field.

Nicholas Anderson, *Baroque Music From Monteverdi to Handel* (London, Thames and Hudson, 1994). An overview for the general reader, fairly short (224 pp.) so inevitably rather superficial. But the account is well balanced between theory, musical developments in different countries, and composer biographies and critiques. Passing references are made to music with recorders, by Monteverdi, Praetorius, Lully, Charpentier and Hotteterre, Vivaldi, Purcell and Handel, and Graupner, J. S. Bach and Telemann.

Twentieth-century recorder music (see Chaps. 9, 11 and 12)

Only one book, but an excellent one: Eve O'Kelly, *The Recorder Today* (Cambridge 1990), revwd Pete Rose *AR* 31/4 (Dec. 1990), pp. 31–2 – 'an essential book both for amateurs and professional players'. DL 94, p. 9.

Four twentieth-century recorder sonatas are discussed in some detail in Rowland-Jones, *PRS* (Murrill, Berkeley, Leigh and Schollum).

AR keeps up-to-date with developments in contemporary recorder music through a lively regular feature, 'The cutting edge', written by Pete Rose. Among Rose's other articles is 'Avant-garde recorder music: an evolutionary view' in *AR* 33/3 (Sept. 1992, pp. 19–22), the last three pages being a pull-out chart covering the period 1950 to 1989. The December 1990 issue (31/4) of *AR* was entitled 'The twentieth-century recorder'.

Malcolm Tattersall has performed the same function in *RV*, with overviews of recent Australian recorder compositions in the March 1984 and June 1987 issues (nos. 1 and 6). See also DL 90, p. 13, and DL 94, p. 11. Benjamin Thorn, composer of 'The voice of the crocodile', wrote in *RV* 10 (Dec. 1989, pp. 5–9) '"New" sounds from old pipes', and *RV*'s November 1985 issue (no. 3) contained an article by a composer, David Worrall, on writing an ensemble piece, *Silhouettes*, for recorders, and another by a performer, John Martin, on preparing Brenton Broadstock's *Aureole 3* (treble and harpsichord) for its first performance. In the *RV* September 1993 issue (no. 17), his last as editor, Malcolm Tattersall wrote 'The recorder in the twenty-first century' (pp. 2–8).

Alan Davis wrote an interesting article, 'Commissioned works for the recorder', including Philip Wilby's *Breakdance*, in *RM* 9/10 (June 1989, pp. 278–81). In the March 1993 issue (13/1, pp. 13–14) John Turner wrote on the rediscovery of Alan Rawsthorne's 1939 recorder *Suite*, and Robert Ehrlich maintained *RM*'s involvement with contemporary recorder compositions in a balanced critical review 'Modern music for solo recorder' (pp. 9–12). It is difficult to find books and articles evaluating rather than merely describing modern recorder music; an exception is Niall O'Loughlin's article 'The recorder in 20th-century music', *EM* 10/1 (Jan. 1982), pp. 36–7 – a 'short and selective' survey of the repertoire through the early 1970s, with an emphasis on post-1945 compositions.

A miscellany

John Solum, *The Early Flute* (Oxford 1992). This attractive book is full of interesting references to our instrument. It has an excellent bibliography, and its music lists provide tempting offerings for the recorder's 'extended repertoire'. The chapter on the renaissance flute is by Anne Smith.

Raymond Meylan, *The Flute*, trans. from German by Alfred Clayton (London, Batsford, 1988). A charming mixture of insights and inaccuracies in the early history, but with some beautiful illustrations.

Related to the above are articles on the voice flute, the recorder with the same range as the baroque flute (ideal for piracy) – Dale Higbee's 'On playing recorders in D' in *AR* 26/1 (Feb. 1985, pp. 16–21), and Douglas Macmillan's 'The recorder in the late eighteenth and early nineteenth centuries' in *The Consort* 39 (1983, pp. 489–97). For references to the Viennese czakan see *PRS*, p. 198, note 45, and Marianne Betz's large-scale study (in German – *DL* 94, p. 32), as well as introductions to LPM Dolce and Moeck edns of czakan music.

Rien de Reede (ed.), *Concerning the Flute* (Amsterdam 1984), includes articles by Jane M. Bowers entitled 'The Hotteterre family of woodwind instrument makers', and by Betty Bang Mather entitled 'The performance of trills in French baroque dance music'.

Van Acht, van den Ende and Schimmel, *Dutch Recorders of the Eighteenth Century* (Celle, Moeck, 1991). Describes in lavish detail and excellent colour seventeen instruments in the Gemeentemuseum collection at The Hague. Revwd Eve O'Kelly, *RM* 11/4 (Dec. 1991), pp. 121–2.

Denis Bloodworth, 'A new design of bass recorder', *RM* 12/1 (March 1992), pp. 3–5, and 'The Lockwood great bass recorder', *RM* 14/1 (March 1994), p. 13. See also his *The Bass Recorder Handbook* (London, Novello, 1986).

Harry Haskell, *The Early Music Revival: a History* (London and New York, Thames and Hudson, 1988). Revwd Brent Wissick, *AR* 12/1 (March 1990), pp. 19–20.

Nicholas Kenyon (ed.), *Authenticity and Early Music* (Oxford 1988). Likely to appeal to those who enjoy controversies. Note Howard Mayer Brown's fine contribution 'Pedantry or liberation: a sketch of the historical performance movement'. See also David Lasocki's 'The great authenticity debate' in *RV* 14 (Dec. 1991), pp. 1–8.

John Caldwell, *Editing Early Music* (Oxford 1985).

Richard Leppert, *Music and Image* (Cambridge 1988). Socio-cultural musical iconography. Leppert's book relates to the eighteenth century. J. M. Thomson's four articles on caricature in music trace its history in the same period (*RM* 3/3–4: Sept./Dec. 1969; and 3/6–7: June/Sept. 1970). These were developed in *AR* (Hogarth, 26/2 (May 1985), pp. 56–61; Rowlandson, 28/3 (Aug. 1987), pp. 96–9; and Callot, 29/2 (May 1988), pp. 48–52). Rowland-Jones wrote 'Renaissance recorders – the pictorial evidence', *RM* 14/3 (Sept. 1994), pp. 76–8. There are references to recorder iconography in Emanuel Winternitz's *Musical Instruments and their Symbolism in Western Art*, Studies in Musical Iconology (New Haven and London 1979 (first edn 1967)) and in the sumptuous catalogue of the Hoogsteder Exhibition of *Music & Painting in the Golden Age* (The Hague, Hoogsteder; Zwolle, Waanders, 1994).

Graham Strahle (ed.), *An Early Music Dictionary* (Cambridge 1995). A dictionary of terms relating to instruments, performance practice, theory and composition drawn from original sources in English during the period 1500 to 1740. It aims to show how musical terminology was understood by players of the time.

Albrecht Dürer (1515), from border decoration f. 34v of Maximilian I's Prayer Book. Will the fox by the skill of his piping lure the cock and hens across the brook to be his companions for supper?

Index

Main references are in bold type. Page-numbers in italics refer to illustrations, music examples and their captions. Publications are normally indexed by authors and composers, not by titles.